Exploring Exodus

The Heritage of Biblical Israel

Nahum M. Sarna

Schocken Books *New York*

We gratefully acknowledge the following permissions:
James B. Pritchard, *The Ancient Near East in Pictures
Relating to the Old Testament,* 2nd ed. with supplement.
Copyright © 1954, 1969 by Princeton University Press.
Scattered selections reprinted by permission of Princeton University Press.

Yohanan Aharoni, *The Land of the Bible: A Historical Geography* (revised
and enlarged edition), translated from the Hebrew and edited by A. F. Rainey.
Copyright © 1962, 1967, 1979 by Yohanan Aharoni.

Map on page 104 reproduced and used by permission of The Westminster
Press, Philadelphia, Pennsylvania and Burns & Oates Ltd., London.

Library of Congress Cataloging-in-Publication Data
Sarna, Nahum M.
Exploring Exodus.
Bibliography: p.
Includes index.
1. Bible. O.T. Exodus—Criticism, interpretation, etc. I. Title.
BS1245.2.S26   1986   222'.1206   85-18445
ISBN 0-8052-0830-5

Design by Thomas Nau

First SCHOCKEN paperback edition published
in 1987

68975

To
Helen

מים רבים לא יוכלו לכבות את-האהבה
ונהרות לא ישטפוה

Contents

the wilderness; Stripping the Egyptians; Signs and wonders; Moses' continued resistance.

ancient Near Eastern laws; The nature of the law collections;
The nature of the Torah's collections of laws; The distinctive
features of Israelite law; *Lex talionis*, or "an eye for an eye";
Lex talionis in the Torah.

Preface

This book is intended primarily for students, teachers, and educated laymen, although it is my hope that the scholarly reader, too, will derive some benefit from it. My aim is to offer a mature understanding of this seminal biblical book. To this end I have attempted to synthesize the rich findings of multifaceted research into the Bible and into the civilizations of the ancient Near East that have a bearing upon the biblical text, much of which is not readily accessible to the nonspecialist. I have tried to integrate the assured results of scholarship into the biblical narrative. Since the Torah is not a book of history, but one that makes use of historical data for didactic purposes, that is, for the inculcation of spiritual values and moral and ethical imperatives, *Exploring Exodus* consistently stresses these aspects of the narratives.

While it is today unassailable that the Sacred Scriptures cannot be adequately understood and appreciated except within the context of the world out of which they emerged, I am not addicted to "parallelomania." I have made my position quite clear in this regard in the introduction to my *Understanding Genesis* (New York: Schocken Books, 1970). It seems to me obvious that contrast is a more important analytical index of cultural configuration than is comparison, and for this reason I have made a point of emphasizing differences at least as much as similarities when drawing upon ancient Near Eastern materials.

Although I take sole responsibility for the entire contents of this book, I must acknowledge my indebtedness to several persons. Ms. Bonny

Fetterman, Senior Editor of Schocken Books, deserves thanks for her advice, patience, and encouragement. I have derived much help and inspiration from my colleagues and friends, Professors Marvin Fox, Michael Fishbane, and Tzvi Abusch. My sons, Professor Jonathan D. Sarna and Mr. David E. Y. Sarna, were helpful in various ways. I am also beholden to Ms. Sheila Mondshein and to Ms. Hadassah Segal. A special debt of gratitude is due to the Institute for Advanced Studies at the Hebrew University where I was privileged to spend the year 1982–1983 as a Fellow, and was enabled to pursue the research for this book without encumbrances. Thanks are due to the staffs of the libraries of Brandeis University and the Hebrew College, Boston, for their unfailing courtesy, kindness, and efficient help. I am most appreciative of the kind permission of the Jewish Publication Society to cite from their new version of the Holy Scriptures, of the consent of the Spertus College of Judaica Press to my reprinting extracts from my article "The Decalogue" in the *Solomon Goldman Lectures: Perspectives in Jewish Learning,* 1982. Princeton University Press was especially generous in allowing me to cite sections of its *Ancient Near Eastern Texts Relating to the Old Testament,* edited by J. B. Pritchard.

Finally, in dedicating this book to my wife, I not only take note of the fact that she typed the entire manuscript and made innumerable improvements in it, but I acknowledge with deep gratitude her happy inspiration, her unceasing and affectionate encouragement, and her unstinting devotion and self-sacrifice, all of which gave me the freedom to study and to write.

N.M.S.

Introduction

Biblical religion revolves around two themes, Creation and the Exodus. The former asserts God's undivided sovereignty over nature, the latter His absolute hegemony over history. These essential themes are inextricably linked, inform one another, and are complementary. A creator-god who withdraws from his creation and leaves his creatures entirely to their own devices is a functionless deity, an inactive being, remote and aloof from the world of men and women. He represents no ideal, makes no demands, enjoins no obligations, provides no moral governance of the world, imposes no moral law. Human strivings rest in no assurance of being other than unreality and futility, and the human race is bereft of ultimate destiny.

Not so the Creator-God of the Bible. He is vitally concerned with the welfare of His creatures, intensely involved in their fate and fortune. An unqualifiedly moral Being, He insistently demands human imitation of His moral attributes. He imposes His law on the human race, and He judges the world in righteousness. History, therefore, is the arena of divine activity, and the weal and woe of the individual and of the nation is the product of God's providence, conditioned by human response to His demands. It is no wonder that the Exodus is the pivotal event in the Bible, and that the experiences connected with it—the slavery of the Israelites, their liberation from Egypt, the covenant between God and His people at Sinai, and the journey in the wilderness

1

toward the Promised Land—all constitute the dominant motif of the Scriptures in one form or another.

Apart from the actual narrative itself, the Exodus theme is referred to about one hundred twenty times in the Hebrew Bible.[1] The Exodus was seen primarily as an event of supreme religious significance, an experience indelibly stamped on Israel's memory and imagination, ineradicably inscribed upon the conscience and understanding of the people. It was never seen just as a historical event of the past, but became a permanent symbol in the Israelite national consciousness. Continually being reenacted, it was ever new, ever imposing itself afresh upon the collective mind and memory, so that the epic of the Exodus nurtured the culture and the religion over the millennia. This remarkable phenomenon is well illustrated by a quotation from the prophet Amos who lived at least five hundred years after that epochal event. Addressing his contemporaries in the name of God, he can meaningfully say, "I brought you up from the land of Egypt and led you through the wilderness forty years to possess the land of the Amorite."[2]

The uses of the Exodus theme

A study of the biblical materials reveals that the Exodus theme is used for theological and didactic purposes in seven ways:

1. It affirms, as in Genesis, that God's sovereignty over nature is absolute. Unlike the pagan gods, the God of Israel does not inhere in nature but exists outside it and above it. This fundamental teaching of the Genesis Creation story is here epitomized through the series of plagues that God visits upon the defiant, tyrannical Egyptian. All the plagues, except the last, have their roots in phenomena of nature upon which God imposes His sovereign will.

2. It demonstrates that human beings cannot successfully defy God's will or effectively thwart His purposes. True, God has endowed man with free will, but the tension between human will and divine will must inevitably resolve itself in the humbling of man. The pharaoh may arrogantly dismiss Moses and Aaron with the derisive proclamation: "Who is the Lord that I should heed Him and let Israel go? I do not know the Lord, nor will I let Israel go."[3] In the end, however, he must ignominiously rise in the middle of the night to summon Moses and Aaron, and to announce his abject surrender:

Up, depart from among my people, you and the Israelites with you! Go, worship the Lord as you said![4]

3. It teaches that history has meaning and purpose. It is not a concatenation of haphazard incidents but rather is the unfolding of God's grand design. The migration of Abraham from Ur of the Chaldeans, the fortunes of Isaac and Jacob and of Jacob's children, the migration of the Israelites to Egypt, are all part of a process that leads up to the Exodus in fulfillment of the divine promise to Abraham recorded in Genesis 15:13–14:

> Know well that your offspring shall be strangers in a land not theirs, and they shall be enslaved and oppressed . . . but I will execute judgment on the nation they shall serve, and in the end they shall go free with great wealth.

4. It illustrates how God is the redeemer from injustice and oppression. The revelation at Sinai opens with God identifying Himself as the One who brought the Israelites out of Egypt and freed them from bondage, not as the One who created the world. Thereafter, this becomes the supreme characteristic attribute of the God of Israel. He is, above all, the great Liberator.

5. The Exodus thus becomes the paradigm of future redemption; it offers a pattern for God's intervention in history in times to come. In periods of national crisis, the Exodus experience of the past serves to strengthen faith in God's redemptive powers, and provides comfort and hope for the future.

6. The religious calendar of Israel and its rituals and practices are all reinterpreted in terms of the Exodus. The New Year is changed to the spring;[5] the weekly sabbath is rationalized as being grounded in the liberation from Egypt rather than in Creation;[6] the great agricultural festivals that relate to the rhythm of nature and the life of the soil are all reinterpreted and historicized in commemoration of the Exodus;[7] even the dietary laws find their ultimate grounding in this momentous event.[8]

7. Finally, with the historicizing of religion comes the ethicizing of history. That is to say, history is used as a source of ethical teachings and as a motive force for social ethics. God's redemptive acts demand

a corresponding imitative human response. A host of biblical passages gives eloquent expression to the idea that the experience of the slavery and the liberation must become the wellspring of moral action. The following quotations amply illustrate the point:

You shall not wrong a stranger or oppress him, for you were strangers in the land of Egypt.[9]

You shall not oppress a stranger, for you know the feelings of the stranger, having yourselves been strangers in the land of Egypt.[10]

When a stranger resides with you in your land, you shall not wrong him. The stranger who resides with you shall be to you as one of your citizens; you shall love him as yourself, for you were strangers in the land of Egypt. . . .[11]

Six days you shall labor and do all your work, but the seventh day is a sabbath of the Lord your God: you shall not do any work—you, your son or your daughter, your male or female slave, your ox or your ass, or any of your cattle, or the stranger in your settlements, so that your male and female slave may rest as you do. Remember that you were a slave in the land of Egypt and the Lord your God freed you from there. . . .[12]

For the Lord your God is God supreme and Lord supreme, the great, the mighty, and the awesome God, who shows no favor and takes no bribe, but upholds the cause of the fatherless and the widow, and befriends the stranger, providing him with food and clothing. You too must befriend the stranger, for you were strangers in the land of Egypt.[13]

If a fellow Hebrew, man or woman, is sold to you, he shall serve you six years, and in the seventh year you shall set him free. When you set him free, do not let him go empty-handed. Furnish him out of the flock, threshing floor, and vat, with which the Lord your God has blessed you. Bear in mind that you were slaves in the land of Egypt and the Lord your God redeemed you; therefore I enjoin this commandment upon you today.[14]

You shall not abhor an Egyptian, for you were a stranger in his land.[15]

You shall not subvert the rights of the stranger or the fatherless; you shall not take a widow's garment in pawn. Remember that you were a slave in Egypt and that the Lord your God redeemed you from there; therefore do I enjoin you to observe this commandment.[16]

When you beat down the fruit of your olive trees, do not go over them again; that shall go to the stranger, the fatherless, and the widow. When you gather the grapes of your vineyard, do not pick it over again; that shall go to the stranger, the fatherless, and the widow. Always remember that you were a slave in the land of Egypt; therefore do I enjoin you to observe this commandment.[17]

The title

The story of the slavery and emancipation of the people of Israel is told in the second book of the Torah or Pentateuch, the Five Books of Moses. It is called in English "Exodus," a title derived originally from the Septuagint, the Greek translation made for the Jewish community of ancient Alexandria in Egypt. It is abbreviated from a fuller title, "The Exodus ["departure"] of the Children of Israel from Egypt," which in turn reflects a Hebrew title current among the communities of the Land of Israel. The most widely used Hebrew name is *Sefer Sh'mot* ("The Book: Names"), taken from the opening Hebrew words of the book, "These are the names of the sons of Israel."

The connection with Genesis

While the book is more or less a self-contained literary unit, it is incomprehensible except as a sequel to the Book of Genesis. The connectives between the two are clear and deliberate. The narratives in Genesis focus upon individuals and the fortunes of a single family; they center upon the divine promises of peoplehood and national territory that are vouchsafed to them. In the Book of Exodus, the process of fulfilling those promises is set in motion. God first reveals Himself to

Moses as the God of the Patriarchs, and the phrase "the Israelite people" appears for the first time.[18] The opening verses of the book list the original seventy pioneers who migrated to Egypt, and the passage clearly derives from Genesis 46:8–27. God's commissioning of Moses at the scene of the Burning Bush directs him: "Go and assemble the elders of Israel and say to them: the Lord, the God of your fathers, the God of Abraham, Isaac, and Jacob, has appeared to me and said, 'I have taken note of you [Heb. *paqod paqad'ti*] and of what is being done to you in Egypt. . . .' "[19] This is a studied echo of Joseph's dying words, "God will surely take notice of you [Heb. *paqod yiphqod*] and bring you up from this land to the land which He promised on oath to Abraham, to Isaac, and to Jacob."[20] Indeed, Joseph's authorship of this phrase is explicitly cited in Exodus 13:19. The threefold reference to Joseph in the initial verses of Exodus is calculated to forge a close and obvious link with the concluding section of Genesis, and to effect the transition from one to the other. It is taken for granted that the reader is aware of who Joseph was and knows the reason for the migration of Jacob and his family to Egypt.

Structure and content

The structure and content of the book are somewhat complicated. On the one hand, the material is presented as one long, continuous, and sequential account, and even legal and ritual matters find expression within a narrative framework. On the other hand, clearly no attempt is made to be comprehensive; only such individual episodes are highlighted as are deemed to be of major significance. This discriminating selectivity is undoubtedly conditioned by didactic considerations.

The work does not easily lend itself to separation into clear-cut major divisions, though a rough arrangement broadly partitions the book into the following sections:

1. Chapters 1–15:21, the story of Israel in Egypt, the oppression, the struggle for freedom, and the final liberation;
2. Chapter 15:22 to Chapter 18, the account of the journey from the Reed Sea to Sinai;
3. Chapters 19–24, the covenant at Sinai and prescriptions of the law;

4. Chapters 25–40, the command to erect the Tabernacle, and its implementation.

The historical background

A vexing question is how to place all these events within the framework of recorded and datable history. In the present state of our knowledge, this cannot be done with any assurance of certainty. This uncertainty flows as much from the problems inherent in the biblical record itself as from the absence of satisfying, direct evidence from extrabiblical sources. One difficulty arises from the fact that the slavery and the liberation are perceived as events of profound religious significance. The emphasis is on the theological interpretation, not on historical detail. The biblical narratives are essentially documents of faith, not records of the past; that is to say, the verities of faith are communicated through the forms of history, but these latter are not presented for their own sake. They are employed only insofar as they serve the purposes of the former. No wonder, then, that solid historical data are so sparse. To cite a case in point: the reigning monarchs with whom Moses contends are simply and uniformly designated "Pharaoh" without any personal identification. All Egyptian kings are so termed, at least from the advent of the New Kingdom in the sixteenth century B.C.E. Another lacuna is the period of time that elapsed between the death of Joseph and the onset of the oppression. After all, it would surely have required the passing of several generations for a mere seventy souls, the stated totality of Jacob's issue that migrated to Egypt, to multiply and increase to the extent that it might be said even hyperbolically that "the land was filled with them."[21]

Another complicating factor is that the meager chronological data that are supplied do not seem to represent a single, uniform, system of reckoning. Exodus 12:40–41 tells us that the time that the Israelites stayed in Egypt was four hundred thirty years.[22] Genesis 15:13 had predetermined a period of four hundred years for the slavery and the oppression, but this is coordinated with no more than four "generations" in verse 16. It is true that a study of the Hebrew word *dor*, usually rendered "generation," and its Semitic cognates, shows that it more accurately means simply "a cycle of time, a life time,"[23] and it is quite indeterminate, so that four generations need not necessarily be incompatible with four hundred years. But the fact of the matter is that Moses is only the great-grandson of Levi who went down to Egypt;[24] also, Jair, great-grandson of Joseph, together with his sons, participated in the wars of conquest and in the settlement of the land.[25] Nahshon, who was a tribal prince at the time of the Exodus, is a fifth-generation descendant of Judah,[26] while Achan, a contemporary of Joshua, Moses' successor, is the fifth generation after Jacob.[27] In other words, no more than a century or a century and a half seems to have elapsed between Jacob's migration to Egypt and the Exodus, a figure that would seem to be incompatible with the four hundred years cited in the text. One biblical text does yield a synchronism. According to 1 Kings 6:1, Solomon built the Temple at Jerusalem in the fourth year of his reign, which is said to have coincided with the four hundred eightieth year after the Exodus.[28] Since this king came to the throne ca. 960 B.C.E., the notice of 1 Kings 6:1 would date the departure from Egypt to around the middle of the fifteenth century B.C.E. This, however, would bring us to the period of the XVIIIth Egyptian Dynasty (ca. 1552–1306 B.C.E.), to the reigns of the powerful kings Thutmosis III (ca. 1490–1436 B.C.E.) and Amenhotep II (= Amenophis; ca. 1438–1412 B.C.E.), both of whom campaigned heavily in Syria and Palestine and asserted strong control over these lands. Thutmosis III extended the empire to the Upper Euphrates. It would have been most unlikely for the Israelite departure from Egypt and the conquest of Canaan to have taken place at this time. The books of Joshua and Judges, in fact, make no mention of Egypt as a factor in the wars of conquest. Apart from this objection, the figure of four hundred eighty years has every appearance of representing schematized chronology, that is, the featuring of neatly balanced segments of time as a way of expressing the idea that what occurs is not happenstance but comes about by divine design.[29] This device is well illustrated in Genesis through, for example, the ten generations between Adam and Noah and between Noah and Abraham, as well as in the number harmony present in the chronologies of the Patriarchs. Thus Abraham lived seventy-five years in the home of his father and seventy-five years in the lifetime of his son. He was one hundred years old at the birth of Isaac and he lived one hundred years in Canaan. Jacob lived seventeen years with Joseph in Canaan and a like number with him in Egypt.

To return to the number 480: it so happens that the sum of the years from the fourth year of Solomon, when he built the Temple, to the last year of the last king in Jerusalem is, according to the biblical sources, exactly 430. If the fifty years of exile are added, the resultant 480 brings us to the Cyrus declaration of 538 B.C.E., which allowed the Jews to return to Zion and to rebuild the Temple. In other words, by having Solomon's Temple building occur in the four hundred eightieth year after the Exodus, the biblical historiosopher may be making that event the central point in the history of biblical Israel. It should also be noted that 480 is the product of 12 × 40, both factors being conventional or symbolic numbers in the Bible and the ancient Near East. The number 40, in particular, designates a fairly long period of time in terms of human experience.[30] All in all, it is highly unlikely that the notice in 1 Kings 6:1 is intended to be an exact, historical time-marker, but is rather a rhetorical statement. As will be seen, to place the Exodus in the fifteenth century B.C.E. is to compound the historical problems.

It is clear that the present state of our knowledge does not permit a definitive solution to the problem. Not until archeological research fortuitously provides us with direct and incontrovertible proof for a specific date will this be possible. In the meantime, by utilizing a few items of indirect evidence we may conclude that the cumulative effect of several lines of approach favors a thirteenth-century B.C.E. dating for the Exodus.

The first item concerns the biblical texts that relate to the area of Israelite settlement in Egypt, all of which point to the eastern part of the Nile Delta. These Scriptural references treat of two different periods: that of Joseph's time, and that of the oppression and Exodus. The message that Joseph sent his father by way of his brothers reads as follows:

> God has made me lord of all Egypt; come down to me without delay. You will dwell in the region of Goshen, where you will be near me. . . .[31]

This means that the royal administration at that time was located nearby. When Jacob traveled to Egypt from Canaan he arrived in Goshen, to which place Joseph rode out in his chariot to meet him, and soon introduced his newly arrived family to the pharaoh. This indicates once again that the palace was within easy access of Goshen, where the king gave them permission to settle.[32] The location of the capital in the northeastern Delta of the Nile in Joseph's day unmistakably indicates the period of the Hyksos invaders, who maintained their royal residence in this region (ca. 1780–1570 B.C.E.). We shall have more to say about them later on.

The second series of texts leads to the same geographic area. According to the story told in Exodus 2:1–10, the daughter of the pharaoh found the baby Moses at a site on the Nile not far from the palace. From here, Moses' sister, Miriam, was easily able to run home and to fetch her mother. In another incident, the pharaoh of the Exodus was able to summon Moses and Aaron to his palace in the middle of the night, which indicates that their domiciles were not too far away.[33]

The Israelites, under the oppression, were conscripted to build the cities of "Pithom and Raamses," and it was from the latter site that the people started their march of liberation out of Egypt.[34] It is known that in the course of the two hundred odd years that elapsed between the collapse of the Hyksos rule over Egypt and the XIXth Dynasty (ca. 1306–1200 B.C.E.), the eastern Delta had been neglected.[35] It was Pharaoh Rameses II (ca. 1290–1224 B.C.E.) who set up his capital here in his newly built city that he named for himself. It is highly significant that Genesis 47:11 equates the area of Israelite settlement with "the region of Rameses," which description is a reflex of a genuine historic reality even though in context it is anachronistic.[36] Finally, Psalm 78:12, 43 locates the Israelites in Egypt in the "plain of Zoan." Now Zoan is none other than Tanis, the modern site of either Ṣan el-Ḥagar or Qantir in the northeastern Nile Delta.[37] The conclusion seems to be inescapable that the oppression, or at least the final and most severe stage of it, took place during the reign of Rameses II. His prodigious building activities, of which more will be said later, provide a convincing backdrop for the biblical narrative. The thirteenth century B.C.E. emerges, therefore, as a very likely candidate for the events described in the Book of Exodus.

This deduction is reinforced by what is known of the political situation in the Near East between the thirteenth and eleventh centuries B.C.E. Following the ten-year rule of Merneptah, immediate successor to Rameses II, Egypt was plunged into two decades of anarchy. Even when Rameses III (1194–1164 B.C.E.) finally secured the throne and established order, he was forced to spend the first eleven years of his reign fighting off the Libyans and "Sea Peoples" who attacked Egypt from the west.[38] After his death, Egyptian rule in Canaan came to an end.

In other words, this period provided an ideal setting for the Israelite conquest of the Promised Land. There were no great powers in the east to interfere, and several other small entities in the area also took advantage of the situation to establish new states, such as the Arameans in Syria, the peoples of Transjordan, and the Phoenician port cities.

There is one document from Egypt that also seems to lend weight to the case for a mid-thirteenth-century B.C.E. date for the Exodus. This is the famous "Stele of Merneptah," often referred to as the "Israel Stele." It consists of a huge inscribed slab of black granite, originally installed by Pharaoh Amenhotep (Amenophis) III in his mortuary temple in western Thebes, on which was carved an account of that king's building activities. Merneptah (ca. 1224–1211 B.C.E.), the successor to Rameses II, had it removed to his own funerary temple that he built to the northwest of the other, and had recorded on its reverse side a lyrical recitation of his great victory over a coalition of Libyans and "Sea Peoples" that invaded Egypt in the fifth year of his reign (ca. 1220 B.C.E.). This battle proved to be the most serious and most threatening situation that Merneptah faced in the course of his years on the throne.

The special interest of this document for students of the Bible lies in its concluding poem that is attached to the main text. This celebrates the pharaoh's role as the protector of Egypt, as evidenced by a successful military expedition into Palestine. It reads as follows:

> The princes are prostrate, saying: "Mercy!"
> Not one raises his head among the Nine Bows.
> Desolation is for Tehenu; Hatti is pacified;
> Plundered is the Canaan with every evil;
> Carried off is Ashkelon; seized upon is Gezer;
> Yanoam is made as that which does not exist;
> Israel is laid waste, his seed is not;
> Hurru is become a widow for Egypt!
> All lands together, they are pacified;
> Everyone who was restless, he has been bound
> by the King of Upper and Lower Egypt. . . .[39]

A few explanatory comments on the text are in order before we analyze the inscription and assess its significance:

The term for "Mercy" is the Canaanite word *shalam*, which is the Hebrew *shalom*; the "Nine Bows" are the traditionally hostile neighbors of Egypt; the Tehenu are one of the Libyan peoples; Hatti is the land of the Hittites, now Asiatic Turkey; Ashkelon and Gezer are two southerly Canaanite towns; Yanoam is a town in the north of the country; Hurru, the land of the Hurrians, who are the biblical Horites, is an Egyptian term for Palestine and Syria.

The historic reality behind this triumphal poem has been questioned, primarily because of the conventional phrasing and because of the omission of any details about the battles, contrary to the usual style of pharaonic campaign inscriptions.[40] Yet it is not unreasonable to assume that the Canaanite city kingdoms took advantage of the massive Libyan invasion, and of Merneptah's preoccupation with the western border of Egypt, in order to revolt, and it is probable that following his victory the king would make a show of force in Canaan. In fact, independent evidence for some military action by this pharaoh inside Canaan comes from an important inscription found in the temple at Amada in Nubia, present-day Sudan. Engraved at the entrance doorway, it celebrates Merneptah's defeat of the invasion of Egypt from Libya in his fourth year, and it accords him the title "Reducer of Gezer."[41] That city is in Canaan, and the epithet proves that this pharaoh did campaign in that land.

The fascination that the "Stele of Merneptah" holds is due to the fact that it features the first mention of the people of Israel to be found in any extrabiblical source, and the only one, so far, to occur in any Egyptian text. It is ironic and instructive that this should be an obituary notice: "Israel is laid waste, his seed is not!" Curiously, the second mention of Israel in any extrabiblical source—that in the triumphal inscription of Mesha, king of Moab—is of a similar character. It pronounces the verdict, in the ninth century B.C.E., that "Israel has perished for ever!"[42]

Be that as it may, the reference has a bearing on the issue at hand. The name "Israel" in the stele is marked with the hieroglyphic determinative or special sign that indicates the class of meanings to which the term so marked belongs—in the present case, that of a people. The other names in the poem bear the determinatives for city or land. It can be safely assumed that no Egyptian scribe would have mentioned such a politically insignificant entity as Israel then was, let alone have placed it in Canaan, unless it reflected reality. Moreover, there are four names listed between the synonymous terms Canaan and Hurru, three of which represent the traditional city-state system characteristic of the country. The cities of Ashkelon and Gezer form a pair, both being situated in the south. Yanoam and Israel are similarly paired, the former lying in the north. Hence, "Israel" must also be in the north, or at least in the central highlands. Accordingly, it may be concluded that ca. 1220 B.C.E. the people of Israel was located in Canaan, but had not yet settled down within definable borders. Its presence there was of recent origin, so that the Exodus would have taken place in the course of the thirteenth century B.C.E.

There is one other line of approach that needs to be considered in attempting to ascertain the most likely date for the Exodus of Israel from Egypt. Clearly, the Israelite conquest and settlement of Canaan have a direct bearing on this subject since only forty years intervened between the departure from Goshen and the beginning of Joshua's campaigns in the land itself. The archeological evidence is by no means either conclusive or consistent, but it, too, does seem to favor a thirteenth-century B.C.E. dating.[43]

Excavations have shown that by the end of the Late Bronze Age, which is generally agreed to cover the period ca. 1550 to ca. 1200 B.C.E., the land of Canaan was in an advanced state of decay. Riven by political fragmentation and chronic disunity, debilitated by economic instability, with their military strength greatly weakened by the successive forays of Egyptian kings, the fortified city-states that made up the country were in a parlous condition. Canaanite culture came to an abrupt end in the course of the second half of the thirteenth century. A significant number of city-states, among them Lachish, Bethel, and Hazor, ceased to exist. All the evidence points to violent destruction caused by human agency.

The old Canaanite culture was replaced by a totally different civilization, no longer based on the city-state system, and giving every appearance of being the work of semi-nomads who were in the early stages of sedenterization. The great city of Hazor exemplifies the process. Excavations there leave no doubt that it was suddenly destroyed by a gigantic conflagration sometime in the thirteenth century. By the year

1230 B.C.E. at the latest, new settlers had begun to inhabit part of the mound. The pottery type used thereafter differs radically from that uncovered in the earlier strata of the city.

In the course of the same century at least a dozen Late Bronze Age cities all over Canaan met similar violent destruction and were succeeded by more primitive and poorer villages on the ruined sites. No extrabiblical evidence has so far turned up to identify the invaders and new settlers with Joshua's armies. But the picture reconstructed by archeological research generally fits biblical accounts of the wars of conquest, and there is no convincing reason not to correlate the one with the other.

To sum up: several diverse and variegated lines of evidence converge to make a very good case for placing the events of the Exodus within the thirteenth century B.C.E.

CHAPTER I

The Oppression

EXODUS 1

The newly founded community of Israelites in Egypt prospered at first, and their numbers grew enormously in the course of the years. The divine promises to the patriarchs that their posterity would be numerous were amply fulfilled.[1] The Israelites had become a "great nation." As the text has it, they "were fertile and prolific; they multiplied and increased very greatly, so that the land was filled with them."[2] The term "land" here most likely refers to the area of their settlement, the region of the eastern part of the Nile Delta, not to Egypt as a whole. This population explosion was perceived as a threat and a danger to the security of Egypt, and when a "new king,"[3] most probably the founder of a new dynasty, took over the reins of power, the situation came to a head.

The Hyksos and their expulsion

If the conclusion reached in the preceding chapter about the date of the Exodus be correct, the development of events becomes intelligible, and the historical background can be plausibly reconstructed. For this we have to go back a few centuries to what is called by historians of Egypt the "Second Intermediate Period," which lasted from the eighteenth to the sixteenth centuries B.C.E. This is the era of the Hyksos, the Asiatics who seized power and ruled Egypt for about a century and a half.[4] The name itself means "Rulers of Foreign Lands," and strictly applied only to the chiefs themselves, but it has long been given a more general application.

15

The Hyksos were not organized invaders. They were rather a con-
glomeration of ethnic groups, among whom Semites predominated,
who infiltrated into the land over a long period of time in ever-increasing
numbers, probably coming from Canaan. By ca. 1720 B.C.E. they were
fully in control of the eastern Delta of the Nile and had established
their capital at Avaris.[5] From this base they expanded southward into
Lower Egypt. By ca. 1674 B.C.E. a Hyksos king with the Semitic name
Salitis had occupied Memphis, the ancient capital of Egypt. The Hyksos
constituted the XVth and XVIth Dynasties, adopting the style and bureaucratic institutions of the traditional pharaohs. Gradually, Semites
replaced Egyptians in high administrative office. The rise of Joseph to
power and the migration of the Hebrews fits in well with what is known
of the era of Hyksos rule. The Second Intermediate Period in Egyptian
history is marked by a strong Semitic presence.

The Hyksos never seemed to have dominated Upper Egypt, where a
native family retained control of that part of the country. It comprised
the XVIIth Dynasty and operated out of Thebes, situated some three
hundred thirty miles (four hundred thirty kilometers) upstream from
modern Cairo. This became the focus of opposition to the Hyksos. One
of the last kings of this dynasty, Seqenen-re II, began to organize the
resistance. From the state of his mummy, which showed that he died
at about the age of forty from a series of horrible head wounds, and
from the fact that he received the title "The Brave," it has been assumed
that he fell in battle with the Hyksos. The struggle was continued by
his son, Kamose, who succeeded in driving the Hyksos out of Upper
Egypt and in recovering Memphis. The final and victorious stage in
the liberation of Egypt was accomplished by Amose, brother of Kamose.
He inflicted a crushing defeat on the Hyksos by capturing their capital
of Avaris and driving them back into Canaan. Amose (ca. 1552–1527
B.C.E.) founded the XVIIIth Dynasty of pharaohs, and inaugurated the
New Kingdom, the period of the Egyptian Empire, in the course of
which the country reached the height of its power and magnificence.

The Hyksos occupation was a shameful humiliation for the Egyptians
that had a profound effect upon the national psychology. About one
hundred years after the liquidation of Hyksos rule, Queen Hatshepsut
(ca. 1480–1469 B.C.E.) had carved above the entrance to the rock-cut
temple she built at Speos Artimedos, (Istabl Antar) in Middle Egypt,

an inscription in which she recalled the ruination of the country caused by these Asiatics.[6]

As late as ca. 300 B.C.E., Manetho, an Egyptian priest who wrote a history of his country in Greek, reports, according to the fragment cited by the Jewish historian Josephus (ca. 38–100 C.E.), that the Hyksos "savagely burnt the cities, razed the temples of the gods to the ground, and treated the whole native population with the utmost cruelty, massacring some and carrying off the wives and children into slavery."[7]

Whether or not these sources truly reflect historic reality is uncertain, but they give expression to the sharp and lasting impact that the episode had on the popular mind. Henceforth, Egypt was acutely conscious of the perils lurking in the outside world. The danger of foreign invasion, especially from Asia via the eastern Delta, haunted her thereafter and could never again be smugly ignored or underestimated. The fact is that the Semitic population was not driven out of that region with the expulsion of the Hyksos rulers, and it continued to reside there during the XVIIIth and XIXth Dynasties.

The enslavement of the Israelites

It is against this background that the opening chapter of the Book of Exodus becomes comprehensible. Quite understandable is the anxiety of the new pharaoh about the rapid growth of the Israelite presence in the strategic Delta region: "Look, the Israelite people are much too numerous for us. Let us then deal shrewdly with them, so that they may not increase; otherwise in the event of war they may join our enemies in fighting against us and rise from the ground."[8]

A close reading of the final pages of Genesis uncovers subtle intimations of a deteriorating situation. The domicile of the Israelites in Egypt is not regarded as something permanent. Before he dies, Jacob recalls the divine promise of national territory in Canaan, and foresees the return of his descendants from Egypt to the land:

I am about to die; but God will be with you and bring you back to the land of your fathers.[9]

Most striking is the contrast between the private funeral and interment of Joseph in Egypt and the public state funeral earlier accorded his father, Jacob, and his burial in his ancestral vault at Machpelah in Hebron. Joseph's family did not have the influence with the Egyptian authorities to be able to secure for him a similar privilege. Moreover, Joseph himself seems to have been aware of the gathering storm clouds, for his dying words are:

> God will surely take notice of you and bring you up from this land to the land which He promised on oath to Abraham, to Isaac, and to Jacob. . . . When God has taken notice of you, you shall carry up my bones from here.[10]

If the anxieties of the authorities were understandable in the circumstances, the reaction to the potential menace posed by the presence of a large foreign population in a strategic area can only be described as iniquitous. The pharaoh took draconian measures to limit the growth of the Israelites, and to this end he cunningly devised that adult males be pressed into slavery.

The pharaoh involved is not identified. The term "Pharaoh" itself simply means in Egyptian "The Great House." Originally applied to the royal palace and court, late in the XVIIIth Dynasty it came to be employed by metonymy for the reigning monarch, just as "The Palace" or "The White House" or "City Hall" would be used today.[11] This is how it is employed in the Bible. If the pharaoh in question belonged to the XIXth Dynasty, the new policy of dealing with the Israelites coincides with known events belonging to this period.

The kings of the XVIIIth Dynasty (ca. 1552–1306 B.C.E.) all lived in Upper Egypt and operated out of Memphis or Thebes. Although they campaigned in Canaan and Syria, they wholly neglected the Delta area, apparently begrudging any expenditure on the region that had been the base of the hated Hyksos foreigners. However, toward the end of this period attitudes began to change. Haremhab (ca. 1333–1306 B.C.E.), the last pharaoh of the dynasty, is known to have renovated the temple of the local god Seth in the eastern Delta. The first effective king of the XIXth Dynasty, Sethos (Seti) I (ca. 1305–1290 B.C.E.), built himself a summer palace just north of Avaris that was intended to form the nucleus of a new suburb. His very name expresses an orientation toward the local deity, Seth.[12] In fact, he was descended from an ancient family that had roots in this region, and that had long supplied the

priesthood of that god. This divinity was heartily disliked by the rival
Thebans from whom the previous dynasty had derived.

Rameses II, successor to Sethos I, wholeheartedly shifted the center
of gravity of Egyptian government to the eastern Delta.[13] Not long after
his coronation, he made a ceremonial visit to his father's freshly erected
palace near Avaris, and announced the foundation of a new capital city
to be built around it. A variety of converging motivations occasioned
this step. He wanted to distance himself as much as possible from the
priesthood of the god Amun centered in Thebes. He, himself, worshipped Seth as the chief god, and adopted him as the divine patron
of Egyptian imperial rule in Asia. Further, by transferring the capital
to the Delta, he was able to shorten the lines of communication and
supplies, and to acquire a more convenient strategic base for his campaigns in Canaan and Syria.

The new capital was named after himself, Pi (Per)-Ramesse, "Domain
of Rameses." The first element was often dropped due to the fame of
this monarch, so that the city was known simply as "Rameses" (Raamses).
Its beauty and glory were extolled in poems that have survived to this
day. One such describes it as being "full of food and provisions. . . .
The sun rises in its horizon and sets within it. All men have left their
towns and settled in its territory. . . . The castle which is in it is like
the horizon of heaven." Another text reports it to be "in [very, very]
good condition, a beautiful district, without its like, after the pattern
of Thebes. . . . The Residence is pleasant in life; its field is full of
everything good; it is full of supplies and food every day, its ponds with
fish, and its lakes with birds. Its meadows are verdant with grass; its
banks bear dates; its melons are abundant on the sands. . . . Its granaries
are so full of barley and emmer that they come near to the sky. Onions
and leeks are for food, and lettuce of the garden, pomegranates, apples
and olives, figs of the orchard, sweet wine . . . surpassing honey. . . .
Its ships go out and come back to mooring so that supplies and food
are in it every day. One rejoices to dwell within it. . . ."[14]

This lavish praise bestowed upon the city of Rameses recalls the words
of Genesis 47:5–6,11:

Then Pharaoh said to Joseph, . . . "the land of Egypt is open
before you: settle your father and your brothers in the best part of
the land; let them stay in the region of Goshen." . . . So Joseph

settled his father and his brothers, giving them holdings in the
choicest part of the land of Egypt, in the region of Rameses. . . .

In other words, Rameses II built his capital in the very area of Israelite
settlement.[15] Not only so, but this pharaoh achieved an unrivalled
reputation as a vigorous builder on a prodigious scale. Monumental
structures, numerous obelisks, colossal statues of himself, magnificent
palaces and temples adorned the land of Egypt, and especially the Delta,
in the course of his sixty-six-year rule.

Such vast public projects required an unlimited supply of labor, a
high degree of organization, and the continuous production of abundant
supplies of brick, masonry, and other building materials. The pharaoh
could find a large pool of manpower at hand in the Delta in the Israelite
population, and he proceeded to exploit it to the full.

So they set taskmasters over them to oppress them with forced
labor; and they built garrison cities for Pharaoh: Pithom and
Raamses.[16]

"Raamses" is, of course, none other than the capital city that Rameses
II built for himself, as discussed above. Its precise location in the northeastern Delta is still a matter of dispute.[17] The district of the modern
villages of el-Khata'na and Qantir now seems to house the most likely
sites.[18] Nearby is probably the old Hyksos capital of Avaris.

"Pithom" is Egyptian P(r)'Itm, "House of [the god] Atum," which
is generally identified with modern Tell el-Maskhuta. The earliest inscriptions found here derive from the time of Rameses II and show that
this place was also that known as Tjeku in Egyptian, and is the biblical
Succoth, the first site on the journey of the Israelites out of Egypt, as
mentioned in Exodus 12:37 and 13:20, and Numbers 33:5–6. This city
is known to have been a center of the cult of Atum.

For his vast building program Rameses II preferred to conscript foreigners in the area, rather than native Egyptians. Such was reported by
the Greco-Roman historian Diodorus Siculus (first century B.C.E.), who
apparently relied on trustworthy Egyptian sources.[19] The enslavement
of the Israelites falls into the category that Diodorus describes. It was
not domestic bondage, the type in which an individual becomes the
chattel of a private master and lives in his household, although this

type of slavery is well attested to in Egypt. There is no evidence that the Israelite women were enslaved or that slavery involved the dissolution of the family unit. In fact, one text shows that the Israelites could live next door to or even in the same house as Egyptians, and maintain social relations with them:

> Each woman shall borrow from her neighbor and the lodger in her house objects of silver and gold, and clothing, and you shall put these on your sons and daughters, thus stripping the Egyptians. [20]

What we are dealing with is state slavery, the organized imposition of forced labor upon the male population for long and indefinite terms of service under degrading and brutal conditions. The men so conscripted received no reward for their labors; they enjoyed no civil rights, and their lot was generally much worse than that of a household slave. Organized in large work gangs, they became an anonymous mass, depersonalized, losing all individuality in the eyes of their oppressors. [21]

They were requisitioned for the maintenance of the irrigation ditches, dikes, and canals, having to clean out the mud deposited by the inundation of the Nile. Agriculture in Egypt is not sustained by rainfall, which is too meager for the purpose, but by the annual rise of the Nile, which is literally the lifeline of the country. A ramified network of ditches and canals conducts the Nile waters into the fields. Unless these waterways are constantly kept in proper condition, the fertile soil becomes barren. [22]

The Israelites were also put to work in the fields to be subject to the unending drudgery demanded by the manifold and arduous tasks of agriculture. [23] Several Egyptian texts shed light on the burdens endured by the agricultural worker, on his wretched condition, and on his low status in Egyptian society. [24] A composition known as "The Satire on the Trades" describes the burdens of the vegetable gardener: "Early in the morning he must water the vegetables and in the evening the vines." Of the farmer it is said that he is "wearier than the wayfarer. . . . His sides ache, as if heaven and earth were in them. When he goes forth from the meadows and he reaches his home in the evening, he is as one cut down by traveling." [25] Another wisdom composition warns the young that labor in the fields "is the toughest of all jobs," [26] and the following citation elaborates on the harsh treatment he receives: "the worm has taken half of the food, the hippopotamus the other half; . . . Poor miserable agriculturist: What was left on the threshing-floor thieves made away with. . . . Then the scribe lands on the bank to receive the harvest, his followers carry sticks and the negroes carry palm rods. They say, 'Give us corn'—there is none there. Then they beat him as he lies stretched out and bound on the ground, they throw him into the canal and he sinks down, head under water. His wife is bound before his eyes and his children are put in fetters."[27] A feel for the unremitting toil to which the workmen were subject is gained from this complaint of laborers engaged in loading heavy sacks of corn onto ships: "Are we then to have no rest from the carrying of the corn and the white spelt? The barns are already so full that the heaps of corn overflow, and the boats are already so full of corn that they burst. And yet we are still driven to make haste."[28]

Brickmaking

The building program inaugurated by Rameses II required an inexhaustible supply of bricks. The lives of the Israelites were "embittered with harsh labor at mortar and brick." From another episode it becomes clear that they were required to manufacture the bricks according to fixed daily quotas.[29]

The Egyptians were among the world's most talented and skilled stoneworkers. Temples, pyramids, funerary monuments, gateways, and other imposing structures made abundant use of stone taken from the great quarries that lay on either side of the Nile Valley.[30] But the common building material was the alluvial mud supplied by the Nile River and shaped into bricks by laborers.[31] The brick walls that encircled towns often reached a height of about sixty feet. The ordinary private dwellings and the administrative buildings were mostly constructed of brick. It is readily understandable that the frantic building activity in the region of the eastern Delta called for the organization of a brickmaking industry of unprecedented dimensions. Egyptian papyri and paintings yield a clear picture of the nature of the work and the techniques involved. The industry would be located within easy reach of a plentiful supply of water, usually a pool or canal. Some laborers would do nothing but cart the water back and forth all day long. Others would be employed in the collection of stubble. The artisan who actually molded the bricks would receive from the workers baskets of water-soaked clay mixed with stubble gathered from the fields. He would then shape the material either by hand or in a rectangular wooden mold. The brick would be left to dry in the sun for about three days and then turned over, so that the entire process took just about a week.

Some idea of the immense quantity of bricks used may be gained from studies done on the pyramids of Sesostris III at Dahshur. It is calculated that it took about 24.5 million bricks to construct. A practiced artisan in present-day Egypt, where the same brickmaking technique as employed from time immemorial can still be observed, is capable of turning out about three thousand bricks in the course of a seven- to eight-hour working day. Such a quota imposed on raw slaves would constitute an intolerable burden. Thirteenth-century B.C.E. inscriptions testify to official concern about maintaining the quotas of brick production. A leather scroll from the fifth year of Rameses II tells of forty men who were each assigned a quota of two thousand bricks, making a total supply of eighty thousand. The text shows that the target was rarely reached by any of them.

Something of the hardships experienced by the brickmaker may be perceived from an inscription accompanying wall paintings from the days of Thutmosis III (ca. 1490–1436 B.C.E.). It depicts, among various scenes of building construction, Asiatics making and laying bricks, and it bears the ominous line from the mouth of a taskmaster, "The rod is in my hand, do not be idle." The afore-cited "Satire on the Trades" has this to say of the brickmaker and the builder: "He is dirtier than vines or pigs from treading under his mud. His clothes are stiff with clay; his leather belt is going to ruin. Entering into the wind, he is miserable. . . . His sides ache, since he must be outside in a treacherous wind. . . . His arms are destroyed with technical work. . . . What he eats is the bread of his fingers, and he washes himself only once a season. He is simply wretched through and through. . . ."[32]

The nefarious scheme of the pharaoh to reduce the male Israelite population through state-imposed enslavement, and its subjection to degrading, exhausting, and backbreaking toil, did not yield the expected results: "But the more they were oppressed, the more they increased and spread out. . . ."[33] Accordingly, the king resorted to more barbarous measures. In order to achieve immediate and certain regulation of the population, he decreed the murder of all new-born Israelite males. The obligation to commit this infanticide was thrust upon the midwives.[34]

The midwives

Midwifery in Egypt was one of the few professions open to women. Its practitioners seem to have been held in esteem, for a popular tale about magicians has three important goddesses practicing the craft on a certain occasion.[35] It must have been a regular institution in Israel to judge by the matter-of-fact way in which the presence of the midwife is mentioned not only here, but also in connection with the birth of Benjamin to Rachel in Genesis 35:17, and of the twins to Tamar in Genesis 38:28. There is no record in the Bible of a male assisting at confinements. From the fore-mentioned Egyptian legend and from Ezekiel 16:4 and other biblical passages, it would appear that in addition to attending the mother at the time of parturition, it was the function of the midwife to cut the umbilical cord, to wash the baby in water, to rub its skin with salt, and to swaddle it. In the case of twins, she had to testify as to which was the firstborn.[36]

The English text in Exodus 1:16 refers to the "birthstool." The exact meaning of the Hebrew *ovnayim* is unclear. The word literally translates "the two stones." Some scholars take the word as a euphemism for the genitals,[37] a glance at which would at once enable the midwife to determine the sex of the baby, and to act in accordance with the pharaoh's decree. The more usual understanding is as an allusion to the custom of women experiencing parturition in a crouching or sitting position. Such a posture is clearly mentioned in 1 Samuel 4:19, " . . . she was seized with labor pains, and she crouched down and gave birth." The birthstool would then be that on which the mother sat during delivery in order to ease the access of the midwife, who sat facing her, to the baby as it emerged from the uterus, while at the same time facilitating passage through the maternal birth canal. The Egyptian hieroglyphic sign for birth was a woman in a kneeling position. One hymn to a goddess reads, "I sat upon bricks like the woman in labor."[38] A similar custom is attested to in Mesopotamian society.[39]

In issuing his decree to the midwives, the king obviously relied upon the ease with which the baby could be killed at the moment of delivery by means not easily detectable in those days. What is not clear is whether these midwives were Israelite or Egyptian women, for the Hebrew text can yield the renderings "Hebrew midwives" and "midwives of the Hebrew women."[40] It would have been strange for the king to have expected the Israelites to kill the males of their own people. Another oddity is that only two midwives are mentioned for such a large population. Either they were the overseers of the practitioners, and were directly responsible to the authorities for the women under them, or the two names, Shiphrah and Puah, are those of guilds or teams of midwives called after the original founders of the order.[41] At any rate, the names are Semitic. Shiphrah is derived from a verbal stem meaning "to be beautiful," and appears in a list of slaves belonging to an Egyptian household.[42] She is marked as being an Asiatic. Puah is the name of the daughter of the hero Danel in Ugaritic literature, and simply means "a girl," apparently originally being a term for a fragrant blossom.[43]

What is remarkable is that the names of these lowly women are recorded whereas, by contrast, the all-powerful reigning monarch is consistently veiled in anonymity. In this way the biblical narrator expresses his scale of values. All the power of the mighty pharaoh, the outward magnificence of his realm, the dazzling splendor of his court, his colossal monuments—all are illusory, ephemeral, and in the ultimate reckoning, insignificant, and they must crumble into dust because they rest on foundations empty of moral content. Seven times in this brief episode the term "midwife" is repeated, an index of the importance that Scripture places upon the actions of the women in their defiance of tyranny and in their upholding of moral principles.

The midwives, fearing God, did not do as the king of Egypt had told them; they let the boys live.[44]

Here we have history's first recorded case of civil disobedience in defense of a moral cause.[45] Be it noted that the motivation of these women in defying the promulgated law of the sovereign is given as "fear of God." This term is frequently cited in biblical texts in relation to situations that involve norms of moral or ethical behavior. It will be recalled that in Genesis 20:11 Abraham justified the tactic he adopted, of passing off his wife as his sister in order to save his life, on the grounds that the local citizenry was not thought to possess "fear of God," and would not therefore have any restraint on committing murder. Joseph sought to convince his brothers of his integrity by appealing to his own "fear of God."[46] In Leviticus 19:14, 32, one is exhorted not to insult the deaf or place a stumbling block before the blind, to rise before the aged and to show them deference—all out of "fear of God." The Amalekites could commit unprovoked aggression against the peaceful Israelites who had just escaped from Egyptian bondage because "they had no fear of God."[47] Job was a perfectly righteous man who eschewed evil precisely because he did "fear God."[48] In short, the consciousness of the existence of a Higher Power who makes moral demands on human beings constitutes the ultimate restraint on evil and the supreme incentive for good.

Faced with an irreconcilable conflict between obedience to the sovereign's depraved law and allegiance to the higher moral law of God, the midwives chose in favor of the transcendent imperative of morality. Their noncompliance with the law, however, was not publicly announced but privately effected on obvious prudential grounds. They could not disclose the truth in response to the pharaoh's interrogation because had they done so, the predictable consequence would have been their removal from a situation in which they could be enabled to save lives.

Thwarted once again in his evil designs, the pharaoh now enlists "all his people," the entire apparatus of the state, in a national effort systematically to annihilate the people of Israel. All new-born males are to be drowned in the River Nile,[49] a decree that is ultimately to turn out as tinged with irony, for the very agency of destruction that he has chosen—water—is eventually to become the instrument of his own punishment.

CHAPTER II

The Birth and Youth of Moses

EXODUS 2

Curiously, the events narrated in the preceding chapter are laid out in the Bible in a very natural manner. Apart from His rewarding the virtuous midwives—in what way remains unclear—God is not said to have intervened. No divine causality is specified. Nevertheless, no reader of the text is left in doubt that the developments described represent, as it were, a contest between God and the pharaoh, in which the human king is worsted on each occasion. The pharaoh "deals shrewdly" in order to curb the fertility of the Israelite community, but his nefarious efforts prove to be wholly ineffectual. The outcome is actually and mysteriously quite the opposite of what is expected. With transparent clarity, the impression is compellingly conveyed, although not articulated, that behind the complex of events seemingly unfolding in a secular and serendipitous way, there is at work the divine will controlling and directing human affairs.[1] Nowhere is this more discernible than in the recounting of the birth and exposure of Moses to the River Nile.

This towering personality, preeminent in the entire cast of biblical characters, appears upon the scene of history unaccompanied by any supernatural phenomena. Unlike, for instance, the cases of Isaac, Jacob, and Samson,[2] there is no prior birth announcement for him who is to be the redeemer of Israel, architect of its religion, consummate political leader, lawgiver, and archetypal prophet.

The birth of Moses

The facts are simple enough. A Levite family has a son. Because of
the pharaoh's decree, the infant is hidden away for three months, but
the situation becomes intolerable and the mother fashions a wicker
basket, caulks it with bitumen and pitch, and places the baby therein
among the bulrushes at the Nile's edge. His sister stands nearby to keep
watch. The pharaoh's daughter happens to come by, notices the basket,
and has it fetched. When opened, it was seen to contain a crying baby,
which the princess recognized at once to be an abandoned Hebrew
child. At that moment the sister approaches and offers to bring a Hebrew
nurse, to which the princess readily agrees. Thereupon the pharaoh's
daughter unwittingly hires the infant's own mother as a wet nurse.
When the child is weaned he is delivered to the princess, who adopts
him and names him Moses.[3]

This simple narrative is spiced with conscious irony directed against
the king. The course of history hinges upon a single event—the rescue
of Moses—and it was brought about by the daughter of the very tyrant
who decreed Israel's extinction! To add to the effect, Moses' natural
mother is actually paid by the palace to rear her own child! In the end,
the Egyptians bestowed their bounty upon the departing Israelites.[4]

Aside from the irony, there are stylistic features that are meant to
arouse immediate associations that disclose a certain understanding of
events. We are told that Moses' mother "saw that he was good (*tov*)."[5]
This phrase is usually taken to mean that he was "a goodly/fine/hand-
some child." Literally, the Hebrew simply translates "She saw him that
he was good." Now this statement recalls a key phrase in the Genesis
creation story—"God saw that it was good"—occurring there seven
times,[6] and one wonders whether, by repeating it here, there is not a
deliberate attempt to stir an echo of that chapter, to inform us that the
birth of Moses is another Genesis, an event of cosmic significance.
What is more, the "wicker basket" in which the baby is placed is called
in the Hebrew, *tevah*. This noun is used again in the Hebrew Bible
only in the story of Noah and nowhere else, and it is employed in that
context because it is an ark, not a sailing vessel; that is to say, like
Noah's ark, our *tevah* is the instrument of salvation in the perilous
waters, though it possesses neither steerage gear nor steersman, being
wholly dependent upon God's benevolent protection for its safety.[7]

The material of which the ark was made is called *gome'*, a word that may well be of Egyptian derivation, and that refers to the papyrus plants. [8] Papyrus belongs to the sedge family, and its technical botanical name is *Cyperus papyrus*. Practically extinct today, it once abounded in the marshlands of the Nile Delta. The papyrus plant was used by the Egyptians for a variety of purposes, the most famous, of course, being writing material. Its huge stems, often more than ten feet high, served as raw material for sandals, cordage, and especially for the construction of light, swift boats. This last function is mentioned in Isaiah 18:2 and Job 9:20. [9]

The container that held the infant Moses was placed among the "reeds," in Hebrew *suf*, a term borrowed from the Egyptian for "papyrus/reed thicket." The idea of the mother was to make sure that the infant would not be carried downstream. It may well be that the rare word *suf* has been selected in the present text because it is allusive, prefiguring Israel's deliverance at the Sea of Reeds (Hebrew: *yam suf*).

The motif of the abandoned hero

The account of the birth of Moses as told in Exodus has often been compared to a well-known class of legends that has as its subject the birth of a national hero and in which the motif of the abandoned child repeatedly recurs. These legends concern both mythology and folklore. Heracles (Hercules) was abandoned by his mother Alcmene; Oedipus, who became king of Thebes, was exposed on a mountain; Romulus and Remus, the legendary founders of Rome, were put in a chest and cast into the Tiber; Cyrus, founder of the Persian Empire, was ordered by his royal grandfather to be left to die on a mountain. The examples could be multiplied; the motif appears in quite unrelated cultures. [10] What has most attracted the attention of biblical scholars is the Mesopotamian version known today as "The Legend of Sargon." [11] He was the third-millennium B.C.E. king who established the first Semitic dynasty based at the city of Akkad, and who founded the first of the great empires of the world. This text purports to be Sargon's autobiographical account in which he ascribes to himself a mysterious origin, according to the preserved portion of the inscription. More likely it was the work of later scribes. The relevant section of the text reads as follows:

Sargon, the mighty king, king of Agade, am I.
My mother was a high priestess, my father I knew not.
The brother(s) of my father loved the hills.
My city is Azupiranu, which is situated on the banks of the Euphrates.
My mother, the high priestess, conceived; in secret she bore me.
She set me in a basket of rushes, with bitumen she sealed my lid.
She cast me into the river which rose not over me.
The river bore me up and carried me to Akki, the drawer of water.
Akki, the drawer of water, lifted me out as he dipped his ewer.
Akki, the drawer of water, took me as his son and reared me.
Akki, the drawer of water, appointed me as his gardener.
While I was a gardener, Ishtar granted me her love,
And for four and . . . years I exercised kingship. [12]

The supposed close affinities between this folkloristic composition and our Exodus narrative are fanciful. [13] In fact, the story of Moses' birth departs from "The Legend of Sargon" and from the genre in general in so many significant respects that one almost gets the impression of a conscious attempt on the part of the biblical narrator to dissociate this narrative from the features otherwise characteristic of the foundling hero motif.

In the first place, Sargon is exposed to the river because he is the unwanted child of an illicit relationship. His mother belongs to a class of priestesses that is supposed to live in chastity, and is forbidden to bear children. [14] She therefore needs to conceal the birth and to dispose of the baby as quickly as possible in order to avoid the shame and disgrace that would be her lot should her offense be uncovered. Moses, by contrast, is the legitimate offspring of a lawful marriage, and his mother tries to keep him as long as possible. She places him by the river as an act of desperation, and this she does with tender loving care—such is the force of the Hebrew verb sim, "to place," used of her action, as opposed to the verb hishlikh, "to abandon," used by the pharaoh. [15] She takes every precaution to ensure his safety and to keep track of his fate.

Another striking distinction lies in the identity of the one who chances upon the foundling. In Exodus the discoverer is a princess, whereas in the Sargon folktale, and generally in this genre of literature, the finder is a person of low social status, or even an animal. Furthermore, the origin of the child is usually unknown, and only later in life is it revealed through detection or recognition on the part of a third person. In Moses' case there is no identity problem. Even the princess recognizes at once that this is a child of Hebrew origin.[16] Then there is the fact that in the story of Moses it is his own mother who nurses him, a circumstance quite alien to the foundling type of story. Finally, attention must be paid to the function of the Sargon and similar legends. Usually the child is the son of distinguished parents, often royalty, and when he ultimately achieves rank and honor it constitutes recognition and confirmation of his true and rightfully deserved status. Not so in the Exodus account. Here the parents of Moses are ordinary folk, albeit Levites, and the son stakes out no claim for himself. The narrative does not serve the political purpose, as it does in the case of Sargon, of legitimating the usurper who has no royal genealogy. Sargon's name, in fact, in Akkadian is *sharru-ken*, which means "the king is legitimate," that is, "the legitimate king."

The role of women

An interesting feature of the Exodus narrative is the favorable light in which the daughter of the wicked pharaoh is portrayed. Her name is not given. If her father was indeed Rameses II, she would have been one of his fifty-nine daughters![17] Her motive for saving the crying baby is sincere and honorable; she is actuated by pity. Indeed, the story is remarkable for the prominent, fateful, and generally noble role played by women—the midwives, the mother, the sister, the Egyptian princess, and soon, Jethro's daughters.

It should not be considered strange that the king's daughter conducts the negotiations and concludes the transaction regarding the care of the infant entirely by herself, without the assistance of husband or other male. The social and legal position of the woman in Egypt was relatively high. Descent was strictly matrilineal, so that property descended through the female line. This meant that the woman possessed inheritance rights and could dispose of property at will. As a result, she enjoyed a certain measure of economic independence.[18]

The particular arrangements that the princess made for the nursing and rearing of the child follow a pattern found in Mesopotamian legal texts that relate to the adoption of a foundling.[19] These "wet-nurse contracts," as they are now called, provide for payment for the services of suckling and rearing the infant in the home of the wet nurse for a specified period, usually two to three years. Following the weaning, the child is returned to the finder, who then adopts it. This deferring of the adoption until after the weaning is probably to be explained by the high infant mortality rate. The Laws of Hammurabi, §194, make provision for just such a contingency—that the baby might die when in the care of a wet nurse—so it could not have been a rare occurrence. The documents dealing with these contracts derive from Mesopotamia, not Egypt. It is probable, though not certain, that there was a common practice in such matters throughout the Near East.

The name "Moses"

The princess named the child "Moses" following her formal adoption of him. She explained, "I drew him out of the water."[20] As is frequently the case in the Bible when names are given an etymological explanation, what we really have is word-play. In the present case, the pharaoh's daughter obviously bestowed an Egyptian name on the child, which has been artfully interpreted as a Hebrew word from the stem m-sh-h, "to draw out (from the water)," itself exceedingly rare in biblical vocabulary.[21] The meaning of the name as a Hebrew verb is "the one who draws out," an active form, whereas a passive, "the one who was drawn out" (Hebrew: mashui), would be expected. We may surmise that once again the narrative is subtly pointing to Moses' destiny as the one who safely led Israel to freedom across the Reed Sea.[22] In actual fact, the name that the princess conferred upon the child is of Egyptian origin.[23] It has as its base the verb msy, "to be born," or the noun ms, "a child, son," frequent elements in Egyptian personal names, usually with the addition of a divine element. Examples are Ah-mose, Ra-mose, Ptah-mose, Thot-mose—in each case meaning "The (god) X is born." Names such as these would be given to babies born on the anniversary of the god's birthday according to the local mythology. Sometimes the second element alone appears as an abbreviated name. A papyrus from the Rameside era records a grievance against a vizier that is lodged before a certain "Mose" who was powerful enough to depose the vizier.[24] Another inscription from the time of the XIXth

Dynasty deals with a court proceeding concerned with land ownership in which the plaintiff's name is Mose.[25] In light of these facts, it is quite clear that the king's daughter gave the Hebrew child an Egyptian name, which the biblical narrator has reinterpreted in terms of a Hebrew verb, thereby hinting scornfully that the pharaoh's own daughter unwittingly has rescued the one who will eventually deliver his people from her father's oppression. She has given him a name that foreshadows his destiny.

Moses' upbringing

The narrative is silent on the years Moses spent in the palace, which is where he undoubtedly passed the formative period of his life. Like the other privileged boys in royal court and bureaucratic circles in Egypt, he would have commenced his education at the age of four, attending school from early in the morning until noonday for about twelve years. Discipline is known to have been exceedingly strict, with corporal punishment the chief means of its enforcement. One notable proverb frames the educational theory thus: "The ears of a boy are on his back; he hears when he is beaten." The school curriculum largely centered on reading, writing, and arithmetic, the second of these subjects receiving special emphasis. The art of penmanship and the cultivation of style were both highly esteemed as the indispensable prerequisites for a sound education. Drill and memorization seem to have been the chief pedagogic techniques.[26]

As far as Moses is concerned, the likelihood of his having received such a conventional education as was achieved by the sons of the privileged is enhanced by the substantial evidence from the period of the Ramesides for the presence of foreigners, especially of Semites, in the royal schools.[27] Notwithstanding the knowledge and the skills that Moses acquired as the adopted son of the Egyptian princess, one thing is certain: it was the values and the beliefs of his parental home that remained paramount in his life. He was seized with the consciousness of his Israelite identity: " . . . when Moses had grown up, he went out to his kinsfolk and witnessed their labors."[28]

Three incidents in his life that occurred while he was still attached to the palace are given prominence in the narrative because they reveal aspects of his character and disclose his commitments. Having "witnessed the labors of his kinsfolk" and become sensitive to their sufferings, he cannot tolerate the sight of an Egyptian beating a Hebrew. This outrage against decency and human dignity spontaneously arouses in him feelings of anger and resentment. He strikes down the oppressor and buries him in the sand.[29] By this act, Moses has decisively thrown in his lot with his suffering people and has psychologically severed his ties to his aristocratic and privileged Egyptian past. His instinctive indignation at the maltreatment of his brethren has effectively overcome his self-interest.

The narrative does not relate to the moral questions that may be raised concerning Moses' fatal blow against the Egyptian oppressor, because the function of the story in the present context is to illustrate prime qualities of Moses' character and personality—his intolerance of oppression and his wholehearted identification with the plight of his people. In any case, the facts are too meager to permit any valid moral judgment. For instance, we do not know whether the Egyptian seemed to be actually beating his victim to death, in which case Moses' intervention was in accordance with the elementary human duty of going to the aid of one whose life is in peril. Significantly, the same Hebrew verb, *hikkah*, "to strike," is used for the action of the tormentor as for the reaction of Moses. Certainly the story does not lend itself to any interpretation that seeks to find in the incident a justification for the use of violence as an instrument to achieve what may be viewed as a desirable end. There is no ideology of protest at work in the story, and Moses is not praised for his deed. There is only a tale about an isolated event, an impetuous and spontaneous outpouring of righteous indignation in response to a specific situation. The counter-assault was directed against the perpetrator of the atrocity, not indiscriminately aimed against anyone who is perceived to be a symbol of the coercive power of the state.[30]

In the second incident,[31] Moses encounters two Israelites who are quarreling, one of whom raises his hand against his fellow. Moses remonstrates with the bully, once again evincing instinctive sympathy for the underdog. However, from the assailant's retort it becomes clear that the story of Moses' attack on the Egyptian is common knowledge. He is now a wanted man, condemned to death by the authorities, and he flees for his life into the wilderness to take refuge in the territory of the Midianites. There he sits down by a well. Wells in the Near East often served as meeting places for shepherds, wayfarers, and townsfolk, and it was natural for a newcomer to gravitate toward them. Abraham's servant had gone straight to the well on arriving at Haran, and Jacob did the same thing at the end of his flight from his brother, Esau, to his Uncle Laban.[32]

Here at the well, Moses experiences the third test of his character. He witnesses rough local shepherds pushing aside a group of girls who were first in line to draw water. Once again he cannot remain indifferent. His spirit rebels against the abuse of the weak by the strong. He cannot tolerate this blatant infringement of the girls' rights, and he immediately rises to their defense, driving off the offending shepherds, and himself watering the girls' flock. Their father, described as "the priest of Midian," invites the rescuer home, and Moses ends up marrying one of his daughters.[33]

The Midianites

The Midianites among whom Moses took refuge were actually a confederation of semi-nomadic tribes, basically five in number.[34] They ranged over a very wide area of the Near East stretching from the eastern shore of the Gulf of Aqaba, up through the Syro-Arabian Desert, and into the border areas of the land of Israel, west and northwest of Elath.[35] The route that Moses took in his flight is illustrated by the story of Hadad the Edomite, who in the days of King Solomon fled in the opposite direction, from across the Jordan to Egypt by way of Midian and Paran, as told in 1 Kings 11:17–18.

The friendly relations between Israel and the Midianites that are reflected in the story of Moses are consonant with the account in Genesis 25:2 that traces the lineage of Midian back to Abraham. They also accord with the later report in Exodus Chapter 18 of Midianite influence upon the organization of the Israelite judiciary system. This amicable situation must be both authentic and quite early because toward the end of the period of the wilderness wanderings, and during the period of the Judges, relations between Israel and Midian were thoroughly hostile.[36] No one, therefore, would likely have invented such stories depicting the Midianites in so favorable a light with very close kinship ties to Israel.

Jethro

Moses' father-in-law is here called Reuel, which means "friend of God." In Exodus Chapter 3, as well as in Chapter 18, this same person is called Jethro, shortened to Jether in Exodus 4:18. To compound the difficulty, he is also named "Hobab son of Reuel the Midianite" in Numbers 10:29, and simply Hobab in Judges 4:11, where he is designated a "Kenite," not a "Midianite." This conforms to Judges 1:16, which refers to the descendants of "the Kenite, father-in-law of Moses." How is all this bewildering variety to be sorted out?

One solution that has been widely accepted in modern times is that we are dealing with different strands of tradition. Another is to understand the phrase "they returned to their father Reuel," found in our narrative,[37] as referring to their grandfather. There is plenty of evidence for the use of "father" and "son" for more remote relationships. For instance, although Laban, uncle of Jacob, was the grandson of Nahor, he is called "son of Nahor." [38] Similarly, in Genesis 46:18, "the sons of Zilpah" number sixteen, but fourteen of them are grandchildren and great-grandchildren. In like manner, Reuel, in our text, could well be the grandfather of the seven girls. This leaves Moses' father-in-law with two names, Jethro and Hobab. It is only with the first of the two that he is designated "the priest of Midian."[39] It is possible, therefore, that "Jethro" was his official priestly title, not a personal name. In fact, the word might mean "His excellency."[40]

As to his being a "Kenite," 1 Samuel 15:6 has preserved a tradition of friendship between the Kenites and the Israelites at the time of the Exodus.[41] In corroboration of a connection between that tribe and the Midianites, one may cite the story of the seer Balaam who was hired by Moabites and Midianites to curse the Israelites in the wilderness. From their territory he was able to observe the Kenites who were nearby.[42] Finally, the name Kenite is actually not an ethnic designation, but signifies the occupation of metal-worker. One is reminded of Tubal-Cain in Genesis 4:22, "who forged all implements of copper and iron." In short, the Kenites were most likely a nomadic clan that specialized in metal-working and that was affiliated with the Midianites in the period of Moses. In the days of Saul they were associated with the Amalekites, but the history of their early agreeable relations with Israel was well preserved. Moses' father-in-law, if he were a member of the Kenite clan, might also be described as a Midianite.

The text tells us that there among the Midianites, a son was born to Moses whom he called Gershom.[43] Various levels of associative meaning blend in this name. Its true etymology is to be sought in the Hebrew stem *g-r-sh*, "to drive off/out," a verb that is at once redolent of the incident with the shepherds who "drove away the girls" and that led to Moses' finding a wife.[44] By the folk etymology given in the story, it also evokes Moses' unhappy personal situation as a fugitive and a man without a country. Finally, the name presages divine promises of Israel's redemption, for this verb is three times employed in Exodus in such contexts to express the breaking of the pharaoh's obduracy. Thus in Exodus 6:1 God assures Moses that the Egyptian king would eventually "drive them from his land," and again in Exodus 11:1 He pledges that the arrogant monarch "will drive you out of here one and all." When the Exodus finally occurs, the text confirms that the Israelites indeed "had been driven out of Egypt."[45]

At this point our attention is once again directed to the wretched condition of the Israelites back in Egypt. After a considerable interval of time, the king of Egypt died.[46] If the change in regime had raised Israelite expectations of relief in their oppression, these were soon dashed. But apparently, as was often the case, when a new king ascended the throne, general amnesty for offenders was granted so that the conditions were ripe for Moses to be able to return to Egypt.

Events are now about to take a dramatic turn. As we have noted earlier, the narrator conveys an impression of a purely temporal succession of events even as he implicitly and subtly communicates a pervasive causation of the divine will. Now the hidden power of God is about to become manifest in the narrative; the silence of God is about to be broken. In their abject misery the people "cried out; and their cry for help from the bondage rose up to God. God heard their moaning, and God remembered His covenant with Abraham and Isaac and Jacob. God looked upon the Israelites, and God took notice of them."[47] The scene is set for the call to Moses.

CHAPTER III

The Commissioning of Moses

EXODUS 3–4

Of Moses' life in Midian, the vicissitudes of time and chance that befell him there, nothing is known except that the urbane Israelite, reared in the royal palace, pursued the shepherd's life just as his ancestors had done. One day in the wilderness, while driving the flock he came to a place called Horeb where there was a mountain, which the text designates "the mountain of God."[1]

Horeb, a word that means "desolate/waste land" in Hebrew, seems to be interchangeable with Sinai. At least no geographic differentiation between the two is discoverable from the texts. It is not uncommon for geographic sites to be referred to by more than one name. In Merneptah's stele, Egypt is referred to under two names: Kemit and Tameri, and Memphis under five different names, while in the prologue to the laws of Hammurabi, the city of Nippur is called Nippur-Duranki (the second element is the ancient Sumerian name for the same city).[2] Hence, Horeb and Sinai may be identical. Alternatively, Horeb may refer to the wilderness region and Sinai to the mountain itself, or vice versa, or Horeb may be a range and Sinai a particular peak within it. The location of the mount cannot be settled with certainty because no early traditions about it have survived, and the folklore that places it where St. Catherine's Monastery is situated is very late, being post Christian, and of little historical value. Clearly, the identification of Horeb/Sinai will depend upon fixing the route of the Exodus, a subject that will be dealt with later.

The epithet "mountain of God" in the present story would, at first glance, imply some prior history of its sanctity, but the narrative shows that Moses knows nothing about this, nor does the Bible afford any information to confirm it. More likely the designation resulted from the divine self-manifestation to Moses that is about to occur or from the great national experience at Sinai following the Exodus. Its use here would be proleptic, that is, anticipating the later event.[3]

The Burning Bush

While alone with his sheep in this desolate wilderness, Moses suddenly beheld an awesome spectacle that defied nature's laws and all human experience. A bush was all aflame yet remained intact, unaffected by the fire.[4] The Hebrew word for bush employed here, s'neh, appears only once more in the Bible, in Deuteronomy 33:16, in an epithet of God who is referred to as "the Presence in the Bush," an unmistakable echo of the present episode. The term seems to have been deliberately selected as word-play on Sinai, an augur of things to come. The bush is most likely the prickly type known as Rubus sanctus,[5] that grows about a yard high beside wadis and in humid soil, and has flowers that resemble small roses and fruit like the raspberry that turns black when it has ripened. The remarkable phenomenon of the bush on fire, yet unconsumed, arouses Moses' curiosity. He approaches to examine it more closely, whereupon he hears a voice issuing from this marvel twice calling his name. Moses responds, "Here I am." At this, he is told to approach no further and to remove his shoes because the site is holy ground.

The "shoes" mentioned here are most likely sandals, which would have been manufactured either from woven papyrus strips or from a single piece of leather cut to the shape of the foot and secured to the leg by straps. In Egypt and the Land of Israel, the common folk generally went about barefoot. A person of means would wear sandals outdoors.[6] In the present scene, it is not clear whether Moses did so after the manner of the Egyptian aristocrat or because the life of the shepherd necessitates the provision of protection from the rugged state of the land and the rigors of the climate. Either way, the sandals accumulated dust and dirt, and were therefore removed before entering the house.[7] For the same reason, it was not considered proper or respectful to come into a sacred place without first casting off one's footgear. To this day,

Muslims follow this practice before entering a mosque. It might be added that Egyptian custom required going barefoot in the presence of a superior, especially the king.[8] Connected with this idea may be the Israelite practice of having the priests perform their sacred duties in the Temple barefoot. At least no mention of footwear is included in the laws concerning the proper attire of the officiating priest.[9]

The site of the bush is described as being "holy ground." As has been noted, Moses knows nothing at all about the sanctity of the environs of the bush that he sees. His amazement at the spectacle, his lack of compunction about approaching it, and about doing so without removing his sandals, all prove his complete ignorance of any special holiness attaching to the place hitherto. This situation is paralleled in Joshua 5:15 where Joshua is suddenly confronted by a "captain of the Lord's host" who tells him, "Remove your sandals from your feet, for the place where you stand is holy." In both incidents the holiness derives solely from the immediacy of the Divine Presence and does not outlast the experience. Significantly, Moses conducts no cultic exercise there, and the site does not become a place of pilgrimage.

The underlying concept of holiness presupposed in these two accounts represents a radical break with accepted pagan notions. In the world of paganism, the holy is such by virtue of the intrinsic "natural" mysterious quality of the object or place that is so revered. In Israelite monotheism, with its fundamental insistence on a God who is outside of and wholly apart from nature, who created nature and who is sovereign over it, there is no room for any possibility of an independent, immutable, and inherent holiness. That which is holy, be it temporal or spatial, possesses that quality solely by divine will.[10] It is no coincidence that in Israel the holiness of a place lies in historic experience, not in mythological justification. The site of the Temple at Jerusalem, the holiest place in the history of Israel, acquired that character only after David's purchase of the land on which it stood and the stationing there of the Ark, and following Solomon's construction and dedication of the Sanctuary at that place, with divine approval. It played no prior role in the cultic or spiritual life of the people, and no "natural" sanctity adhered to it. The polar contrast between Israelite and pagan concepts is vividly illustrated by the fact that the Mesopotamian "creation epic" known as *Enuma elish* closes with the building of a temple to the god Marduk, that is, with the sanctification of space.[11] In the Scriptural creation story, it is the sanctity of time—the Sabbath—that is first celebrated.[12] The sanctity of space appears explicitly for the first time here in Exodus, and it is a one-time phenomenon, the duration of which is limited to the period of the revelatory experience itself.

The pictorial detail of the scene of the Burning Bush has been understood in two different ways. Most commentators see in the fire that is self-sufficient, self-perpetuating, and wholly unaffected by its environment, a symbol of the transcendent, awesome, and unapproachable Divine Presence. The Scriptures afford ample justification for this interpretation. In the "Covenant between the Pieces" in Genesis 15:17, God is represented by "a flaming torch." In the Exodus and wilderness wanderings traditions He is symbolized by a "pillar of fire."[13] The prophet Ezekiel, in his opening visions of the celestial chariot, also depicts the Divine Presence in the symbol of fire.[14]

The persuasiveness of the suggestion is further enhanced by the prominence given to the symbol of fire in the descriptions of the great national theophany—the divine self-revelation at Sinai. There, in Exodus 19:18, the Lord is said to have come down upon Mount Sinai "in fire," and the imagery is even more explicit in Exodus 24:17: "Now the Presence of the Lord appeared in the sight of the Israelites as a consuming fire on the top of the mountain." In Deuteronomy 4:11–12 the theophany is described as follows:

> The mountain was ablaze with flames to the very skies, dark with densest clouds. The Lord spoke to you out of the fire; you heard the sound of words but perceived no shape—nothing but a voice.[15]

Another line of interpretation sees in the lowly bush a symbol of the pathetic state of the people of Israel in Egyptian bondage while the fire represents the forces of persecution. Just as the bush remains unconsumed, so Israel will not be crushed by its tormentors. This rendering by no means excludes the other, for the biblical text can simultaneously accommodate multiple levels of meaning.[16]

Overcome with irresistible fascination at the astonishing scene, yet now profoundly sensible of the divine potency with which the place is charged, Moses' attention shifts from the visual to the aural. The sight of the Burning Bush fades away and is mentioned not again. Its place is taken by the Divine Voice. Here, too, a transformation takes place. The imperious Voice, commanding and admonishing, gives way to softer tones of pathos, concern, and tidings of liberation.

The "God of the Father(s)"

The opening words of the divine address are: "I am the God of your father, the God of Abraham, the God of Isaac, and the God of Jacob."[17] This self-characterization must have been particularly meaningful to Moses, the Israelite who had been brought up in the Egyptian royal palace, yet who had identified with his people's sufferings, who was now a fugitive in Midian and had married the daughter of the high priest of that land, and who seemingly had lost all contact with his family and his people. The mention of his father and his forebears must have had a stunning effect on Moses, jolting him into renewed consciousness of his Israelite heritage and into the sudden realization of his true and inescapable identity. At the same time, by recalling the three Patriarchs, God implicitly evokes the promises of redemption He had made to them.

The stylistic formulation of the divine self-identification is also of historical import. The introductory phrase "I am . . ." is characteristic of the communications with the Patriarchs, as well as of many royal inscriptions and divine declarations generally in the ancient Near East. In the "Covenant between the Pieces" in Genesis 15:7, God commences His self-disclosure with "I am the Lord who brought you out from Ur of the Chaldeans," and later He says: "I am El Shaddai" ("God Almighty").[18] This latter statement is also found in a theophany to Jacob in Genesis 35:11. Isaac, too, was addressed in a similar manner: "I am the God of your father Abraham." [19] At the great vision experienced by Jacob at Bethel, as described in Genesis 28:13, God begins with "I am the Lord, the God of your father Abraham and the God of Isaac. . . ." When that Patriarch paused to worship at Beer-sheba on his way to Egypt, God responded with the selfsame identification: "I am God, the God of your father."[20] The Ten Commandments, it will be remembered, likewise begin in this manner: "I the Lord am your God. . . ."[21]

Moses himself is once again to experience this "I am . . ." statement in God's self-manifestation in the land of Egypt.[22]

This mode of introducing a solemn declaration is an example of the divine "speaking in human language."[23] It has its source in the conventional rhetoric of royal proclamations in the northwest Semitic area of the ancient Near East, of which there are numerous examples. A celebrated ninth-century B.C.E. inscription from the land of Moab across the Jordan opens with "I am Mesha, son of Kemosh[yat] King of Moab."[24] A series of royal inscriptions in the Phoenician language ranging from that of Kilamuwa in the second half of the ninth century B.C.E.[25] to Azitawadda of Adana a century later,[26] to the sepulchral admonition of Tabnith of Sidon at the end of the sixth century B.C.E.,[27] and the votive text of Yehawmilk of Byblos in the fifth or fourth century B.C.E.[28]—all commence with the "I am . . ." formula. The eighth-century B.C.E. royal inscriptions from Syria in early Aramaic from the hands of Zakkur of Hamat and Lu'ath,[29] of Panamu of Sam'al,[30] and of his son Barrakab,[31] do likewise.

The function of this introductory, self-identifying formula is everywhere to emphasize effectively the unimpeachable authority behind the ensuing declaration. In the case of the passage under discussion, the scene at the Burning Bush, it serves, in addition, to establish an unbroken historic continuity between the present experience of Moses and the revelation received by his forefathers the Patriarchs, beginning with Abraham. The God who revealed Himself to them, and who made them promises of redemption for their posterity, is the same God who now addresses Moses. He is about to fulfill those promises, and is soon to choose Moses as the one through whose agency this will be achieved.

The epithets by which God here designates Himself are of particular interest on other grounds. They conform to what is one of the distinctively characteristic features of the narratives about the Patriarchs found in the Book of Genesis, namely, the use of the title "The God of my/ your/his father," which frequently includes the proper name of the Patriarch as well.[32] In addition, one encounters the epithets "God of Abraham," "God of Isaac," and "God of Jacob," as here. Of course, the variety of names does not imply a variety of deities. This phenomenon of the multiplicity of designations for one and the same deity is well known in the ancient world.[33] One may cite the evidence from the Ugaritic texts in which, for instance, the god Baal is variously referred to also as Hadad and as Aliyn Baal ("Baal the Mighty"), as *zbl b'l arṣ* ("Prince, lord of earth"), and as *rkb 'rpt* ("Rider of the clouds"). Similarly, the craftsman-god Kothar ("The skillful one") is frequently termed *Kothar-w-Hasis* ("Skillful and clever"), as well as *Hayyin* ("Deft").[34] In Mesopotamian religious texts, examples of variant or multiple names and epithets for a single god are legion.[35]

The specific title "God of my/your/his father" is not exclusive to Israel, and is, in fact, widely documented outside the Bible.[36] It occurs in nineteenth-century B.C.E. tablets from old Assyrian trading colonies in Cappadocia in east-central Asia Minor,[37] as well as in correspondence from the king of Qatna in southern Syria, found in the archive at Mari about fifteen miles (twenty-five kilometers) north of the present-day Syrian-Iraqi border, deriving from a century later.[38] It also occurs in a fourteenth-century B.C.E. letter found at Tell el-Amarna in Egypt,[39] as well as in Ugarit near present-day Latakia (Ras Shamra) on the Syrian coast.[40] In these texts, the "god of the father(s)" is sometimes named, sometimes not. Thus we find phrases like "Ashur the god of my father," "Ashur and Amurrum the gods of our father," "Ashur and Amurrum and the Ishtar-star, gods of our fathers," "Ilaprat god of our father," "Shamash the god of my father," and an oath "by the name of the god of my father."

This title undoubtedly expresses special intimacy between the devotee and the deity who is his patron, protector, and benefactor. It is of paramount significance for evaluating the biblical texts to note that the formula is never employed by or in reference to Abraham. It is only by and to Isaac and Jacob that we find it. In other words, the narratives implicitly recognize that the advent of Abraham constitutes a break with the past, religiously speaking.[41] By the same token, the disappearance of the singular "God of the father" epithet following the Exodus constitutes tacit but irrefutable evidence that a new stage in the history of Israelite religion commences with the commissioning of Moses. In the formative period of Israel's history, as it is portrayed in the Scriptures, the narratives center around the lives of individuals. It is fitting, therefore, that the leading designation of God be one that conveys the personal, individual, familiar, and elective relationship between Him and the Patriarch who is promised posterity. In the new stage, it is the fortunes of the people that are the focus of interest, so that the old epithet is no longer adequate.[42] For the first time we now find the title "God of your Fathers," the plural comprehending all three Patriarchs and forging the link and continuity with the past. But henceforth the dominant name of the God of Israel, the one that gives voice to the national relationship, to the collective experiences of the people with God, is to be what is transcribed in the Hebrew text by the four consonants YHVH (the "Tetragrammaton"), the certain pronunciation of which has long been lost, and which in Jewish tradition has been replaced by the surrogate 'adonai, "My Lord," or ha-shem, "the Name," that is, the ineffable Divine Name.

The immediate, instinctive reaction of Moses to the divine speech is to hide his face, "for he was afraid to look at God," that is, further to observe the spectacle of the Burning Bush. The overwhelming, awesome intensity of the experience of the encounter with the Divine Presence typically, in the Bible, evokes trauma and dread. Following Jacob's struggle with the angel at Penuel, the Patriarch says, "I have seen a divine being face to face, yet my life has been preserved."[43] At one point in the wilderness wanderings, God Himself says to Moses, " . . . man may not see Me and live."[44] Gideon, in the time of the Judges, exclaims after his encounter with the angel, "Alas, O Lord God! For I have seen an angel of the Lord face to face," to which God responds, "All is well; have no fear, you shall not die."[45] In similar circumstances, Manoah, father of Samson, declares, "We shall surely die, for we have seen a divine being."[46] Always, the unique, transcendent, supernal holiness of the Divine Presence is an experience felt to be almost beyond the human capacity to endure.

The Divine Voice continues to impart the message to Moses:

I have marked well the plight of My people in Egypt and have heeded their outcry because of their taskmasters; yes, I am mindful of their sufferings. I have come down to rescue them from the Egyptians and to bring them out of that land to a good and spacious land, a land flowing with milk and honey, the region of the Canaanites, the Hittites, the Amorites, the Perizzites, the Hivites, and the Jebusites. Now the cry of the Israelites has reached Me; moreover, I have seen how the Egyptians oppress them. Come, therefore, I will send you to Pharaoh, and you shall free My people, the Israelites, from Egypt.[47]

"A land flowing with milk and honey"

The foregoing declaration contains several interesting features. The description of the singular fertility of the Promised Land has not appeared hitherto in the Bible. Strangely, none of God's solemn pledges to the Patriarchs recorded in the Book of Genesis ever mentions the "land flowing with milk and honey." Yet hereafter this epithet is reproduced again and again in biblical literature, about twenty times altogether. In striking contrast, the Patriarchs repeatedly encountered famine in the course of their peregrinations in the land. Ironically, it was famine in Canaan that set in motion the train of events that resulted in the migration of the Israelites from the land, their original settlement in Egypt, and their subsequent enslavement.[48] It would seem that the "milk and honey" motif has been deliberately avoided in the promises to the Patriarchs. For these elect individuals, abiding and implicit faith in God's word was the lodestone of their lives; trial and tribulation was to be their lot. However, for an entire people suffering slavery in Egypt, emphasis on the fertility and attractiveness of the Land of Promise plays an important role in fortifying their morale, in raising their spirits, and in sustaining their courage in the face of adversity.

The description itself bears examination in light of some extrabiblical references. The classic tale of the adventures of an Egyptian courtier named Sinuhe yields an interesting comparison. This official lived during the reigns of Kings Amenemhet I (d. ca. 1960 B.C.E.) and his successor, Sen-Usert I (ca. 1971–1928 B.C.E.). For political reasons, he felt constrained to flee his native Egypt for exile into Canaan and Syria. The composition contains valuable information about these lands. One celebrated excerpt reads as follows:

> It was a good land. . . . Figs were in it, and grapes. It had more wine than water. Plentiful was its honey, abundant its olives. Every [kind of] fruit was on its trees. Barley was there, and emmer. There was no limit to any [kind of] cattle.[49]

A half a millennium later, the annals of the military campaigns in Asia of Thutmosis III (ca. 1490–1436 B.C.E.), carved on the walls of the Temple of Karnak, mention the spoils of "grain, wine, and large and small cattle" that he brought home. From the town of Megiddo this king took 1,929 cows, 2,000 goats, 20,000 sheep, and over 207,300 sacks of wheat, which amount to about 450,000 bushels. Concerning the Phoenician coast, he reports that "every port town which his majesty reached was supplied with good bread and with various [kinds of] bread, with olive oil, incense, wine, honey, fruit. . . . They were more abundant than anything, beyond the experience of his majesty's army, without equivocation."[50]

Texts such as these show that the phrase "a land flowing with milk and honey" as a metaphor of fertility is well grounded in ancient historic reality. The Book of Deuteronomy, which employs the phrase several times, also describes the Promised Land in the following detail:

> For the Lord your God is bringing you into a good land . . . a land of wheat and barley, of vines, figs and pomegranates, a land of olive oil and honey. . . .[51]

The above-cited texts, and the approximately fifty biblical passages in which honey is mentioned, testify to the popularity of that product and to its abundance as a food and as a sweetener for other foods. It was also valued for its supposed medicinal properties, as Proverbs 16:24 shows: "Pleasant words are like a honeycomb, sweet to the palate and a cure for the body." However, while substantial evidence is at hand for the practice of beekeeping in Egypt, Mesopotamia, and Asia Minor, the Scriptures are silent on the subject. Bees' honey, as such, is mentioned only once, when Samson found a swarm of bees and honey in the carcass of a lion.[52] It is all but certain that Jonathan, son of King Saul, together with his troops, came across bees' honey on the eve of their battle with the Philistines.[53] But these cases refer to wild honey, not to the cultivated variety. The same applies to the biblical expressions "honeycomb" and "honey from the rock."[54] Accordingly, it is extremely likely that Hebrew *devash*, "honey," actually means what its Arabic equivalent *dibs* signifies to this day, the sweet syrup produced from the juice of the grape and especially the date. This better fits the context than does bees' honey in the list of the most characteristic agricultural products of the land of Israel given in the passage in Deuteronomy 8:8 just cited.[55]

The ethnic complexity

Apart from the description of its fertility, the Promised Land is also defined in ethnographic terms, as the home of an assortment of six different peoples. In Genesis 15:19–21, as many as ten resident peoples are recorded, and the several lists scattered over the Pentateuch and other biblical books offer varying numbers. This remarkable ethnic diversity is matched by the extraordinary political fragmentation. Joshua found no fewer than thirty-one royal city-states in this tiny land west of the Jordan.[56] Such an amazing situation can be explained only by the singularity of geographical position and physical features.

First of all, Palestine lay at the convergence of the major sea and overland routes of the ancient world. The main arteries of intercontinental communications flowed through it. This meant that the population was always exposed to multifarious and powerful influences from outside, particularly from the great river civilizations situated at either end of the Fertile Crescent, Egypt and Mesopotamia, but also from the Mediterranean islands.

Then, the astonishing contrasts in the physical configuration of the land proved to be a potent factor in promoting centrifugalism. The distance from Dan in the north to Beer-sheba in the south is only about one hundred sixty miles, while from the Mediterranean coast to Rabbath-Ammon across the Jordan in the east is only ninety miles. Yet within this small area of about 10,150 square miles can be distinguished several diverse parallel zones that extend the entire length of the country from north to south. The coastal plain gives way to the central hill regions that include Galilee, Samaria, and Judea. This is followed by the great Rift of the Jordan that encompasses the Dead Sea depression and the Aravah Valley. The plateaux of Transjordan come next, and merge into the deserts. Within these broad regions, there are a large number of subregions that create astonishing extremes of altitude. The level of the Dead Sea is thirteen hundred feet (four hundred meters) lower than that of the Mediterranean, thereby creating the deepest continental depression on earth.

These extreme contrasts in physical features are matched by a wide range of climatic conditions—Mediterranean, steppe, and desert—and by a corresponding diversity in vegetation caused by differences in soil, the intensity and direction of the winds and air movements, the seasonal rainfalls and deposits of dew, and the daily variations in temperature. All these are subject to considerable regional fluctuation. It is as though the accidents of geography, topography, and environmental conditions all conspired to produce irresistible centrifugal forces that could not but make for a maximum of ethnic diversity, for the intensification of the rivalry of political and strategic interests, and for the interpenetration and interweaving of religions and cultures

The foregoing information provides the necessary background for the understanding of the inclusion of the list of nations in God's theophany to Moses at the Burning Bush. It means that the people of Israel is destined to defy and to overcome all these powerful disintegrative forces that created thirty-one city-states and that made the land a home to so many diverse ethnic groups. It is surely an astonishing phenomenon that in the course of the entire history of the Promised Land, down to our own day, Israel alone of all the peoples of the earth succeeded in imposing a unity upon that country from within.

Moses' reluctance

The man who is to initiate this process, through whose instrumentality the liberation of Israel is to be effectuated, is Moses. He is now commissioned to become the emissary of God to the court of the pharaoh. His spontaneous reaction, however, is to recoil from the task, and to assert his personal inadequacy.[57] This sudden, unexpected, and wholly unprepared-for encounter with God, the summons to heed a divinely designated calling, the natural reluctance of the individual concerned, and his eventual surrender to God's overwhelming persuasiveness, all form the characteristic constituents of the later classic prophetic tradition in Israel.

Amos, who describes himself as a "cattle breeder and tender of sycamore trees," testifies that God took him away from the flock, and ordered him: "Go prophesy to my people Israel"; and Amos confesses: "My Lord God has spoken, who can but prophesy?"[58] Isaiah protested that he was "a man of unclean lips"[59] and thus unworthy to fulfill the prophetic role. Jeremiah, on receiving the divine call, replied: "Ah,

Lord God! I don't know how to speak, for I am still a boy,"[60] and in
the anguish of his soul, he revealingly confesses:

> You enticed me, O Lord, and I was enticed;
> You overpowered me and You prevailed.
> I have become a constant laughingstock,
> Everyone jeers at me. . . .
> I thought, 'I will not mention Him,
> No more will I speak in His name'—
> But [His word] was like a raging fire in my heart,
> Shut up in my bones;
> I could not hold it in, I was helpless.[61]

In the present narrative, there now ensues a prolonged dialogue
between God and Moses, in which the man resists and God insists and
gradually wears down Moses' reluctance and overcomes his hesitancy.
To Moses' objection that he did not feel worthy of undertaking the
mission thrust upon him, God responds with a promise to "be with"
him, that means, to lend encouragement and to restore self-confidence.
The Hebrew verb "to be" used here—h-y-h[62]—is an intimation of the
next point made by Moses, which relates to God.

The Divine Name

Moses asks: "When I come to the Israelites and say to them 'The
God of your fathers has sent me to you,' and they ask me, 'What is His
name?' what shall I say to them?"[63] This question raises all sorts of
of perplexities. God has said nothing about addressing the people, only
about sending him to the pharaoh. A query about the king's reaction,
not the people's, would have been expected. But Moses realized at once
that he could not effectively represent Israel at the Egyptian court without first receiving a mandate from the people. He therefore anticipates
their response to his announcement of his mission. Quite naturally,
they would want to know in whose name he comes with his message
of redemption. Still, why is not the claim to speak in the name of "the
God of your fathers" sufficiently acceptable? As we have seen, this
epithet was fairly common in the ancient Near East, sometimes used
anonymously, sometimes attached to the personal name of a deity. Just

because it was a generalized epithet, applicable to any god, the people might expect specific identification of this particular "God of your fathers" whom he invokes.

This, however, does not exhaust the problematics of Moses' question. The answer that he receives clearly points to the use of the peculiarly Israelite personal name of God, written *YHVH*, and known as the Tetragrammaton. There are varied strands of tradition in the Torah relating to its history.[64] According to Genesis 4:26, men first "began to invoke the Lord [*YHVH*] by name" in the days of Enosh, grandson of Adam. In other words, it had its origin in the primeval, pre-Patriarchal period. Consistent with this tradition is the frequent use of *YHVH* throughout the Patriarchal narratives. On the other hand, the present text of Exodus 3:14–15 implies a new departure, for Moses himself does not know this Name. But he assumes that the people do; otherwise, why should they find Moses' reply either meaningful or acceptable? How would it authenticate him in their eyes if they were ignorant of it?

Still another text, Exodus 6:2–3, has a bearing on this subject. There, God says to Moses: "I am the Lord (*YHVH*). I appeared to Abraham, Isaac, and Jacob as El Shaddai, but I did not make Myself known to them by My name *YHVH*." The strand of tradition represented by this passage seems to suggest that El Shaddai was the name of the "God of the Fathers" most familiar to the Patriarchs. That title is usually rendered "God Almighty" in the English translations, but its true origin and meaning have been entirely lost.[65] At any rate, it is the most common of the divine names in the Genesis narratives that are compounded with the initial element *El*.[66] Outside that book, El Shaddai appears only in poetic texts. This phenomenon testifies to the great antiquity of the appellation since Hebrew poetry characteristically preserves archaisms, or survivals of the forms of language common in an earlier age that fell into disuse. Another support for the above-cited tradition of Exodus 6:2–3 is the extreme rarity of biblical personal names constructed of the element *Shaddai*. There are, in fact, only two certain examples: Zurishaddai[67] and Ammishaddai,[68] and both belong to persons born in Egypt. Curiously, the second of these two names has turned up in a hieroglyphic inscription on a sepulcher as the name of a petty official in fourteenth-century B.C.E. Egypt.[69]

The reverse side of the evidence for the pre-Mosaic antiquity of the divine name El Shaddai and of its popular replacement by YHVH in Moses' day lies in the telling fact that the first biblical personage to bear a name compounded of a divine element derived from this Tetragrammaton is, fittingly, Jochebed, mother of Moses.[70] Thereafter, such names predominate in the Israelite onomasticon, or thesaurus of names. The conclusion is inescapable that the Tetragrammaton only comes to the fore as the dominant personal name of the God of Israel beginning with the new era of Israelite monotheism inaugurated by the advent of Moses.

Whatever be the true etymology of the Tetragrammaton, and to this day it remains an enigma, God's response to Moses' question—'Ehyeh-'Asher-'Ehyeh—reflects a popular understanding that YHVH is to be interpreted in terms of the Hebrew stem h-y-h, "to be."[71] Clearly, the name is not meant to be a mere identifying label. Such was not the main function of names in the ancient Near East. Rather, the name is intended to connote character and nature, the totality of the intricate, interwoven, manifold forces that make up the whole personality of the bearer of the name. In the present case, therefore, God's reply to Moses means that the Tetragrammaton expresses the quality of Being. However, it is not Being as opposed to nonbeing, not Being as an abstract, philosophical notion, but Being in the sense of the reality of God's active, dynamic Presence. Whether it means "I Am That I Am," or "I Am Who I Am," or "I Will Be What I Will Be"—and it can mean any of these—God's pronouncement of His own Name indicates that the Divine Personality can be known only to the extent that God chooses to reveal His Self, and it can be truly characterized only in terms of itself, and not by analogy with something else. This is the articulated counterpart of the spectacle of fire at the Burning Bush, fire that is self-generating and self-sustaining. Furthermore, since in the ancient world there existed the notion that name-giving communicates superiority and power over the recipient of the name, it is self-evident that God's name must proceed from Himself, and cannot be conferred by man. This explains why God uses the first person—'Ehyeh—instead of the regular third-person form of this verbal name—YHVH. Finally, in Exodus 3:15 God reaffirms the identification of YHVH with the God of the Patriarchs, and declares, "This shall be My Name forever, This My appellation for all eternity." The character of God as just explained to Moses is absolute and unchanging. This immutability provides inflexible reliability that the promise of redemption will be realized.

The elders

God now orders Moses to go and assemble "the elders of Israel," that is to say, to return to Egypt and to contact the "elders" of the people, to convey the tidings of freedom to them, and to enlist their support and presence when he stands before the pharaoh. In this way, the pharaoh will know that Moses is not some eccentric individual acting on his own, but is truly representative of the people of Israel.

These "elders" actually constitute a kind of representative judicial body in Israel. Some light has been shed on this institution by the archive discovered at Mari, modern Tell Hariri, near the present Syrian-Iraqi frontier. These documents are an important source of information about the tribal organization of western Semites. We learn that the Council of Elders (*shibuti*) exercised authority in the government of the tribe, and represented it before the urban authorities.[72] Except for Egypt, throughout the ancient Near East the "elders" functioned as an entity that represented specific social groupings, and often assumed judicial and advisory responsibility.[73] The term itself originated in tribal societies where advanced age and rich experience in life were valued assets that qualified one for leadership. In the course of time, the term lost its primary meaning, and evolved into a title for a holder of office, an official representative. The identical process can be registered in respect of the Akkadian *shibutum*, the Greek *gerousia*, or "Council of Elders" at Sparta made up of *gerontes*, the Roman "senators," and the Arab *sheikh*. Each of these terms goes back to a word connected with old age.

The "elders" whom Moses is bidden to assemble and instruct frequently appear in the Exodus narratives, especially at crucial moments.[74] They are mentioned in particular in connection with the paschal lamb, the production of water out of a rock in the wilderness, the sacrificial meal held for Moses' father-in-law, the revelation at Sinai, and the execution of the covenant between God and Israel. However, in all these events they are entirely passive, and never exhibit any signs of leadership, initiative, or independence. It is not simply that they are overwhelmed and intimidated into acquiescence by the powerful personality of Moses. It must not be overlooked that Moses himself is portrayed in all his actions as the agent of God whose orders and directions he carries out. The Exodus episode throughout is presented as the direct and personal intervention of God in history. He is the sole, effective actor, the single controlling force, manipulating events toward their predetermined climax.

In accordance with this orientation, we now find Moses being dictated the precise language that he is to use before the pharaoh. He is to say, "The Lord, the God of the Hebrews, manifested Himself to us. Now therefore, let us go a distance of three days into the wilderness to sacrifice to the Lord our God."[75]

"Hebrews"

One of the singular features of the Exodus narratives thus far has been the repeated use of the term "Hebrew" ('ivri).[76] Mention has been made of "Hebrew midwives," "Hebrew women," "a child of the He-brews," "a Hebrew nurse," "an Egyptian beating a Hebrew," "two Hebrews fighting," and now "the Lord, the God of the Hebrews," an epithet that is to be repeated again and again in communications to the pharaoh. Always "Hebrew" is employed to designate the Israelites as opposed to another ethnic group.[77] The same holds true for the other two narrative contexts in which there are clusters of this term, the Joseph stories[78] and the wars with the Philistines recorded in the Book of Samuel.[79]

Attempts have been made to find the origin of "Hebrew" in the phenomenon of the Ḥab/piru or 'Apiru documented over a long period of time and in a wide variety of texts deriving from all over the ancient Near East stretching from Egypt through Canaan into Syria and the Hittite sphere and down into Mesopotamia.[80] For about a thousand years covering the entire second millennium B.C.E., these people, wherever and whenever they appear, constitute an alien, inassimilable element in the population. They share in common an inferior social status. They may be mercenaries, slaves, marauding bands; only occasionally do they hold important positions. Certainly, the term Ḥab/piru or 'Apiru has no ethnic coloration, and the names they bear betray widely varying linguistic and cultural connections—Akkadian, Hurrian, West Semitic, and others. The term is overwhelmingly derogatory, and in cuneiform texts it is often written as SA.GAZ, which syllables are associated with murder, robbery, and razzia. From all this it is clear that there is no connection between the biblical "Hebrews," who constitute a distinct ethnic group, and the Ḥab/piru or 'Apiru, unless the term simply indicates social elements marginal to a society.

A widely held view of the origin of the biblical term "Hebrew" is to derive it from 'eber, "beyond, across," and to connect it with the phrase 'eber ha-nahar, "Beyond the River (Euphrates)," whence the ancestors of Israel came.[81] This is how the Greek translation of the Bible known as the Septuagint seems to have understood "Hebrew," for it renders it "the one from beyond," "the wanderer." Still a third explanation traces it to Eber, ancestor of Abraham.[82] Both these attempts have the disadvantage of not being able to account for the biblical restriction of "Hebrew" to Israel, to the exclusion of the other ethnic groups that descended from Abraham or from Eber. Abraham's family in Aramnaharaim are "Arameans,"[83] while the other descendants of Eber are simply b'nei 'eber, literally, "sons of Eber."[84] Until further evidence is at hand, the origin and significance of the term "Hebrew" must remain a mystery.

Worship in the wilderness

A strange feature of the theophany to Moses is the instruction to ask the pharaoh not for the emancipation of the enslaved Israelites and permission for their emigration from Egypt, but for his consent to their traveling a three-day journey into the wilderness in order to celebrate a sacrificial festival to the Lord. This is precisely what Moses requests in his first audience with the king, and the demand is repeated after the fourth plague, and becomes a factor in the course of the negotiations with the pharaoh as the plagues continue to increase in severity.[85]

Strictly speaking, the pretext that is given to the king is the truth, for earlier, in the encounter at the Burning Bush, God had told Moses that when He freed the people from Egypt they would worship God at that site. But it leaves the impression that when the festival is over the people would return to Egypt, and certainly that was not intended. Undoubtedly, the formula is a stratagem designed to outmaneuver the pharaoh's intransigence, the only device available to a helpless people, wholly subject to a tyrant's will. As a matter of fact, the request for

temporary relief from drudgery in order to celebrate a religious holiday
was not something unreasonable or exceptional in the Egyptian system
of state-imposed servitude. This is shown by the account of one su-
pervisor of a gang of workmen, for instance, who kept a log in which
he recorded the work habits of his forty-three laborers. He included the
days of the month on which they were absent, as well as their excuses.
While "illness" and "laziness" account for most failures to appear,
"sacrificing to the god" is also given as a reason. One log reports that
laborers building the royal necropolis enjoyed four days of holiday in
order to celebrate a religious festival.[86] In making his request, therefore,
Moses could invoke the support of established precedent, and was not
asking for a special privilege. By restricting his petition to this limited
and reasonable item, rather than demanding the wholesale and permanent release of the people, Moses might succeed in outwitting the
pharaoh. The immediate and outright rejection of even this modest
request exposes the true character of this monarch. No wonder, then,
that the divine proclamation to Moses introduces a note of caution.
The one called to be the liberator of Israel is forewarned of the implacable obduracy of the king of Egypt. Moses must be prepared at the
outset of his new career for a long series of disappointments and failures
in his dealings with the pharaoh. It is as though he is being told to steel
himself against falling prey to despair. The mission will require a sustained effort. However, the inevitability of ultimate success is assured
because the liberation of Israel belongs to the divine plan of history.
The pharaoh's intransigence will be eroded by God's forceful measures.
Moreover, Moses is promised that when the exodus from Egypt finally
arrives, the people will not leave "empty-handed," but the Egyptians
themselves will provide the Israelites with " 'objects of silver and gold,
and clothing . . . thus stripping the Egyptians.' "[87]

Stripping the Egyptians[88]

This last item has its inspiration in the original covenant that God
made with Abraham, as related in Genesis 15:13–14. There, God fore-
tells the future enslavement of Abraham's descendants, and pledges that
He would "execute judgment on the nation they shall serve, and in
the end they shall go free with great wealth." Indeed, when the time
comes for practical preparations to be made in anticipation of the last

of the plagues to be inflicted on Egypt, Moses is instructed to tell the people "that each man shall ask of his neighbor and each woman from hers, objects of silver and gold."[89] Then we are informed that the people did "Moses' bidding and asked of the Egyptians objects of silver and gold, and clothing. And the Lord had disposed the Egyptians favorably toward the people, and they let them have their request; thus they stripped the Egyptians."[90] This motif of bespoiling the oppressors is mentioned once again in the homiletic historical sermon that is Psalm 105: "He led them out with silver and gold" (verse 37). Clearly, tradition saw in this development a matter of importance. Naturally, the notion that the tyrannical oppressors are not only forced to free their victims, but even yield their possessions to them, appealed to national pride. The Israelites escaped from Egypt with their dignity intact. The text is obviously conscious of the seeming implausibility of such a development, which is why it is emphasized that what happened was the result of God's causing the Egyptians to be favorably disposed toward Israel.[91] The implication is that the Egyptians obviously would not have been prompted by such generous impulses of their own accord. As to the significance of the payments, they have been variously interpreted as restitution for the deprivations of slave labor, or as being in accordance with Israelite provisions for the emancipated slave:

> When you set him free, do not let him go empty-handed: Furnish him out of the flock, threshing floor, and vat, with which the Lord your God has blessed you. Bear in mind that you were slaves in the land of Egypt and the Lord your God redeemed you; therefore I enjoin this commandment upon you today.[92]

It is also possible that the motif of bespoiling the Egyptians functions to explain how it came about later that the Israelites in the wilderness were able to erect a sanctuary and to furnish it with all kinds of precious materials.

Signs and wonders

Regardless of God's assurance about the certainty of success in his mission, Moses still resists the divine call. His concern is not with the pharaoh but with his own credibility in the eyes of the people. It is all very well to claim to speak in the name of the Lord-YHVH; but how to prove the reality of the revelation he received? How can he authenticate his mission to the satisfaction of the masses? In response, God prescribes three "signs" that are to function as authenticating the legitimacy of Moses as a divinely sent emissary to effect the deliverance of Israel: Moses' rod will turn into a snake when thrown on the ground and will revert to its normal state when he grasps it by the tail; his hand will suddenly be afflicted with severe dermatitis, which will as suddenly disappear; and water taken by him from the Nile will turn to blood when poured on the dry ground.[93]

At first sight, these "signs" appear to belong to the realm of wonder-working magic so well known from polytheistic cultures. Egypt, especially, was the classic land of magic, which played a central role in its religious life. In fact, magic permeated every aspect of life. The number of gods in Egypt was almost unlimited. One version of the Book of the Dead mentions over five hundred.[94] This prodigious multiplicity of divine beings in itself meant that no god could be either infinite or absolute. Moreover, the inherence of the gods in nature, their dependence upon the physical and the material for their continued existence, further limited their scope. They, like human beings, were deemed to be subject to superior forces inherent in the primordial realm of existence, a meta-divine realm from which the gods themselves derive. Human destiny was thought to be controlled by two distinct forces, the gods and the powers beyond the gods.[95] Neither of these was necessarily benevolent. In fact, antagonism and malevolence were considered to be characteristic of the divine relationship with man.[96] Inevitably, religion became increasingly concerned with the elaboration of ritual designed to propitiate or neutralize the numerous unpredictable powers that be. Man had to be able to devise the means whereby those powers inherent in the meta-divine realm could be activated for his benefit. Magic thus became an integral part of religion.[97] Even the gods were believed to resort to magic against one another. The magician was an important, indeed indispensable, religious functionary. He possessed the expertise necessary for the manipulation of the mysterious powers. These skills included the spoken word such as spells and utterances, the use of magical objects such as charms and amulets, and ritual practices. A considerable body of magical literature grew up, including popular tales and short stories about the wonder-working magicians.

In light of all this, the performance of signs and wonders in Egypt on the part of Moses, and the high concentration of this motif in the story of the Exodus, admirably suit the social and religious milieu. Yet appearances are deceptive. While the actions of Moses appear to belong to the same category as those of the Egyptian practitioners, in actual fact the comparison is superficial. Several subtle and striking distinctions separate the two, and stamp the Israelite phenomenon as partaking of quite a different order of religious thinking.[98]

In the first place, Moses' wonder-working functions solely to establish his credibility in the eyes of the people as the authentic instrument of divine will. It is precisely because he is not a magician, because he neither possesses nor is endowed with any supernatural or occult powers, that this is possible. God's question "What is that in your hand?" and Moses' reply "A rod" mean that the object he is holding is a plain, ordinary stick such as any shepherd would have. It is not a wand and contains no magical properties. Moses is completely taken by surprise at the unexpected development and recoils from the snake into which the rod is transformed. He personally has no control over events. No snake-handler would pick up a reptile by its tail, but Moses does so at the divine behest, an act that expresses unquestioned faith and perfect confidence in God.

Then it should be noted that whenever in the course of his career as the leader of Israel he resorts to wonder-working, it follows a crisis that he himself cannot handle, and he must receive specific instructions from God. Each instance relates to a particular end or to the purpose at hand. Invariably, the initiative for action comes from God. Moses knows no techniques, recites no spells, utters no incantations or magical formulae that are supposed to be automatically efficacious. He cannot perform wonders at his own discretion.[99] As a matter of fact, on the one occasion that he attempts to do so, striking a rock to produce water, as is related in the narrative of Numbers 20:1–13, he comes to grief. Of course, the religion of Israel excludes the possibility of magic because the fundamental belief in one absolutely omnipotent God who is sovereign over nature leaves no room for the existence of any meta-divine realm or of any external, independent forces that need to be manipulated. In Egypt the magician manipulates the divine; in Israel it is the one God who manipulates man and nature.

An obvious question that asserts itself is why just the three "signs" given, out of numerous possibilities, were selected for the particular purpose. Here one can only resort to conjecture. Generally, with biblical "signs" that are intended to be corroborative of something, it is less the form and content and more the function that is of importance.[100] Nevertheless, it is quite likely that what Moses is told to do is invested with special symbolism.

The rod, in the Bible, is frequently emblematic of royalty, power, and authority.[101] As a scepter, it belonged to the ceremonial insignia of Egyptian kings. Sometimes the pharaohs hold a serpent staff in their hand. The uraeus or stylized representation of the sacred cobra, patron goddess of Lower Egypt whose chief shrine was in the marshes of the Delta, was worn by all the pharaohs on the forehead as the symbol of imperial sovereignty, and as an omen of death to the enemies of the monarch.[102] Accordingly, the feat that Moses is told to perform may well have signified his being endowed with leadership and authority, thus enabling him to handle effectively the mighty power of the Egyptian crown.

The second "sign" was that Moses' hand became encrusted with snowy scales. The Hebrew term for the affliction, *tsara'at*, is often rendered "leprosy" in English translations, but in actuality it does not refer to the dread disease known by that name today, also called "Hansen's disease." The Hebrew is a generic term covering a group of diseases described in Leviticus Chapters 13–14. Apart from attacking the human body, *tsara'at* may also affect clothing and the walls of a house. The biblical malady is curable, and some of the symptoms described in the sources do not correspond to those characteristic of true leprosy.[103] At any rate, whatever be the disease's real identity, the Bible often portrays it as a sign of divine displeasure in reaction to human offense.[104] It is this association that may well be significant in the present context. The affliction would be a warning sign to Moses that he is approaching the moment of God's impatience at his continued evasion of the call to leadership. At the same time it would serve as an omen to the people of the serious consequences that would ensue should they reject Moses.

The third and last "sign" is the turning of the Nile water into blood. Here the meaning is clear. The Nile is the life blood of Egypt, and God can impose His will upon nature and through it upon the Egyptian state.

Moses' Continued Resistance

In disregard of all that he has heard and seen at the Burning Bush, Moses remains stubbornly unmoved and continues to resist the divine call. He now offers what seems to be a plausible excuse. He who would be a leader of people, a spokesman who has to negotiate with the Egyptian court, must possess oratorical skills. But Moses feels himself to be inadequate to the task. He lacks persuasive eloquence.[105] Whether the text means that he literally suffered from some speech defect or that after the passage of years away from Egypt his fluency in the language of the land had deteriorated, or whether he simply asserts his inexperience and native reserve regarding the art of public speaking, it is hard to say.[106] He certainly does mean that he cannot express himself clearly and effectively enough to gain attention and acceptance. To this, God replies with what in effect is a statement that epitomizes the essence of the phenomenon of biblical prophecy.[107] The chosen messenger conveys not his own word but the word of God, and he does so because he is irresistibly compelled to by a Force and a Will more powerful than his own. Prophetic eloquence is not a matter of native talent, but of revelation that derives from the supreme Source of truth that is external to the speaker. The facile talker, the golden-tongued, the consummate demagogue, is not the recipient of the prophetic word or the vehicle of its transmission. Prophetic eloquence is a divine gift bestowed for the purpose on him who is elected, often against his will, to be the messenger. In these circumstances, experience and talent are irrelevant qualities.

Having exhausted all the arguments he can muster, Moses makes one final desperate plea: "Please, O Lord, make someone else Your agent."[108] With this, the limits of divine tolerance have been reached. Moses cannot escape his destiny, but the way will be eased by enlisting the help of his brother, Aaron, who has already earned a reputation for eloquence. The message that God reveals to Moses will be mediated to the people and to the pharaoh through Aaron. At this, Moses succumbs to his ineluctable fate, rejoins his family, and receives his father-in-law's consent to return to Egypt.

The record of this phase of the life of Moses closes with the report that he and his brother, Aaron, assembled the elders of the Israelites, to whom Aaron related the tidings of impending liberation and before whom he performed the signs to verify the legitimacy of Moses' mission. The people were convinced, and accepted the leadership of Moses. Thus the indispensable condition for the next stage in Moses' career now exists. Moses can now approach the Egyptian authorities with a mandate from the people.

CHAPTER IV

The Ten Plagues

EXODUS 5–11

The hardening of the heart

At the scene by the Burning Bush, God shared with Moses His foreknowledge that the pharaoh would reject the call for the release of the Israelite slaves: " 'I know that the King of Egypt will let you go only because of a greater might.' "[1] The clear implication of these words is that the man is possessed of a ruthless and stubborn character, and is devoid of all compassion. He will eventually yield, but reluctantly, and only under compulsion of overwhelming force. However, toward the end of the revelation to Moses, a new and seemingly contradictory note is introduced. God makes the startling declaration that He Himself will harden the heart of the king so that he will not let the people go.[2] The pharaoh's obstinate resistance to Moses' demands actually appears to be attributed to divine causality! Moreover, the theologically disturbing perplexities produced by such a statement are intensified by a repeated observation of the narrator. In the course of the description of the series of punitive disasters that befall the Egyptians, he tells us unambiguously that God indeed "hardened Pharaoh's heart."[3]

Before examining this problem in detail, it is useful to discuss the idiom itself. Generally in the Bible, physical sensations are expressed in terms of the actions of the specific part of the body with which they are believed to be associated. Thus, bowels were thought to be the seat of strong emotions. When Jeremiah cries out in anguish, "My bowels, my bowels!"[4] he is really saying, "O my suffering, my suffering!" and when he speaks of Ephraim as God's beloved son, and declares, "My bowels are troubled for him,"[5] he means that he is filled with longing for him. In like manner, the elegist who laments the fall of Jerusalem in the Book of Lamentations can proclaim that his "liver spills on the ground"[6] over the ruin of his people. When the psalmist confesses that his kidneys afflict him,[7] he is suffering the torments of conscience; and when God "probes the kidneys,"[8] He subjects to searching scrutiny the innermost thoughts of a human being. So it is that the heart (Hebrew lev[av]) only rarely in the Bible refers to the physical organ as such. Mostly it is as the vital principle, the controlling center of human actions, the seat of the inner life, that "heart" is used. Man's thoughts, his intellectual activity, the cognitive, conative, and affective aspects of his personality, are all regarded as issuing from the heart. The state of the heart defines, then, the essential character of a person.[9] Its "hardening" connotes the willful suppression of the capacity for reflection, for self-examination, for unbiased judgments about good and evil. In short, the "hardening of the heart" becomes synonymous with the numbing of the soul, a condition of moral atrophy.

The motif of the hardening of the pharaoh's heart occurs precisely twenty times in one form or another within the scope of the Exodus story between Chapters 4 and 14. Intriguingly, the distribution of the motif is exactly equally divided between the pharaoh and God as the direct cause of the hardening. Ten times it is said that the pharaoh hardened his own heart,[10] and ten times the hardening is attributed to God.[11] Furthermore, it is not until the advent of the sixth plague that divine intervention begins.[12] For the first five plagues the pharaoh's obduracy is the product of his own volition. This is crucial to the theological issue, for it stamps the king as a callous, evil-minded person who must bear full responsibility for his iniquitous acts freely and knowingly perpetrated. The pharaoh's culpability is established beyond doubt. He is not an innocent, blameless individual whose integrity is compromised, and finally subverted, by the intervention of Providence. He exhibits an obvious and willing predisposition to cruelty. Accordingly, the king's continued intransigence from the sixth plague on cannot be said to be involuntary, a point that is carefully made in the narrative by its twice stressing that the pharaoh's obstinacy after the seventh plague was again self-willed.[13] He was not one to be constrained by moral principles, and he cannot be excused from criminal liability. In brief, the idea of God's hardening the pharaoh's heart is that He utilizes a man's natural proclivity toward evil; He accentuates the process in furtherance of His own historical purposes.[14]

There is one other point to be made in this connection. The theology and political theory of ancient Egypt stressed the literal divinity of the living pharaoh. His will was law, his word absolute. By reinforcing the pharaoh's stubbornness, thereby making him a prisoner of his own irrationality, God deprives the "god" of his freedom of action. The pharaoh can no longer control his own will and his so-called divinity is mocked.[15]

Bricks without straw

As was foreseen, the first encounter between Moses and the pharaoh was a failure. Not only did the king summarily reject the Israelite petition, modest as it was—restricted to a plea for permission to have three days of respite in order to celebrate a religious festival in the wilderness—but he arrogantly disdained even to recognize the God of Israel. "Who is the Lord that I should heed Him and let Israel go? I do not know the Lord, nor will I let Israel go,"[16] he defiantly avowed. In addition, he gave orders that henceforth the government would no longer issue straw for the manufacture of bricks. The laborers would have to provide their own and still meet the same fixed daily production schedule as before.

The manufacture and role of the brick in the architecture and construction work of ancient Egypt has been discussed in Chapter One. Here the emphasis is on the straw or stubble gathered from the fields, chopped and mixed in with the water-soaked clay. This substance played a crucial role in the brickmaking process. Its function was not just to act as a binding element. Through the action of the acid in the vegetable matter that was released in the course of chemical decay, the strength and plasticity of the brick were greatly enhanced. Without the addition of the chopped straw, the bricks would shrink, develop cracks, and lose their shape.[17] That is why the straw looms so large in our story.

Demoralization

The pharaoh's new draconian decree imposed one more intolerable hardship on the long-suffering people. The Israelite foremen of the labor gangs, who were responsible to the Egyptian taskmasters, obviously could not supply the assigned quotas, and were administered beatings in punishment for their failure to do so. They organized a protest and sent a delegation to the court, but it met with unfeeling rebuff and harsh insult. The unfortunate foremen happened to encounter Moses and Aaron as they emerged from the palace, and they vented their anger and frustration upon the two. "May the Lord look upon you," they shouted, "and punish you for making us loathsome to Pharaoh and his courtiers—putting a sword in their hands to slay us."[18] Profoundly discouraged and disillusioned, Moses cried out, "O Lord, why did You bring harm upon this people? Why did You send me? Ever since I came to Pharaoh to speak in Your name, it has gone worse with this people; and still You have not delivered Your people."[19] In this moment of acute distress, the Lord does not rebuke Moses for lack of faith, but instead reassures him as to the ultimate success of his mission.

Now ensues the second great revelation that Moses experiences.[20] Aspects of its form and content have been discussed in the previous chapter. On this occasion, unlike before, the message is directed first to the people of Israel, not to the pharaoh. They have become demoralized as a result of Moses' disastrous encounter with the king, and their spirits need to be raised. God therefore reiterates His solemn pledge to redeem them from slavery, to which He now adds a promise of severe punishment for the Egyptians. He will enter into a covenant with Israel, and He will bring them into the land He swore to give to the Patriarchs.

Moses conveys the message to the Israelites, but it falls on deaf ears. Crushed by the cruel bondage to which they were subjected, and given the awesome power at the disposal of the Egyptian state, the people understandably regarded the utopian declaration as being utterly irrational. It would henceforth be the task of Moses to convince them that what seemed to be irrational would inevitably become a reality.

Signs before the Pharaoh

The pharaoh denied any knowledge of the Lord (*YHVH*), the God of Israel.[21] In accord with the concept of the time, if Moses claims to be the divine spokesman, he must be able to prove the reality of this God by performing wonders in His name. Moses and Aaron are therefore told to appear before the pharaoh and to throw down the rod that will turn into a serpent. This is the same "sign" that Moses had earlier performed when he needed to prove his own legitimacy before the people as the messenger of God. It is likely that the symbolism we there read into the act applies here too. On the present occasion, however, it is Aaron, not Moses, who enacts this feat of turning a rod into a snake. The reason is that in this way Moses tacitly asserts his equality of status with the Egyptian king. He comes to negotiate with the pharaoh as the dignified representative of the people of Israel. Just as the pharaoh has his magicians, so Moses has his assistant. As a matter of fact, in the subsequent narratives, detailing the ten plagues, Aaron is active only so long as the Egyptian magicians are present. Once their ingenuity fails them and they appear no more, then Moses' personally serves as the instrumentality of the plagues.

Apart from the symbolism involved in the turning of the rod into the serpent, it is also probable that the selection of this particular marvel to impress the pharaoh was conditioned by the fact that it has a distinctly Egyptian background. [22] Among the popular tales that have survived from the period of the Middle Kingdom (twenty-first to eighteenth centuries B.C.E.) are those about "King Cheops (Khufu) and the Magicians." One such tells of the wife of the "chief lector" of King Nabka who had an affair with a townsman. When her husband discovered the perfidy, he modeled a crocodile out of wax, recited the appropriate magic formula, and ordered his steward to throw it into the lake as his wife's lover went to bathe there. When this was done, the wax crocodile was transformed into a live one, which then dragged the offender under the water. When the husband seized the crocodile, it reverted in his hands to its original wax state. [23]

When Aaron performed his wonder at the court, the king summoned his magicians, who were able to duplicate it. The text says that they did it "with their spells," [24] which means that the trick was a standard item in their professional repertoire. Egyptian scarabs, those engraved ceramic or stone amulets or ornaments having the shape of a beetle, depict the magician performing the feat of holding a snake that is as stiff as a rod. This trick is reproduced in Egypt to this day by native snake charmers, and has often been described and photographed. [25] The secret has been revealed as depending on the particular species of Egyptian cobra known as the *naja haje*. Its distinctive feature is that it can be rendered totally immobile and absolutely rigid through the skilled application of great pressure to one of the nerves at the nape of the neck. When it is thrown to the ground, the jolt causes it to recover and the snake wriggles away.

The ability of the Egyptian magicians to reproduce Aaron's feat of course robbed the latter of its evidential function. Moses and Aaron had apparently failed. At that moment, however, something unexpected happened that was not in the magicians' script. Aaron's rod swallowed the rods of the Egyptians. The text does not record that Moses or Aaron did or said anything. It simply occurred, and it signalled a humiliating defeat for the Egyptians. Within the religious context of the times, what took place should normally have been interpreted as vindication of the God of Israel. But the pharaoh's stubbornness of heart would not permit him to acknowledge the truth. Nevertheless, the first chink in the king's wall of obduracy had been made. A new stage in the struggle for the liberation of Israel is about to commence. The entire people of Egypt is to be brought into the scope of God's punitive and coercive operations. In the biblical view, society as a corporate entity cannot evade responsibility for the follies and evils committed in its name, and it cannot escape the consequences thereof. Egypt is about to suffer a concentrated succession of disasters.

The Plagues[26]

The coercive measures taken by God to break down Egyptian resistance to His demands took the form of ten plagues: the River Nile turned to blood; it then swarmed with frogs that invaded the land; lice infested man and beast; the land was overrun with swarms of insects; pestilence struck the livestock in the field; man and beast suffered inflammation of the skin that broke out in boils; devastating hail lashed the countryside; locusts descended in destructive swarms; Egypt was plunged into darkness for three days; all the male firstborn of Egypt perished at midnight.

It will surely be noted at once that there is nothing inherently mythological or supernatural about the first nine plagues. They can all be explained within the context of the familiar vicissitudes of nature that imperil the Nile Valley and elsewhere from time to time. Some of the plague types appear as items in ancient Near Eastern literature. Thus the changing of water into blood is said in our narrative to have been duplicated by the Egyptian magicians "with their spells." This implies that it, like the snake trick, was part of their professional stock-in-trade. A popular Egyptian story has come down in a late manuscript emanating from Roman times but purporting to center on Prince Khamwas, the fourth son of Rameses II. This young man was a magician who, before entering a contest, told his mother, "Should I be defeated, then when you drink water it will become the color of blood." [27] An ancient Egyptian composition from either the First Intermediate Period (twenty-second to twenty-first centuries B.C.E.) or the late Middle Kingdom times (twenty-first to eighteenth centuries B.C.E.) known as "The Admonitions of an Egyptian Sage," supposedly reported on conditions of social, economic, and political chaos in the land. The speaker, Ipuwer by name, states that the River Nile was blood, and that he who attempted to drink from its waters balked at human contact and went thirsty. [28] The earliest reference so far to a plague of this kind is found in the Sumerian myth "Inanna and the Gardener." [29] The goddess, "queen of heaven," punished men with plagues, the first of which was blood. She filled all the wells of the land with blood, and she saturated all the hedges and the gardens of the land with blood. The slaves collecting firewood drank nothing but blood; the female slaves who came to draw water drew nothing but blood.

The nature of the fourth plague, called in Hebrew 'arov, has been variously identified as wild beasts and as flies. The Egyptian composition known as "The Prophecy of Nefer-Rohu," or "The Prophecies of Neferti," supposedly tells of the reestablishment of law and order by Amenemhet I after the collapse of the Old Kingdom. Among the misfortunes that befell the land is an invasion of wild beasts before which the citizens were powerless. [30] The Atra-ḥasis epic from Mesopotamia seems to indicate that a plague of flies was narrowly averted. [31]

Of course, it hardly needs mentioning that pestilence, the fifth plague, was one of the most dreaded and most widespread scourges to ravish civilization until fairly recently. The same may be said of locusts. The biblical text vividly depicts this eighth plague. "Locusts invaded all the land of Egypt and settled . . . in a thick mass; They hid all the land from view, and the land was darkened; and they ate up all the grasses of the field and all the fruit of the trees . . . so that nothing green was left . . ."[32] This description of a locust plague is elaborated in the biblical Book of Joel, and is no hyperbole. The swarms that periodically invade territories in Africa, southwestern Asia, and southern Europe may number up to ten billion individual locusts and cover areas as large as four hundred square miles. A flight of locusts across the Red Sea in 1889 was estimated to be two thousand square miles in size.[33]

The ninth plague, three days of darkness, is described as "a darkness that can be touched,"[34] that is to say, it was so profound as to be tangible. Nothing is said about the withdrawal of the sun. A perfectly natural explanation lies at hand in the dry, southerly, sand and dust storms, known as *khamsin*, that sweep in each year in the spring.[35] The atmosphere becomes hazy and heavy, a condition that may last for a few days and that keeps people indoors. The above-mentioned Egyptian "Prophecies of Neferti" reports, "The sun-disc is covered over. It will not shine [so that] people may see. No one can live when clouds cover the sun."[36]

The descriptions of the plagues in Exodus do not yield any hint of a consistently logical order or of any necessary link between one plague and another. One scholar, Greta Hort, has propounded a theory of a chain of direct causal connections to explain the nature and sequence of the majority of these calamities, and their concentration within the limited duration of about twelve months.[37] (Such a time span can be deduced from the notations of Exodus 7:7, and Deuteronomy 34:7 to the effect that Moses was eighty years of age at his first audience with the pharaoh, and was one hundred twenty years old when he died after spending forty years in the wilderness leading the people to Canaan.)

This theory of the plagues is based upon the assumption of an uncommonly heavy rainfall in the East African Plateau, the Highlands of Ethiopia, and the southern parts of the Nile Valley, such as occasionally occur. As a result, the annual rise of the river that starts in July and reaches its peak in mid-September brings catastrophe instead of the usual blessings. The soil in the basin of the Blue Nile and its tributary, the Atbara, is tropical red earth. This continues along much of the course of the inundation so that an excessive amount of red sediment would be discharged into the Nile by the abnormal floods. It would be carried down the entire length of the river, and would be too much to be neutralized, as it is in the normal volume of flow. This would have led to discoloration of the waters "throughout the land of Egypt," so that they gave the appearance of being blood red. That is how the first of the plagues is explained.

As to the stench emitted and the death of the fish, these would have been caused by the super-abundance of flagellates and purple bacteria brought down from the high mountain lakes. The oxygen balance in the water would have been upset, thus giving rise to the two by-products of the plagues, at the same time intensifying discoloration. All this explains why the first plague was not abruptly terminated by Moses as were many of the others. The ecosystem of the Nile was gradually and naturally restored as the rains lessened and the flagellates were swept out to sea.

The second plague, the swarms of frogs, struck soon after the first, according to Exodus 7:25–29. Normally these amphibians become terrestrial with the fall of the Nile in September-October, but in that year the frogs, exceptionally, invaded the land during the inundation period. This is to be explained, according to the Hort theory, by the pollution of the natural habitat of the frogs caused by the dead fish. The creatures were therefore unseasonably driven to seek refuge on dry land where, however, they would have been infected by the *Bacillus anthracis*, an organism that forms highly resistant spores and that is transferred by insects. The masses of decomposing fish would have provided an excellent breeding ground for the disease, which would have accounted for the wholesale dying of the frogs.

The third plague, called in Hebrew *kinnim/kinnam*, is identified by Hort as mosquitoes. These bloodsuckers are regularly quite abundant in Egypt during the October-November period. The unusual flooding of the Nile would intensify the phenomenon. These insects are prolific breeders. Here again, the plague is not stated to have ended abruptly. It apparently subsided gradually, as would be expected.

The fourth plague, the swarms of insects, is associated by Hort with the fly *Stomoxys calcitrans*, or stable fly, a vicious, blood-sucking variety. It multiplies suddenly and vanishes just as suddenly in tropical and subtropical regions. This would explain why Goshen was exempt from it; its climate is not tropical but Mediterranean.

The fifth plague consisted of pestilence that struck the livestock in the fields, but also did not reach Goshen. It must have occurred early in January, when the subsiding of the flood waters allowed some of the cattle to pasture in the open. The cause of the disease in question would have been the *Bacillus anthracis* mentioned earlier. The cattle of the Israelites, who lived in the Delta region, would not have been affected because the fields here would have been waterlogged longer than usual, thus not permitting open-field pasturing. Also, Mediterranean rain squalls would have washed away the surface bacilli.

The inflammation that was the sixth plague would have been anthrax transmitted by the *Stomoxys calcitrans* of the fourth one. Here again, Goshen would have remained unaffected.

The seventh plague consisted of singularly destructive hailstorms. The note in Exodus 9:31–32 that the flax and barley were ruined, but not the wheat and emmer, or spelt, gives a clue to what happened. In Upper Egypt, hail and thunderstorms occasionally occur, but in no particular season. In the north, a Mediterranean climatic zone, these happen exclusively in late spring and early fall. Between November and March, Goshen would not experience storms of this kind. Now flax is normally sown in Egypt early in January, and it flowers three weeks later. Barley is ordinarily sown in August and harvested in February. Wheat and spelt were sown in August and harvested toward the end of March. Due to the abnormally heavy inundation, the crops would all have been sown late that year, and would have been tardy in ripening. However, in early February the flax and barley would have been sufficiently advanced to be imperiled by the large hailstones, whereas the wheat and spelt would not yet have developed to that stage.

The eighth plague was locusts, a visitation quite common in Egypt, but this time occurring in unprecedented swarms. This may be explained as follows. In February-March, the locusts that hatch during the winter months usually migrate to Palestine and Egypt, depending on the prevailing winds. They invade both countries from March till early May. A strong "east wind" would indeed have brought the locusts upon Egypt. The strong "west wind" that is said to have removed them from the borders of Egypt is, as the Hebrew literally means, "a sea wind," that is, a storm coming in from the Mediterranean and blowing the locust swarms down into the Nile Valley and into the south, out of the land.

The ninth plague, darkness for three days, was the first *khamsin* of the season, which happens early in March. As explained above, this is the hot southerly Egyptian wind that blows in from the Sahara Desert carrying with it sand and dust. In that particular year the cumulatively devastating effects of the previous plagues on the soil meant that the matter released into the atmosphere would have been extraordinarily dense and abundant, blocking out the sun. A *khamsin* of two or three days' duration is not unusual. Since the Israelites were largely domiciled in Goshen, which is the Wadi Tumilat, they would have been little affected by such a *khamsin* from the south, because this region is at right angles to the narrow Nile valley.

The literary form

Hort's theory has been attacked on several grounds, though the facts given in the fields of geology and microbiology have not been challenged. However, apart from the prose narrative in the Book of Exodus, two other accounts of the plagues have been preserved in the Bible in poetic form in the Book of Psalms.

In Psalm 78:42–51 we read as follows:

> They did not remember His strength,
> or the day He redeemed them from the foe,
> how He displayed His signs in Egypt,
> His wonders in the plain of Zoan.
> He turned their rivers into blood;
> He made their waters undrinkable.
> He inflicted upon them swarms of insects to devour them,
> frogs to destroy them.
> He gave their crops over to grubs,
> their produce to locusts.
> He killed their vines with hail,
> their sycamores with frost.
> He gave their beasts over to hail,
> their cattle to lightning bolts.
> He inflicted His burning anger upon them,
> wrath, indignation, trouble,
> a band of deadly messengers.
> He cleared a path for His anger;
> He did not stop short of slaying them,
> but gave them over to pestilence.

He struck every first-born in Egypt,
the first fruits of their vigor in the tents of Ham.

In Psalm 105:27–36 the events leading up to the Exodus are celebrated
this way:

> They performed His signs among them,
> His wonders, against the land of Ham.
> He sent darkness; it was very dark;
> did they not defy His word?
> He turned their waters into blood
> and killed their fish.
> Their land teemed with frogs,
> even the rooms of their king.
> Swarms of insects came at His command,
> Lice, throughout their country.
> He gave them hail for rain,
> and flaming fire in their land.
> He struck their vines and fig trees,
> broke down the trees of their country.
> Locusts came at His command,
> grasshoppers without number.
> They devoured every green thing in the land;
> They consumed the produce of the soil.
> He struck down every first-born in the land,
> the first fruit of their vigor.
> He led Israel out with silver and gold;
> none among their tribes faltered.
> Egypt rejoiced when they left,
> for dread of Israel had fallen upon them.

It will be seen at once that these passages differ from the account in
the Book of Exodus and from each other in the number and order of
the plagues, and to a certain extent, also in their content. A glance at
Table 4.1 clarifies the variant traditions.[38]

It is clear that multiple traditions concerning the plagues circulated
in ancient Israel, in which the conventional numbers, ten and seven,
were used symbolically, each signifying the idea of totality. To base a

Table 4.1   A Comparison of Accounts of the Plagues

Exodus	Psalm 78:42–51	Psalm 105:28–36
1. Blood	1. Blood	1. Darkness
2. Frogs	2. Insects	2. Blood
3. Lice	3. Frogs	3. Frogs
4. Insects	4. Locusts	4. Insects and lice
5. Pestilence striking livestock	5. Hail	5. Hail striking the trees
6. Boils hitting man and beast	6. Pestilence striking livestock	6. Locusts
7. Hail striking man, beast, agriculture, and trees	7. Pestilence striking firstborns	7. Killing of firstborn
8. Locusts		
9. Darkness		
10. Killing of firstborn of man and beast		

theory on only one of these traditions invites hesitation about the validity of its application. Further, many scholars claim that the version in the Book of Exodus is itself a composite, which, if proven, would undermine Hort's theory's usefulness. On the other hand, it could be argued that Hort's explanations support the unity of the narrative and undermine the claim that the Exodus version is a combination of traditions. It might also be maintained that the arrangements in the Psalms are later poetic reworkings of the primary prose version. More to the point is the objection that extraordinary high rises of the Nile obviously have occurred periodically in Egyptian history, yet the native literature leaves no trace of the chain of dire consequences here alleged.

In truth, the biblical narrative says nothing about causal connections or about an abnormal inundation of the river. It does insist that the series of plagues was the product of divine deliberation. It is the implicit presupposition of all that is described that the guiding hand of Providence is detectable, less in the nature of the calamities than in their terrifying intensity, their timing, their concentrative force, and above all, in the shielding of the Israelites from their effects. The entire account

Table 4.2 The Literary Structure of the Plagues Narrative

	Plague	Exodus source	Forewarning	Time indication of warning	Instruction formula	Agent
First series	1. Blood	7:14–24	yes	"in the morning"	"Station yourself"	Aaron
	2. Frogs	7:25–8:11	yes	none	"Go to Pharaoh"	Aaron
	3. Lice	8:12–15	none	none	none	Aaron
Second series	4. Insects	8:16–28	yes	"in the morning"	"Station yourself"	God
	5. Pestilence	9:1–7	yes	none	"Go to Pharaoh"	God
	6. Boils	9:8–12	none	none	none	Moses
Third series	7. Hail	9:13–35	yes	"in the morning"	"Station yourself"	Moses
	8. Locusts	10:1–20	yes	none	"Go to Pharaoh"	Moses
	9. Darkness	10:21–23	none	none	none	Moses
Climax	10. Death of Egyptian firstborn	11:4–7 12:29–30	yes	none	none	God

has a didactic and theological purpose, not a historiographic one. In order to underline and emphasize these points, the narrator has devised a literary structure of impressive artistry.[39]

The plagues are arranged in the form of three series of calamities comprising three afflictions in each series. The tenth is climactic and lies wholly outside the series in that it, alone, has no grounding in natural events. It belongs to the realm of the supernatural. Within each series, the first two plagues are each preceded by divine forewarning, while the third strikes each time unheralded. Again, in the case of the first plague in each series Moses is bidden to confront the pharaoh "in the morning," but no time indication is given in respect of the other two. Also common to the first, fourth, and seventh plagues is the manner in which God's instruction to Moses is formulated. He is told, "Station yourself" before the pharaoh; the verbal stem *y-ts-b* is used each time. The second, fifth, and eighth plagues share the introductory formula "Go to Pharaoh," in which the verb *b-w-'* is uniformly employed. The third plague in each series has no common instruction formula. Finally, the entire first series of the three plagues is wrought through the instrumentality of Aaron, the entire last series is accomplished through the agency of Moses. The middle series has no pattern. Table 4.2 illustrates the literary structure of the narrative.

It is worthy of note that a similar kind of literary symmetry and schematized arrangement is employed in the Genesis Creation story and in the opening prose narrative of the Book of Job. In the former, the creative process is laid out as a systematic progression from chaos to cosmos through a series of six successive units of time culminating in a climactic seventh that pertains solely to God. The creative acts are arranged in two corresponding groups, each comprising four productions within three days, while the third day each time witnesses two creations. Within each of the parallel groups, the movement is from heaven to terrestrial water to dry land. Further, the creations of the first three days become the resource to be utilized by the corresponding creature in the second group. The recurring use of fixed verbal formulas rounds out the literary design.

In the Book of Job, the series of misfortunes that beset the hero is presented in three groups of two afflictions each, in which the first blow falls on livestock and the second on human beings. The cause of each series is alternately human and divine, and the whole culminates in a climactic, divinely wrought, seventh calamity. Here, too, there are fixed literary formulas punctuating the series.[40]

The meaning and function of the structural symmetry is always to emphasize that what has occurred is the vindication of God's active presence in the life of the world. In the case of the plagues, in particular, precisely because the first nine are rooted in familiar afflictions, the literary presentation stresses that they are not a fortuitous succession of random, senseless visitations of Nature's blind fury, but the calculated, purposeful, directed, and controlled workings of the Divine Intelligence. Just as God may use a person's fundamentally evil character to further His own objectives, as in the case of the pharaoh's obstinacy, so may He employ the vagaries of Nature to achieve His historical goals.

This explains why the climactic tenth plague must be wholly outside of human experience, and must defy any rational explanation. It must be clear to all, and beyond the possibility of misinterpretation, that what took place can only have emanated from a divine source.

Judgments on the gods of Egypt[41]

In two passages in the Torah the plagues are understood to be as much judgments on the Egyptian gods as on the Egyptians themselves. In the words of Exodus 12:12, the Lord declared, "I will mete out punishments to all the gods of Egypt, I the Lord." The historical summary of Numbers 33:4 distinctly states that "the Lord executed judgment on their gods." The meaning of these assertions is not spelled out, and the motif is again mentioned in the Bible only in Jeremiah 46:25. The Hellenistic-Jewish work known as "The Wisdom of Solomon" that is included in the extrabiblical collection called the "Apocrypha," understood the plagues to be a mockery of Egyptian paganism.[42]

It is not possible to account for each and all the ten plagues in this manner, but in the case of some of them an explanation of this kind makes sense.[43] The opening and closing calamities of the threefold series assail the two great pivotal fundamentals of Egyptian life—the Nile and the sun—both of which were personified as deities in the Egyptian religion.

The densely populated valley of the River Nile, flanked by deserts to the east and west, is desperately dependent for its fertility upon the life-giving waters produced during the few months of the river's annual inundation as it surges northward through the valley and drains into the Mediterranean Sea. The classic dictum of Hecataeus, cited by Herodotus, that Egypt is the gift of the Nile, aptly epitomizes the reality of Egyptian life and culture. As the vital artery of the land, the Nile is the obvious and most vulnerable target. Therefore, the first two plagues center upon the river. They seriously affected the entire hydrography of Egypt and polluted the existing sources of water supply. Insofar as the Nile was deified by the Egyptians as Hapi the Nile god, and its inundation was viewed as a manifestation of the great god Osiris, the plague of blood had to be locally interpreted as a diminution of the powers of these two gods.[44]

The sun too was of paramount importance in the culture of Egypt. It was regarded as the first king of the land from whom all the pharaohs were descended. They were considered to be his successors on earth, and their rule was the image of the reign of the sun. The sun was a god, Re, and also Amon-Re, and the worship of the sun god pervaded the official ritual of the palace. As the source of heat, light, and creativity, as the symbol of the cosmic order, his divinity exceeded that of the other gods of the pantheon. The plague of darkness, therefore, would have been regarded as the humiliation of the sun god. This is all the more likely in light of the powerful Egyptian cosmogonic myth relating to the monstrous serpent Apophis.[45] This creature symbolized darkness and was viewed as the embodiment of all that is terrible. The sun's journey across the sky was thought to involve a mighty struggle between it and Apophis that ceaselessly attempted to destroy it. Each morning's rising sun represented the defeat of the forces of darkness. A plague of three days of darkness would surely have been taken by the Egyptians as the vanquishing of the sun god by Apophis, as the triumph of demonic and chaotic powers, and as a portent of incipient horrors.

In addition to the first and ninth plagues, the visitation of frogs, the rotting, foul masses of them, might well have been regarded as a mocking of the well known frog goddess Heqt, who was the consort of the god Khnum, the one who fashioned humans out of clay at the potter's wheel. Heqt was fancied as assisting women in labor.[46] One wonders whether the affliction of the waters of the Nile and the plague of frogs might not have been construed by the biblical narrator as a kind of retribution for the decrees of the pharaoh ordaining the killing of male Israelites at birth, and then their drowning in the Nile.

Finally, it must be remembered that the entire story of the plagues is about a contest between the will of the pharaoh and the will of the God whom only the Israelites recognized. The pharaoh was a self-proclaimed god, the object of worship by his subjects. The theory of his divinity was sustained by the religious and political institutions of the Egyptian state. Consequently, the plagues, the ignoble defeat, and the ignominious end of the god-king constitute a saga that breathes contempt for Egyptian paganism.

Whether or not any or all of the foregoing interpretations are valid, the fact remains that here we encounter for the first time a new development in the religion of Israel. The text unequivocally speaks of judgments upon the gods of Egypt. The Book of Genesis ignores the theme of the struggle against paganism. The Patriarchal narratives exhibit no tension between the religion of the founding fathers and that of the nations with whom they come in contact. Only oblique hints of difference are occasionally perceptible, such as when Jacob swears "by the Fear of his father Isaac" while Laban, the Aramean, takes an oath by his ancestral deities;[47] or when Jacob demands that the members of his household rid themselves of the "alien gods" in their midst.[48] The notion of a war on polytheism, however, is first found here in our Exodus narrative, and it becomes henceforth one of the Bible's major themes. Apart from the explicit statement of Exodus 12:12 and Numbers 33:4, and the nature of some of the plagues, it also finds subtle expression in other ways in the plagues narrative. The inability of the magicians to reproduce the plagues after a while,[49] the transcendent ability of God to manipulate nature in order to realize His purposes, and the protection from the effects of the plagues that He bestows upon Israel—all are calculated to undermine faith in what the Egyptians accepted as divinities. Without doubt, the Israelite war on polytheism begins with the advent of Moses as liberator from Egyptian bondage.[50] Its ultimate formulation will appear in the Ten Commandments: "You shall have no other gods besides Me."[51]

CHAPTER V

The Passover and the Exodus

EXODUS 12–13:16

The calendar

The capitulation of the pharaoh following the culminating and inexorably decisive blow—the death of the Egyptian firstborn—is now at hand. Between the prediction of the impending climax and the account of its realization, the narrative interposes detailed instructions to the Israelites in preparation for their liberation from slavery. A people newly freed must henceforth be sustained by its own native resources if it is to achieve true national independence, if it is no longer to be a passive object of history, subservient to a dominant but alien culture. A liberated people must evolve and stress its own distinctive autonomous culture, devise its own structures of national existence, and forge its own institutions. One of its first desiderata is the establishment of a uniform calendar. Such an institution is a powerful instrument of societal, cultural, and religious cohesion.

This being so, the Israelites are informed that the month of liberation, the springtime of nature and now the springtime of Israel as a free people, is henceforth to be the start of the year. "This month shall mark for you the beginning of the months; it shall be the first of the months of the year for you."[1] We know nothing of Israel's earlier calendar, but the phrasing unmistakably points to an innovation, to a break with the past.

In Egypt, not surprisingly, the river and the sun controlled the pattern of calendrical observances. The seasons of the year were named in connection with the agricultural conditions caused by the inundation and subsidence of the Nile. There were three such seasons: "The Season of Inundation," in June-July when the river overflowed the fields; "The Season of Coming Forth," when the arable land emerged and could be worked; and "The Season of Deficiency," that is, the period when the Nile was at its lowest ebb. Throughout most of Egyptian history the calendar was a solar one, based upon a highly complicated calculation connected with the heliacal rising of the "Dog Star," Sirius. The festivals fell into three categories: the festivals of the gods, the festivals of the king, and the festivals of the dead.[2]

The new calendar of Israel is to be completely different. It is to be a lunisolar one. That is, it is to be regulated by the positions of both the moon and the sun. The month begins with the new moon, but the first month of the year is to fall in the spring.[3] The entire gamut of religio-national calendrical observances is to be oriented to the great act of divinely wrought liberation of Israel from Egypt.

Four liturgical calendars are listed in the Torah, and each commences with the Passover.[4] The months of the Israelite year have no names. However, there are traces of a very ancient system. Apart from the "month of Abib,"[5] there are also the "month of Ziv"[6] (the second month), the "month of Ethanim"[7] (the seventh month), and the "month of Bul"[8] (the eighth month). Significantly, these ancient Hebrew names, the only such preserved in the Bible, represent the two months of the spring and the two months of the fall, that is, the two equinoxes. It is not known whether any other months had names.[9] The predominant system in biblical literature of the pre-exilic period is to designate the months by the ordinal numbers. Wherever it can be controlled, it turns out that the enumeration is based on a spring New Year reckoning. To give just a few examples, in the Book of Jeremiah it is related that King Jehoiakim of Judea ordered the scroll of the prophet's oracles to be fetched and read to him. After the completion of every three or four columns, the king took a knife, cut them from the scroll, and threw them into the fire. The date of this event is given as the "ninth month," and it is explained that "the king was sitting in the winter house, with a fire burning in the brazier before him."[10] This makes sense only if the enumeration of the months of the year commenced with the spring.

Another incident related in the Book of Jeremiah tells of the ap-

Table 5.1 The Hebrew Liturgical Calendar

Month	Ancient Hebrew name	Post-exilic name (Babylonian)	Season	Festivals	Biblical source
1	'Aviv (Exod. 23:15)	Nisan	March/April	14 Passover sacrifice	Exod. 12:11; Lev. 23:5; Num. 28:16; Deut. 16:1–2
				15–21 Feast of Unleavened Bread	Exod. 12:17–20, 23:5, 34:18; Lev. 23:6–8; Num. 28:17–24; Deut. 16:3–5, 8
				16 First sheaf of harvest	Lev. 23:10–15
2	Ziv (1 Kings 6:1, 37)	'Iyyar	April/May	14 Later Passover	Num. 9:9–11
3		Sivan	May/June	6 Pentecost—Feast of Weeks	Exod. 23:16, 34:22; Lev. 23:10–21; Num. 28:26–31; Deut. 16:9–12
4		Tammuz	June/July	[17] Fast Day	Zech. 8:19
5		'Av	July/August	[9] Fast Day	Zech. 7:3–5, 8:19
6		'Elul	August/September		
7	'Ethanim (1 Kings 8:2)	Tishri	September/October	1 Day of Sounding of Shofar	Lev. 23:24–25; Num. 29:1–6
				10 Day of Atonement	Lev. 16:29–34, 23:27–32; Num. 29:7–11
				15–21 Tabernacles—Feast of Ingathering	Exod. 23:16; Lev. 23:34–36; Num. 29:12–34; Deut. 16:13; Neh. 8:14
				22 Solemn Assembly	Lev. 23:36; Num. 29:35–38; Neh. 8:18
8	Bul (1 Kings 6:38)	Marḥeshvan	October/November		
9		Kislev	November/December	[25 to 2 Tevet Hanukkah]	[1 Macc. 4:52–59]
10		Tevet	December/January	[10] Fast Day	Zech. 8:19
11		Shevat	January/February		
12		'Adar	February/March	14 Purim	Esther 9:21–28

pointment of Gedaliah, son of Ahikam, as governor of Judea immediately after the destruction of the Temple by the Babylonians in the
fifth month. It was the season of the harvesting of wine, figs, and oil.[11]
Once again, this is feasible only if the fifth month occurred in the
summertime.

When the Jews returned to Zion after the Babylonian Exile toward
the end of the sixth century B.C.E., they brought back with them the
Babylonian names for the months of the year, and these gradually
displaced the numerical system. The Babylonian names have remained
normative in the Jewish religious calendar ever since. This development
is reflected in the Scriptures that derive from post-exilic times in which
seven of the twelve Babylonian names appear, often glossed by a note
giving the numerical equivalent based on the spring New Year. Several
examples are featured in the Book of Esther: "In the tenth month, that
is the month of Teveth," "in the first month, that is the month of
Nisan," "in the twelfth month, that is the month of Adar,"[12] and so
forth.

On the other hand, there are several biblical passages that indicate
an autumnal New Year. For instance, a phrase like *yoreh u-malkosh*,
"the early rain and the late," in Deuteronomy 11:14 and Jeremiah 5:24,
shows that the order is determined by the agricultural year that takes
its bearings from the fall. This fits in with a formula like "the Feast of
Ingathering at the end of the year," and with the dating of this same
festival "at the turn of the year."[13] One of the earliest Israelite inscriptions, the tenth-century B.C.E. agricultural calendar found in the city
of Gezer,[14] commences the annual cycle of a farmer's tasks with the
"Ingathering" and closes with the "summer fruit." Since this is hardly
a natural order, it must be assumed to reflect a civil year that began in
the autumn. Undoubtedly, the year was reckoned to begin at different
dates for different purposes. This is well illustrated by the opening words
of Mishnah Rosh Ha-Shanah, which lists "four New Years." These are
enumerated as follows: the first of Nisan, in the spring, marks the regnal
New Year, and the base for reckoning the cycle of religious festivals;
the first of Elul, the sixth month, is the New Year for purposes of paying
the tithe of cattle; the first of Tishri, the seventh month, is the beginning
of the civil New Year, and of the sabbatical and jubilee year, and is a
significant deadline in connection with the three-year prohibition on
the fruit of a newly planted tree[15] and with the obligation of the tithe

on vegetables. There are variant traditions regarding the "New Year for trees," that is, the deadline for tithes on fruit, as either the first or fifteenth of Shevat, the eleventh month.

As was noted above, the phrasing of the prescription of Exodus 12:2 ordaining a spring New Year shows it to have been an innovation in Israel. Although the celebration of a festival at this season was quite common in the Near East, the Israelite version belongs to a wholly different category from its contemporaries in that the New Year is now grounded neither in nature's renewal nor in mythology, such as an event in the life of a god, but in a historic event—the liberation of a people from national oppression. Such a revolutionary phenomenon is without analogy in the ancient world.

The paschal lamb and the unleavened bread

The declaration instituting a new calendar is followed by careful instructions about the paschal offering. On the tenth day of the month the animal victim is to be set aside and kept in readiness. No explanation for the choice of this day is forthcoming, but the tenth day of the month in which the New Year falls must carry special significance, though in what way presently eludes us.[16] Joshua chose that day forty years later to cross over into the Promised Land,[17] and the most sacred day in the liturgical calendar, Yom Kippur, also falls on the tenth day of the month, though in the autumn,[18] as does the opening of the jubilee year.[19]

The animal offering was to be restricted to an unblemished one-year-old male lamb or kid. On the fourteenth day of the month it was to be slaughtered at twilight. Some of its blood was to be daubed on the two doorposts and the lintel of the houses. The flesh was to be roasted over the fire, and eaten together with unleavened bread and bitter herbs. No other mode of preparation was allowed. Preferably, it should all be consumed at the festal meal, but should there be any leftovers, they had to be burned the next morning.[20]

The sacrificial meal is the prelude to the Exodus. Therefore, although it will be eaten in haste, the Israelites were to be already fully dressed and ready for the flight from Egypt. No one was to leave home until instructed to do so. What is of particular interest is that the sacrificial meal is termed "a passover offering to the Lord."[21] The text uses the

Hebrew *pesah* as though it is something well known, not a new coinage. Similarly, the unleavened bread is called *matsot* (sing. *matsah*) without further definition,[22] again assuming immediate comprehension on the part of the people. This implies that the two technical terms, *pesah* and *matsah*, preexisted the Exodus association and do not derive their origins from it. In the case of the *matsah*, the Torah itself confirms its prehistory, for it is recounted in the Book of Genesis how Lot, Abraham's nephew, hastily baked unleavened bread (*matsot*) for his two unexpected guests.[23] Two other biblical narratives also suggest that *matsot* were the kind of cakes that one would customarily bake at any time for unexpected guests. Gideon, who was to become one of the judges of Israel, quickly prepared them for the messenger who visited him.[24] The witch of Endor hastily slaughtered a calf, took flour and kneaded it, and baked some unleavened bread for King Saul, who had been fasting since the preceding day.[25] Moreover, *matsot* are not uniformly identified in the Bible with the Exodus. Several ritual texts include them as an ingredient of various offerings that are unconnected with the Passover.[26]

The requirement to eat the paschal lamb together with unleavened bread was obviously ordained long in advance of the actual Exodus. Hence, *matsah* cannot really have its origin in the hasty escape from Egypt. Indeed, no reason for its inclusion in the last supper taken before leaving the country is given in the text of Exodus 12:8. Without doubt, the *matsah* here referred to is the kind of flat cake made from unleavened flour and water that the Bedouin bake to this day.

A strange aspect of the term *matsah* is the lack of any satisfactory etymology either in Hebrew or in any other Semitic language.[27] An attempt to connect it with the Hebrew stem *m-ts-ts*, "to squeeze," puts a strain on the imagination, nor is a supposed association with the Greek *matsa* any more helpful. That noun means specifically "barley bread," as distinct from "wheaten bread," and the verbal form means "to knead barley cake." An allied verb, *masso*, "to knead, press into a mold," is also used especially of barley cakes, of the kind eaten without being baked![28] Moreover, the derivation of the Greek *matsa* itself remains enigmatic and may well be a borrowing into that language from a Semitic source.[29] The one intriguing point of connection with the Greek, apart from the similarity in sound, is that the month of Abib, the month of the festival, is the month in which the barley ripens.

The Hebrew term *pesah* has come to be uniformly rendered "passover" in English usage. It is taken for granted that the name is derived from the verbal form found three times in Chapter 12, which in turn is assumed to convey the idea that God "passed over" the houses of the Israelites when He smote the Egyptian firstborn.[30] However, we have already seen that the noun *pesah* was something previously known and that antedated the Exodus. To this item must be added the interesting fact that the rendering "pass over" is only one of several venerable traditions about the meaning of the verb, and a minority one at that.[31] Further to complicate the matter is the curious lack of internally consistent translations within the ancient versions themselves. Rabbinic tradition too has preserved a variety of interpretations. In brief, the verb *p-s-h* has been understood in three different ways: "to protect," "to have compassion," and "to pass over." It was through the influence of the Latin Vulgate version that "pass over" became the predominant English rendering, even though it seems to be the least likely of the three possibilities.

There is another aspect of the use of *pesah* in the Bible that needs to be stressed, and that is that the term refers exclusively to the paschal sacrifice and encompasses only the fourteenth day of the month and not the entire week following. It is quite clear that there were two distinct festivals. The first, one-day, celebration was known as *pesah* or "the Festival of the Paschal Sacrifice," as Exodus 34:25 has it. From the fifteenth of the month on there was a separate "Festival of Unleavened Bread"—*matsot*. Three biblical texts express this differentiation explicitly. Leviticus 23:5–6 reads: "In the first month, on the fourteenth day of the month, at twilight, there shall be a passover offering to the Lord, and on the fifteenth day of that month the Lord's Feast of Unleavened Bread. You shall eat unleavened bread for seven days." The prophet Ezekiel similarly declares "On the fourteenth day of the first month you shall have the passover sacrifice; and during a festival of seven days unleavened bread shall be eaten."[32] Finally, it is related in Ezra 6:19–22 that the returned exiles from Babylon "celebrated the Passover on the fourteenth day of the first month," and then "joyfully celebrated the Feast of Unleavened Bread for seven days." It is this original separation of the two festivals that explains why Exodus 13:6–8 can mention only the seven days of eating unleavened bread, and can say nothing of the Passover.

A close look at the *pesah* regulations shows that, typologically, the institution belonged to the spring rituals characteristic of the life of the pastoral nomad.[33] All the detailed instructions of Exodus Chapter 12 point in that direction—the restriction of the sacrifice to a lamb or a kid of the goats, the barbecuing of the meat and its seasoning with pungent herbs accompanied by unleavened cakes, its celebration at the time of the vernal equinox when lambing occurs and when the movement of livestock to summer pastures begins, the family nature of the celebration, the dispensing with priest and altar, the unique eating of the entire sacrifice without any part of it being a gift to the Lord or an emolument of the priest, the nighttime observance of the ritual when the shepherd is free of his cares and duties, and on the days of the full moon to provide sufficent natural light for the occasion. All these items are well documented as being the characteristically common heritage of the pastoral nomad.

The "Feast of Unleavened Bread"—matsot—is in sharp contrast to the pesah. The springtime in the Land of Israel is the season of the barley harvest. The chronological connection between the new harvest and the Passover is given in the liturgical calendar of Leviticus Chapter 23.[34] There it is laid down that one may not partake of the new crop until the first sheaf has been brought to the priest, who performs a ritual waving. The prescribed animal sacrifice, meal offering, and libation then take place. All this is done "on the day after the sabbath," the context leaving no doubt of the connection with the Passover. In other words, the seven-day festival of matsot celebrated the spring harvest, and was an agricultural festival. Abib, the name of the month in which it occurs, means "fresh, young ears of barley."

A few biblical texts illustrate how the original springtime agricultural festival came to be reinterpreted in terms of the circumstances of the Exodus. In Exodus 13:8, 23:15, and 34:18, the matsot are simply integrated into that event without any rationalization, but Exodus 12:34 and 12:39 give a reason for the association: "So the people took their dough before it was leavened, their kneading bowls wrapped in their cloaks upon their shoulders" and "they baked unleavened cakes of the dough that they had taken out of Egypt, for it was not leavened, since they had been driven out of Egypt and could not delay. . . ." This explanation clearly underlies the summary in Deuteronomy 16:3: "You shall not eat anything leavened with it; for seven days thereafter you shall eat unleavened bread, bread of distress—for you departed from the land of Egypt hurriedly—so that you may remember the day of your departure from the land of Egypt as long as you live."

The pastoral nomad follows a lunar calendar; the agriculturist goes by a solar one. Following the Exodus and the conquest of Canaan, the people of Israel changed from being pastoral nomads to being farmers. The revised Israelite calendar reflects the mixing of the old with the new reality, and is therefore lunisolar. The transmutation of the original nomadic rite is also effectuated in the case of the paschal lamb. The pagan shepherds offered the animal in order to ensure the fecundity of the flocks, just as the rites of the spring harvest festival were intended to secure the fertility of the soil. In Israel, each rite was severed from its magical and mythical roots. The close proximity in time between pastoral and agricultural festivals, and their coalescence with the events of the Exodus of Israel from Egypt, easily led to the amalgamation and integration of all the varied elements. The entire complex was divested of the former meanings and completely reinterpreted. Invested with radically new significance, it was historicized and transformed into a revolutionary new creation in commemoration and celebration of God's mighty deeds in liberating His people from Egyptian tyranny. As such, it lost its time-bound nature, and became the perennial source and unfailing inspiration for fresh creativity.

Leaven

The requirement to eat unleavened bread—*matsah*—is supplemented by a strict prohibition on the retaining and eating of leavened bread during the annual festival:

Seven days you shall eat unleavened bread; on the very first day you shall remove leaven [*se'or*] from your houses, for whoever eats leavened bread [*hamets*] from the first day to the seventh day, that person shall be cut off from Israel.[35]

No leaven [*se'or*] shall be found in your houses for seven days. . . . You shall eat nothing leavened; in all your settlements you shall eat unleavened bread.[36]

Throughout the seven days unleavened bread shall be eaten; no leavened bread [*hamets*] shall be found with you, and no leaven [*se'or*] shall be found in all your territory.[37]

Two Hebrew terms are used to designate leaven: *se'or* and *hamets*. The first refers to the leavening agent, which was a piece of old dough that had been allowed to reach a high state of fermentation. This is known as sourdough. The verb "to eat" is never used in connection with *se'or* because the product is quite inedible. The second, and the most frequently employed, term is *hamets*. This is, strictly defined, the freshly prepared mixture of flour and water to which the fermented old dough is added and is kneaded along with it, thereby accelerating the rising of the dough. According to rabbinic tradition, codified in law, the fermentation process is characteristic of only five types of grain: wheat, barley, spelt, rye, and oats.[38] Other grains, like rice and millet, rot but do not ferment.

In considering the origin and meaning of this proscription of leaven during the festival, account must be taken of the generalized ban on leaven within the sacrificial rituals. "You shall not offer the blood of My sacrifice with anything leavened. . . ."[39] "No meal offering that you offer to the Lord shall be made with leaven, for you must not turn into smoke any leaven or any honey as an offering by fire to the Lord."[40] ". . . [I]t shall be eaten as unleavened cakes. . . . It shall not be baked with leaven. . . ."[41] The exceptions to this rule are the sacrifice of well-being that is brought as a thanksgiving offering,[42] and the wave offering.[43] The reason for these exclusions from the ban is that these two offerings were eaten by the worshipper or the priest, and were not offered up to the Lord upon the altar.

Because the prohibition on leaven has wider application than the Passover, it is likely that the process of fermentation was associated with decomposition and putrefaction, and so became emblematic of corruption. Accordingly, it would be inappropriate to associate such a symbol with a sacrificial ritual whose function was to effect conciliation between man and God and to raise man to a higher level of spirituality. In like manner, the ban on leaven during the Passover week signifies that national liberation also involves moral and spiritual rejuvenation, and must not be tainted by moral corruption. Admittedly, there is no hard evidence from the Hebrew Scriptures themselves that fermentation was indeed associated with corruption, but this notion certainly appears in later Judaism. Rabbi Alexandri, a third-century c.e. Palestinian sage, is said to have concluded his daily prayers as follows: "Sovereign of the Universe, You know full well that it is our desire to fulfill Your will; but what prevents us from doing so?—The yeast in the dough. . . ."[44] That is to say, the impulse to evil in humankind acts as a fermenting and corrupting agent. This figurative synonymity of leaven with corruption is also found in the New Testament.[45] Plutarch (d. ca. 120 c.e.) as well explicitly states that "leaven is itself the offspring of corruption and corrupts the mass of dough with which it has been mixed."[46]

Bitter herbs

This constituent of the Passover meal, prescribed in Exodus 12:8, is repeated in Numbers 9:11 but is not otherwise mentioned in any of the references to the festival celebrations. No reason for its inclusion is given in the text. We have already noted above the pastoral nomad's practice of seasoning his roasted lamb with pungent herbs. It may be taken for granted, however, that unless the bitter herbs (*merorim*) were invested with some particular significance, they would hardly have merited special mention as a mere popular condiment among the solemn instructions about the paschal lamb. The only other reference to bitter herbs appears in the Book of Lamentations 3:15, "He has filled me with bitterness (*merorim*), sated me with wormwood."[47] Here the word is clearly a figure of speech expressing cruel suffering, and it is likely that a similar symbolic meaning was given the bitter herbs from the beginning, even though this interpretation is first articulated by Rabban Gamliel in the Mishnah Pesaḥim 10:5. He cleverly points to the word play between *merorim* (sing. *maror*) and the description of the sufferings of the Israelites at the hands of the Egyptians recorded in Exodus 1:14, "they made life bitter for them with harsh labor . . ." in which the same stem *m-r-r* is employed.

What specific herbaceous plant is intended by *merorim* is hard to say. The word is probably generic rather than specific. Mishnah Pesaḥim 2:6 enumerates five kinds of herbs that are subsumed under the heading *maror*, not all of which can be identified today.[48] The most widely used since the times of the Talmud is lettuce, called in the Mishnah *ḥazeret* and otherwise known as *ḥassa*. This vegetable was cultivated in ancient

Egypt. The name *hassa* gave opportunity for word-play with the Hebrew-Aramaic verb *h-w-s*, "to have compassion," so that the bitter herb not only symbolized the intense suffering of Israel but also became a reminder of God's compassion upon His people in rescuing them from slavery.[49] It will be remembered that one of the early traditions about the meaning of the stem *p-s-h* is "to have compassion" (*h-w-s*).

The blood

Among the several instructions given in preparation for the departure from Egypt is the indispensable requirement to daub with a bunch of hyssop some of the blood of the paschal lamb on the doorposts and lintel of the houses in which the Israelites were gathered to partake of their last meal on Egyptian soil.[50] The purpose of this procedure is so that "the blood on the houses where you are staying shall be a sign for you: when I see the blood I will pass over [protect] you, so that no plague will destroy you when I strike the land of Egypt." Again, "when the Lord goes through to smite the Egyptians, He will see the blood on the lintel and the two doorposts, and the Lord will pass over [protect] the door and will not let the Destroyer enter and smite your home."[51]

These passages make clear that the blood was simply to function as an outward, visible sign, a marker identifying the occupants as Israelites. It had no apotropaic role; that is to say, it is not considered to possess properties that would automatically and efficaciously provide protection against malign forces. This point deserves to be stressed vigorously because once more it illustrates the transformation that the religion of Israel wrought in the belief and practices of the times. There is good reason to believe that spring rites of the pastoral nomads were essentially magical in nature, and intended to ward off the dangers to the tribe and the flocks arising from the activities of evil spirits. The time of the full moon, at the vernal equinox in particular, was thought to be fraught with the greatest peril. Now, in the new religion of Israel, the entire procedure is demythologized, emptied of any magical content, and historicized. There are no independent demonic forces—only the one God exacting retribution from the intransigent, ruthless exploiters of other human beings. The sign on the doorpost is now an identity symbol; the entrance to the house with such a symbol is now a portal of freedom.

The choice of blood to signify the Israelite houses was probably determined by practical considerations. It was a coloring agent ready at hand. But it may also have absorbed symbolic meaning in that, in the Israelite way of thinking, blood was identified with vitality, and was, in fact, regarded as constituting the life essence. This idea finds explicit mention in the Bible several times.[52] In other words, the daubing of the blood simultaneously indicated both Israelite identity and the preservation of the occupants for life.[53] This use of blood to symbolize divine protection of the Israelites also carries with it a certain ironic resonance. The pharaoh had ordered the shedding of the blood of all their newly born males in order to curb the Israelite population growth; God's punishment of the Egyptians therefore began with a plague of blood, and blood became emblematic of the deliverance of their victims.

The blood was to be applied with a bunch of hyssop. This plant is frequently used as an applicator in purificatory rites.[54] It is almost certainly to be identified with Syrian hyssop, known botanically as *Origanum syriacum l.*[55] To this day the Samaritan sect uses this plant to sprinkle the blood of their passover sacrifice.

The death of the firstborn

We have previously drawn attention to the fact that each of the nine plagues was rooted in a natural phenomenon with which Egyptian history was quite familiar. From a theological perspective, they are the instances of God's harnessing the forces of nature for the realization of His own historic purpose. The tenth and final visitation upon the pharaoh and his people is the one plague for which no rational explanation can be given. It belongs entirely to the category of the supernatural: "In the middle of the night the Lord struck down all the first-born in the land of Egypt, from the first-born of Pharaoh who sat on the throne to the first-born of the captive who was in the dungeon, and all the first-born of the cattle."[56] The Israelite firstborn, however, remained entirely unscathed. In consonance with its miraculous nature, the instrumentality is no longer Moses and Aaron but is said to be God Himself. The plague demonstrates the absolute sovereign power of God of whom the pharaoh had denied all knowledge.

The selection of the firstborn as the target of the sudden, virulent, and swiftly death-dealing contagion is to be understood against the concept and status of the firstborn in ancient times.[57] Like the firstling of livestock and the first fruits of the soil,[58] so the firstborn of the mother's womb was considered rightfully to belong to God in gratitude for His bounteous gifts to humankind.[59] By virtue of this, all three firsts—of the soil, of domestic animals, and of the womb—enjoyed a certain status of sanctity and preciousness. In law and society the firstborn son had preference in inheritance and the right of succession.[60] He often assumed the responsibility of trusteeship of property and of adjudicating disputes. All the foregoing provides the background for the use of the term "firstborn" in a metaphorical, spiritual sense to describe God's special relationship with the people of Israel. The prophet Jeremiah expresses the same sentiment through the imagery of the first fruits: "Israel was holy to the Lord, the first fruits of His harvest. All who ate of it were guilty; disaster befell them."[61]

At the outset of his career, Moses was forewarned about the pharaoh's stubbornness, and was told to admonish the king in these words: "Thus says the Lord: Israel is my first-born son. I have said to you, 'Let My son go, that he may worship Me,' yet you refuse to let him go. Now I will slay your first-born son."[62] This address presaged the final plague and supplied in advance a justification for it. The death of the firstborn is viewed as a kind of measure for measure, as making the punishment fit the crime. The pharaoh sought to destroy God's people, His firstborn, as it were, so the firstborn of Egypt, in whose name he speaks and acts, will suffer the fate that had been planned for Israel.

The plague of the firstborn finally broke the will of the pharaoh. The once-proud monarch was utterly humbled. He summoned Moses and Aaron in the middle of the night and announced his unconditional acceptance of their terms. The all-powerful king-god pathetically implored the leaders of his subject people, "may you bring a blessing on me also!"[63] Urged on by the native populace, the Israelites left Egypt with everything they possessed, not to mention what they received from the Egyptians themselves. The Israelites were free at last.

"Six hundred thousand men on foot"

The totality of Israelites who left Egypt is given as "about six hundred thousand men on foot, aside from children" and womenfolk.[64]In addition, "a mixed multitude"[65] left with them. This last must have comprised a variety of non-Israelites who, taking advantage of the confusion in the Egyptian administration, fled the country.

The figure of six hundred thousand grown men "able to bear arms" would presuppose an Israelite population, at a conservative estimate, of well over two million persons, given the average distribution by age and sex. Six hundred thousand is also cited by Moses in Numbers 11:21, and the first census taken in the wilderness in the second year after the Exodus disclosed 603,550 able-bodied men, excluding the Levites.[66] This same number of males each contributed one-half shekel of silver for the building of the Tabernacle.[67] A second census taken nearly forty years later in the Plains of Moab revealed 601,730 males twenty years of age and up.[68] This is consistent with the data in Joshua 4:13–14, where we are told that two and one-half tribes could muster an army of about forty thousand "shock troops."

All this accords with the repeated assertions in the Exodus narrative about the extraordinary fertility of the womenfolk in Israel. It is said that "the Israelites were fertile and prolific; they multiplied and increased very greatly, so that the land was filled with them."[69] The pharaoh observed that "the Israelite people are much too numerous for us,"[70] and the text asserts that "the more they were oppressed, the more they increased and spread out."[71] The midwives declared the Hebrew women to be more vigorous than their Egyptian sisters: "Before the midwife can come to them, they have given birth."[72]

Such descriptions give the appearance of being hyperbole,[73] of featuring an extravagance of language designed to emphasize God's providential care of His people in their adversity. Yet there is nothing in the narrative to suggest that what is stated is other than what is considered to be factual. Nevertheless, the figure of over two million Israelites confronts us with a complex of well-nigh invincible problems. It hardly accords with there being just two midwives for such a multitude, although, admittedly, as we have earlier suggested, the two mentioned may simply have been the superintendents or guild heads of a much larger corps. Far more difficult is the story of Moses' acting as the sole judge in Israel until a judiciary was organized on the advice of his father-in-law.[74] Further, if the Israelites actually numbered more than two million souls, it means that the original community of seventy souls had grown into that phenomenal figure in the course of their sojourn in Egypt. The number 70, given in Genesis 46:26–27, and repeated in Exodus 1:5 and Deuteronomy 10:22, is a typological or symbolic one in the Bible, and expresses the idea of totality. The lists in the first-cited source do not include the wives of Jacob's sons and grandsons or their daughters. It is inconceivable that Jacob's twelve sons should have had fifty-three male offspring in all, but no daughters. In other words, the Patriarch's entourage comprised far more than seventy persons. The period of time spent in Egypt, a problem discussed above in the Introduction, will obviously be relevant to the issue. Did it extend over four hundred thirty years as Exodus 12:40 says, or did it cover only four or five generations, as the genealogical lists indicate?

If the former be historical, then such a natural multiplication of the kind described in the biblical narrative is theoretically feasible. It is known that a fertility rate of 2.5 percent represents a doubling of the population within a single generation. Any given population would increase sixfold each generation if all the married couples were to procreate at about a natural rate throughout the entire period of the woman's childbearing years.[75] It has been estimated that, on the assumption of an average of eight children per family, the small group of initial settlers could indeed have expanded to over two million in the course of four centuries. By another reckoning, it has been figured that in ten generations covering four hundred thirty years, forty-one men could multiply into 478,224 males above twenty years of age if for the first six generations each couple yielded three sons and three daughters, and if for the last four generations each had two sons and two daughters.[76] Even if the length of stay in Egypt be reduced to the two hundred fifteen years implied in the texts of the Samaritan and Greek Septuagint versions, it has been estimated that the total number of Israelites could have reached one million[77]—still a considerable number. The experience of the French Canadians might present a modern analogy in that an original community of three thousand around the year 1660 naturally increased to several million within three centuries.[78] Another analogy is provided by the example of nineteenth-century Russian Jewry. Between 1825 and 1900 the Jewish community, which was a "closed population," increased from 1.6 million to 5.175 million, an annual growth rate of 1.8 percent.[79] Of course, one would need to have statistics—which are wholly unobtainable—on the infant mortality rates, on longevity, and on many other factors that bear directly on the subject of population increase, before concluding that such an extraordinary natural multiplication as the Bible presupposes was not just theoretically possible, but also realizable in practice. Thus one scholar has computed on the basis of the annual rate of increase per thousand of the population of Egypt between the years 1907 and 1937, as determined by the official decennial censuses for that period, that an original seventy Israelites would have become no more than 10,363 at the end of four hundred thirty years.[80] The problem becomes far more complicated and, in fact, intractable if the computations hinge upon the generational data instead of the time span given in years. After all, Moses was only the great-grandson of Levi, who was among the pioneers of the settlement in Egypt.[81]

Another question that needs be tackled if the Israelites actually numbered over two million is their relationship to the total native Egyptian population. The size of the latter can only be very approximately estimated. The Jewish historian Josephus wrote that in his day, which fell within the last quarter of the first century C.E., there were 7.5 million inhabitants of Egypt exclusive of Alexandria.[82] The Greek historian Diodorus Siculus (mid-first century B.C.E.) reports seven million inhabitants, and he states that it was "of old" about the same.[83] Modern scholars cautiously estimate a population of between four and five million in the ancient period.[84] The point is that the Israelites would have constituted an extraordinarily high percentage of the population of Egypt. Such, indeed, is the impression conveyed by the above-cited biblical passages. But then the question may be posed as to how a minority of such considerable proportions could have allowed itself to have been enslaved and to have remained in that condition for so long. In this case, however, the history of slavery belies the implication of the query. At the end of the fifth century B.C.E. in Athens, slaves constituted 30 percent of the population, and in Italy at the end of the Republic the proportion of slaves was 35 percent. In 1860 the slaves comprised 33 percent of the population of the southern states of the U.S.A.[85]

More serious is the objection that the "land of Goshen," identified by most scholars with Wadi Tumilat, west of Ismailia, where the Israelites were concentrated, could not possibly have supported a population of the size implied. About thirty-eight miles (sixty kilometers) long and less than three miles (four kilometers) wide, it was not suited for agriculture on a large scale in ancient times. Equally critical is the problem as to how the slender resources of the Sinai Peninsula could have sustained over two million people on the move for forty years. In this case, the biblical narrative is quite aware of the difficulty and has the Israelites provisioned by supernatural means, by manna and quails.[86]

There are still other perplexities that are generated by the population figure given in the Book of Exodus. According to nature's usual distribution by sex, it has to be assumed that the number of firstborn females was about the same as that of the males. Now in the census reported in Numbers 3:43 there were 22,273 firstborn sons aged one month and up, so that there must have been at least 44,546 mothers, since the likelihood is that there was an equal number of firstborn girls. (It must be remembered that only the firstborn of the mother, not of the father, was counted.) In other words, only one in about fourteen women over age twenty were mothers! To make matters worse, the ratio of firstborn sons to the whole male population is generally one to four. Here, however, we have a ratio of one to forty-five. This would imply that each married man fathered between thirty-nine and forty-four sons![87] One suggested solution to these disparities is that the census of firstborn males only applied to those born after the Exodus, although the text does not say so.

The actual departure from Egypt provides another difficulty. It was effected in the course of a single day. To move out of Egypt, on foot, over two million persons, including the aged and the children, as well as livestock, in that limited period of time would be nothing short of miraculous. Similarly, the crossing of the Reed Sea by a population of this size that was fleeing the pursuing Egyptian army equipped with chariots, is another feat that can be explained only in supernatural terms.

In order to overcome the problems inherent in the huge figures, various suggestions have been made that hinge upon a reinterpretation of the Hebrew term *'elef*, usually rendered "a thousand." The size of the Israelite population is thereby reduced to what is regarded as credible, without tampering with the traditional text.

It has been noticed that several biblical passages employ *'elef* for a subsection of a tribe. This is the case in Numbers 1:16, which refers to "the elected of the assembly, the chieftains of their ancestral tribes" who are also designated "the heads of the clans of [*'alfei*] of Israel." The identical meaning is to be sought in Joshua 22:14, which speaks of the chieftains "from each ancestral house of each of the tribes of Israel; they were every one of them heads of ancestral houses of the clans ['*alfei*] of Israel." Perhaps the best example of this usage is in the speech of Gideon, who protests, "Why, my clan ['*alpi*] is the humblest in Manasseh and I am the youngest in my father's house."[88]

Taken in this sense, the "six hundred '*elef*" could, it is asserted, mean "six hundred family units." On the surface, those census lists of Numbers Chapters 1 and 25 can be interpreted in this way. Thus instead of Reuben's "46,500 grown males," there would be forty-six units, namely, five hundred persons; Simeon's count would be fifty-nine units corresponding to three hundred persons; and so forth for each of the tribes. According to this theory, an '*elef* represents a tent group averaging nine persons per group made up of two grandparents, two parents, three children, and two additional persons. The sum total of the census would be 598 units, which corresponds to 5,550 persons.[89]. The unit figure is thus practically identical with the 600 "units" who departed from Egypt, so that the entire population of Israel would have been about 5550.

This ingenious theory founders on the inexactitude and variability in the composition of the '*elef*. It cannot explain the number 22,273 given for the sum of the firstborn sons in Numbers 3:43. There, the context is decisive for the literal meaning. The same applies to the number of Levites, given there as amounting to 22,000 (verse 39). The 8,580 males between the ages of thirty and fifty mentioned in Numbers 4:48 is quite proportionate to the total.

An attempt to refine this theory also sees in '*elef* a subsection of a tribe, but with the specific reference to the military unit that went to war under its own commander.[90] The number of men to be recruited from each tribe would differ according to the circumstances, but the sum total of the units column would truly represent the number of '*alafim* into which each tribe was subdivided. The defects of this proposition are, first, that wherever it is controllable, '*elef* encompasses the entire clan and not just those recruited for military duty or *corvée*, and, second, that we would be left with no information whatsoever about the population of Israel at the time of the Exodus, which appears to be contrary to the intent of the text.

Clearly, quite a different approach is called for in the resolution of these quandaries. The foregoing inconsistencies pose problems to modern readers because we tend to treat the data in isolation from the larger purposes of the narrative. We take for granted that the historical consciousness of the narrator requires a presentation of statistical "facts" specific to a certain time-bound context. We are predisposed to equate "truth" with literalism. All these presuppositions are grounded in misunderstanding. The structures of thought within which the biblical writers operated permitted them to conceive of reality in ways quite different from our own. The individual ingredients of the narrative constitute integral elements of the whole, and are in turn informed by that totality. The whole possesses an inner logic of its own because it is not meant to be history writing in the modern sense of that term, but a historiosophical understanding of a complex of events that happened in historical time. Historical time is seen in terms of an era, an extended period, that is characterized by a distinctive development.

The first thing to remember, therefore, is that the departure from Egypt cannot be isolated from the era that it inaugurated and that came to a close with King Solomon's erection of the Temple in Jerusalem. That is why this latter is the only event in the Bible that is dated according to the passage of years from the Exodus.[91] This idea that the building of the Temple is the supreme consummation of the Exodus era actually finds expression in the "Song at the Sea" in Exodus Chapter 15. That poem celebrates the deliverance of Israel from the pharaoh's armies. It concludes (verse 17) with the following phrases:

> You will bring them and plant them in Your own mountain,
> The place You have made to dwell in, O Lord,
> The sanctuary, O Lord, which Your hands established.

The same idea is behind the following passage in Moses' farewell address:

> . . . because you have not yet come to the allotted haven that the Lord your God is giving you. When you cross the Jordan and settle in the land that the Lord your God is allotting to you, and He grants you safety from all your enemies around you and you live in security, then you must bring everything that I command you to the site where the Lord your God will choose to establish His name. . . .[92]

Unmistakable echoes of this theme are found in the story of Solomon's decision to build the Temple. When he wishes to engage the services of Hiram, king of Tyre, he sends him this message:

> You know that my father David could not build a house for the name of the Lord his God because of the enemies that encompassed him, until the Lord had placed them under the soles of his feet. But now the Lord my God has given me respite all around; there is no adversary and no mischance. And so I propose to build a house for the name of the Lord my God. . . .[93]

Similarly, in his address at the dedication of the completed Temple, King Solomon cites a divine oracle, "Ever since I brought My people Israel out of Egypt, I have not chosen a city among all the tribes of Israel for building a House where My name might abide . . ." and he concludes with this doxology: "Praised be the Lord who has granted a haven to His people Israel, just as He promised."[94]

The point of all this is that the building of the Temple is conceived as being the culmination of God's great acts of redemption that began with the Exodus. The edifice itself is the material symbol of the full realization of the original divine promise of redemption to the people of Israel. From the perspective of the biblical narrator, the time span involved in the Exodus events is therefore not restricted to the forty years of wilderness wanderings, but encompasses the period from Moses to Solomon. This is the Exodus era.

Another phenomenon that has to be considered is the conception of that entity called Israel. The people are organized along tribal lines, each tribe featuring its respective leadership and administrative organs. Yet the pan-Israelite orientation of the narrative has all but effaced the discrete tribal histories. Israel is not portrayed as a collection of individual tribes but as a corporate national entity, a psychic collectivity. It is as though all those living at the time of the building of the Temple themselves experienced the events of the Exodus. It is apparent that such a conception of Israel is the correlative of the preceding one that views the Exodus in terms of an era.

We are now in a position to return to the problem of the six hundred thousand adult males who are said to have left Egypt. This population figure more or less represents the historic reality of the period of the united monarchy, the period of David and Solomon.[95] Just as a twentieth-century Christian or Muslim leader might declare of his respective coreligionists that they are all "children of Abraham," and just as a convert to Judaism may sincerely recite in his or her prayers the formula "Our God and God of our fathers," and just as each July 4th a citizen of the United States of America may wholeheartedly celebrate the achievement of independence from the British irrespective of his or her ancestral origin, so the Israelites at the time of the Temple building could see themselves as having come out of Egypt. Viewed from this perspective, the Exodus population problem loses its severity because the figure of six hundred thousand takes on quite a different connotation.[96] It represents the Israelite population at the time of David and Solomon, which was seen to be the culmination of the Exodus era that began with the liberation from Egyptian slavery. This era constitutes, in the mind of the narrator, a continuum in which variation in time and content is effaced as being meaningless.

CHAPTER VI

From Egypt to Sinai

EXODUS 13:17–18:27

The route of the Exodus

It is easier to delineate the route that the fleeing Israelites avoided than to chart the course they actually took to their destination, the land of Canaan. This is because the narrative tells us clearly that "God did not lead them by way of the land of the Philistines, although it was nearer; for God said, 'The people may have a change of heart when they see war, and return to Egypt.' " At the same time, it is related that "God led the people roundabout, by way of the wilderness at the Sea of Reeds."[1]

The "Way of the land of the Philistines" can be traced on the map; the "Way of the Wilderness" lends itself to a variety of possibilities, and the "Sea of Reeds" lacks specificity. To add to the difficulties, the biblical data are sometimes fragmentary, most of the place-names can no longer be identified (a modern name, even if similar in sound, is not necessarily a reliable index to an ancient location), and it is not certain that preserved biblical traditions are all consistent one with another. Moreover, a few of the place-names were coined by the Israelites *ad hoc* in response to some incident that occurred at a given site in the course of the wilderness wanderings. They were not the native names and did not outlast the forty years of the Israelite peregrinations.

The shortest, most convenient, and most direct route from Egypt to Canaan more or less parallels the Mediterranean coastline. Traversing

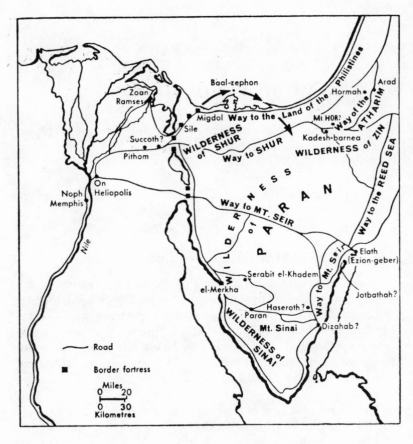

The Exodus and the Desert Routes

the northern part of the peninsula of Sinai, this highway has been one of the most important arteries of international communication throughout history. It was invariably the route taken by the great Egyptian kings in their military campaigns into Asia.[2] The army of Thutmosis III covered the distance from the frontier of Egypt to Gaza, about one hundred fifty miles (about two hundred forty kilometers), in ten days.[3]

The country's vulnerability on its northeastern borders led the pharaohs of all periods to secure this highway against hostile incursion. As early as the days of Amenemhet I (1991–1962 B.C.E.), a line of border fortifications was built along the isthmus of Suez. This defense line is known in several Egyptian texts as the "Wall of Horus," that is, the "Wall of the Ruler," for the reigning pharaoh was supposed to have been the incarnation of the god Horus. That Wall is most likely what is referred to in the Bible as Shur, which literally means a "wall,"[4] and is mentioned, among other contexts, in Genesis 16:7 in connection with Hagar, the Egyptian maidservant of Sarai (Sarah), who was doubtless fleeing to her native land.[5] The Egyptian story of Sinuhe, a court official who fled to Canaan, has the hero report: "I came up to the Wall-of-the-Ruler, made to oppose the Asiatics and to crush the Sand-crossers."[6] The "Prophecy of Nefer-Rohu" (or Neferti) predicts: "There will be built a Wall-of-the-Ruler . . . and the Asiatics will not be permitted to come down into Egypt."[7]

The route that is termed in Exodus 13:17 the "Way of the land of the Philistines" is what is called in Isaiah 9:1 the "Way of the Sea," which corresponds to the Latin name Via Maris, used since Roman times. Two detailed descriptions of this road are extant in Egyptian sources.[8] One consists of the reliefs found on the exterior walls of the columned hall of the temple of Atum at Karnak built by Seti I at the end of the fourteenth century B.C.E. The other is the Papyrus Anastasi I from the time of Rameses II. It is clear that several Egyptian forts, way stations, and watering places were located along this vital route from Egypt to Canaan. More than twenty such sites are named, but only a few can be identified with certainty. The lists start with Tjel or Sile on the frontier near modern Qantir (Al-Qantarah). Important cities like Raphia, Gaza, Ashkelon, Ashdod, and Ekron were Egyptian garrison towns. Recent excavations at Deir el-Balaḥ in the Gaza Strip, the southern coastal plain of Israel, have uncovered a city, a large Egyptian cemetery, a fortress, and a reservoir, all of which served an important Egyptian administrative center situated there in the period of the New Kingdom. In general, the fortress is strikingly reminiscent of those shown on the Karnak reliefs. All in all, recent excavations have unearthed six Egyptian fortresses along this coastal road.[9] The wisdom of having the Israelites avoid the "Way of the land of the

Philistines" and of not exposing them to inevitable warfare is patently obvious.

Incidentally, the biblical designation of that highway signifies the area that later was to come under Philistine domination. At the time of the Exodus, the Philistine invasion of that coastal region had not yet taken place. This people is never included in the several biblical lists that enumerate the various ethnic groups that inhabited Canaan in pre-Israelite times. The earliest historical reference to the Philistines so far discovered stems from the reign of Rameses III (1183–1152 B.C.E.). This king defeated a group of "Sea Peoples"[10] who invaded Egypt from the Cretan-Mycenaean region,[11] although they may have originated in the Anatolian-Aegean area. Following their failure to establish a beachhead in the Egyptian Delta, they settled along the Mediterranean coast of Canaan in that segment of land that roughly corresponds to what is today known as the Gaza Strip. There they were mercenaries of the Egyptian administration. In the course of time they established a confederation of powerful independent city-states that were long to constitute a grave menace to Israel. The name "Way of the land of the Philistines," and the reference to the Sea of Philistia ("Sea of the Philistines") in Exodus 23:31 for that section of the Mediterranean that was adjacent to their shore, constitute emphatic testimony to the important role that this people played in the history of Israel, at least until the time of David, who finally broke their power.

If the coastal road to Canaan was ruled out, the only alternative routes by land traversed the wilderness. As the text says: "God led the people roundabout by way of the wilderness at the *yam suf.*"[12] The Hebrew term for wilderness is *midbar*, which has a broad range of meanings that include uncultivated pastureland as well as arid, desolate wastes and rocky plateaux.

The Yam Suf

This Hebrew term has generally been translated "Red Sea" in the English versions until recently. This tradition goes back to the Latin Vulgate's "Mare Rubrum" and "Mare Erythraeum," which in turn derive from "Erythra Thalassa" of the Greek Septuagint version produced by the Jews of Alexandria. How the Red Sea got its name is itself a mystery, as is also why the Hebrew, which literally means "Sea of Reeds," was connected with that body of water.

The usual theories about the name are not very persuasive, not that based on the supposedly red corals that lie along its shores and bed, or the one that derives the term from the color of the mountains of Edom and Arabia that flank its eastern shores. More convincing is the explanation that rests on the presence of a certain kind of alga that thickly populates that strip of water. The genus *Trichodesmium*, which floats on the surface, gives rise to a reddish-brown discoloration of the water as the algae die off.[13]

Yam suf in the Hebrew Bible presents a problem. Because it literally means "Sea of Reeds," it would be expected to apply only to a body of water that is characterized by the lush growth of the papyrus plants or reed thickets. The Hebrew *suf* is generally taken to be a borrowing from the Egyptian *twf*, "papyrus,"[14] "reed thicket," so that the designation *yam suf* would seem to rule out the possibility of identity with what is traditionally known as the Red Sea. The reason is that the *suf* flourishes in freshwater marshes, which are found only in the Delta region in the north of Egypt. The Red Sea, on the other hand, is saline, and contains no *suf*. This would seem to be decisive for a northern location of the *yam suf*, except that there are biblical passages in which *yam suf* must refer to the traditional Red Sea. Such is the case with 1 Kings 9:26: "King Solomon also built a fleet of ships at Ezion Geber, which is near Eloth [= Elath] on the shore of the *yam suf*, in the land of Edom." Here the Gulf of Aqaba is indubitably intended. The same is true in the oracle in Jeremiah 49:21, where the prophet also mentions *yam suf* in the context of Edom, Teman, and Bozrah. Other pertinent texts are Exodus 23:31 and Numbers 21:4. In the first, the boundaries of the Promised Land are laid out as running "from the *yam suf* to the Sea of Philistia and from the wilderness to the Euphrates. . . ." The second text states, "They set out from Mount Hor by the road to the *yam suf* to skirt the land of Edom." The contexts in both passages point to an identification of *yam suf* with the modern Red Sea.

Apparently, the designation "Sea of Reeds" was applied comprehensively to the entire network of lakes that skirted the wilderness in the northeast Delta region, as well as to the long, narrow strip of water that extends southeastward from Suez to the Straits of Bab el-Mandeb, and that separates the coasts of North Africa to the west from the Arabian Peninsula, including the two northern gulfs, Suez to the northwest and Aqaba to the northeast. It is worth noting that this curious lack of differentiation between what to us are discrete bodies of water has its counterpart in Egyptian writings in which both the Mediterranean Sea and the Red Sea can alike be designated the "Green Sea."[15]

Of course, the idiosyncratic use of *yam suf* in the Bible complicates the problem of retracing the route of the Exodus. One scholar has noted that the *yam suf* that the Israelites crossed has been variously identified as no fewer than nine different bodies of water in locations that are to be found along the Mediterranean coast, the Suez Canal, and the Gulfs of Suez and Aqaba, while thirteen distinct sites have been suggested for Mount Sinai in widely separated regions of the Sinai Peninsula and even in Moab and Edom.[16]

What concerns us at present is the initial phase of the journey out of Egypt. Here the text is clear that the rallying point for the departing Israelites was "Raamses," the city they had built for the pharaoh as forced laborers at the beginning of their oppression (its location was discussed in Chapter One). From here they marched to Succoth. This in all probability is the frontier fortress of Tjeku or Theku, often mentioned in Egyptian sources. The next march brought them to a locality called Etham—still unidentified—described as being "on the edge of the wilderness." Here they were suddenly told to pull back and encamp before Pi-hahiroth, which lay "between Migdol and the sea, before Baal-zephon."[17]

The first of these three sites is otherwise unknown. The construction of the name conforms to that of other Egyptian place-names like Pi-Rameses ("House of Rameses"), Pithom (P[r] Tm, "House of [the god] Atum"), Pi-beseth ("House of [the goddess] Bastet").[18] The initial element is the word for "house/temple." Pi-hahiroth might be a Hebraized word-play for Pi-Hathor ("House of [the goddess] Hathor") mentioned in several Egyptian documents. The Hebrew form would suggest a contrived meaning "Mouth [i.e., opening] of freedom."

Migdol is pure Semitic and means "tower/fortress." It was a loanword in Egyptian, and also came to be used as a place-name for several sites.[19]

Baal-zephon has an interesting history.[20] Baal was the name of the foremost god of the ancient Canaanites. His abode and chief cultic center was situated on Mount Zapan (Zephon), which was thus the Mount Olympus of the Canaanites. Its location is present-day Jebel al-Aqra' at the mouth of the Orontes River, some nineteen miles (thirty kilometers) north of the city of Ugarit near Latakia–Ras Shamra by the Syrian coast. In Hittite and Akkadian texts it is called Khaz(z)i, which gave rise to Mons Casius in classical sources. During the period of the Empire, Semitic gods penetrated Egypt, especially the Delta region, and Baal was the most prominent of them. He was, in fact, identified with the Egyptian god Seth. The place-name Baal-zephon testifies to a temple to this god in the eastern Delta. An extant sixth-century B.C.E. letter sent from Tahpanhes to Memphis carries this line: "I wish you blessing from Baal-zephon and from all the gods of Tahpanhes."[21] This last-named is the modern Tell Daphneh, about twenty-seven miles (forty-three kilometers) south-southwest of Port Said. The phrasing of the letter suggests that Baal-zephon was close-by, if it was not actually identical with Tahpanhes. Another possibility is that the Greco-Roman Casium, which is modern Ras Kasrun, lying about forty-three miles (sixty-nine kilometers) to the east of the eastern branch of the Nile at Pelusium, and backed by Lake Sirbonis, was the Egyptian Mons Casius.

It is possible that the Israelites encountered some obstacle at Etham, perhaps an Egyptian garrison that blocked further advance in that direction. At any rate, the turnabout was reported back to the court by Egyptian intelligence. The assessment in high circles was that the Israelites were disoriented and trapped in the wilderness. Thereupon the pharaoh mustered his infantry and chariot corps, and set out in hot pursuit in order to retrieve his erstwhile slaves. The realization of the damage done to the Egyptian economy by the sudden loss of a most valuable labor resource had now registered.[22] Meanwhile the Israelites were encamped near Pi-hahiroth when the Egyptians espied them. The sight of the advancing enemy forces at once dispirited the Israelites. Hemmed in by the enemy on one side and the sea on the other, they viewed the prospect of Egyptian slavery to be preferable to certain death in the wilderness. At this moment of supreme crisis, Moses rallied the people and encouraged them with calming and reassuring words: "Have no fear! Stand by, and witness the deliverance which the Lord will work for you today; for the Egyptians whom you

see today you will never see again. The Lord will battle for you; you
hold your peace!"[23]

The pillar of cloud and the pillar of fire

Up to this point, the movement of the story describing the actual
departure from Egypt has proceeded in a natural and realistic manner.
But every stage of development is determined by divine edict. To the
biblical narrator, the escape of the Israelites from involuntary enslavement in Egypt is not an instance of a slave rebellion, albeit on a large
scale, in which the fugitives flee en masse.[24] Such have occurred now
and again in the course of the melancholy history of the human race.
However, behind the events that unfold in the Book of Exodus is a
grand plan of cosmic significance in which God plays the central role.
The thrust of the entire narrative is to bring into sharp focus the active,
dynamic presence of God in the life and history of His people. In a
monotheistic religious literature, such a task poses a problem. How
does one express God's immanence, His indwelling Presence in the
world, without in any way compromising His transcendence, that is,
His being wholly other than what is perceived or presented by human
experience? The tension that is generated by this inherent dilemma
surfaces again and again in biblical texts.

At the moment of supreme crisis and extreme peril for the Israelites
in the wilderness, it was necessary for there to be some visible symbol
of God's protective Presence. So we are told:

> The Lord went before them in a pillar of cloud by day, to guide
> them along the way, and in a pillar of fire by night, to give them
> light, that they might travel day and night. The pillar of cloud
> by day and the pillar of fire by night did not depart from before
> the people.[25]

When the Egyptians overtook the Israelites, "The angel of God who
had been going ahead of the Israelite army, now moved and followed
behind them; and the pillar of cloud shifted from in front of them
and took up a place behind them, and it came between the army of
the Egyptians and the army of Israel."[26]

The foregoing picturesque imagery is the only way in which the dilemma is here resolved. The visible emblem of God's invisible Presence is an ever-present columnar cloud. It is seen as such in the daylight hours, but with the onset of darkness it becomes luminous, "a pillar of fire." It expresses the idea of the Divine Presence's extending to His people unfailing guidance and protection. Thereafter, throughout the wilderness wanderings, the cloud with its nocturnal luminosity functions, in particular, to signal the time for and extent of the people's journeying and its interruption.

Scholars have sought to identify the setting in life that might have inspired the particular imagery described in the narrative on the reasonable assumption that what betokens God's Presence must be something that was familiar and readily intelligible, something that was already evocative of such an association. Some have pointed to the military use of smoke and fire signals, especially to the practice of fastening a burning brazier onto a long pole that was carried in front of the army. The troops took their cue as to movement and direction from the smoke and the fire. [27]

Another approach leads to a literary context rather than a natural analog. In the figurative language of the ancient Near Eastern religions, a theophany, or the sudden self-manifestation of the god, is frequently expressed in terms of storm phenomena. In the Bible this kind of figurative language is largely restricted to poetic compositions. The most outstanding example is Psalm 29. Unmistakable echoes of the same literary tradition are featured in the Song of Habakkuk and in Psalm 18, among others. In Habakkuk we find the following lines:

> You make the earth burst into streams,
> The mountains rock at the sight of You,
> A torrent of rain comes down
> Loud roars the deep. [28]

In Psalm 18 the imagery is even more powerful:

Then the earth rocked and quaked;
The foundations of the mountains shook. . . .
He bent the sky and came down,
Thick cloud beneath His feet.
He mounted a cherub and flew,

Gliding on the wings of the wind.
He made darkness His screen.
Dark thunderheads, dense clouds of sky were His pavilion around Him. [29]

Of course, in biblical poetic texts this highly figurative language has been cut loose from any pagan moorings, emptied of mythic content, and monotheized. This is one of the remarkable characteristics of biblical literature: it can employ literary fragments, images, and phrases that are meaningfully literal in pagan compositions, and it can transform them and reuse them as mere colorful poetic imagery. In the present instance of the cloud that symbolizes the Divine Presence, it has been argued that it is actually the objectification and historicization of an ancient literary device. [30] Of special interest in this connection is the mention of the word '*nn* (pl. '*nnm*), "cloud," in early Canaanite literature, where it several times refers to divine attendants or messengers. In Ugaritic literature, the gods Asherah, Baal, and Mot all have their "cloud-messengers." This might have served as the symbolic model for the wilderness cloud. Indeed, Psalm 104:3–4 shows that a similar poetic notion of the phenomena of nature serving as divine escorts and messengers also existed in Israel. This text reads:

He sets the rafters of His lofts in the waters,
Makes the cloud His chariot
Moves on the wings of the wind.
He makes the winds His messengers,
Fiery flames His servants.

Still another approach, and perhaps the most fruitful in the attempt to uncover the source of the cloud imagery, leads to a cultic background, namely, the cloud of incense or column of smoke that arises from the incense altar or burner. [31] Among the prescriptions for the expiation rituals on the Day of Atonement set forth in the Book of Leviticus Chapter 16 is the statement: "Tell your brother Aaron that he is not to come at will into the Shrine behind the curtain, in front of the cover that is upon the ark . . . for I appear in the cloud over the cover" (Leviticus 16:2). It is quite clear from verse 13 that the cloud of incense is meant: the high priest "shall put the incense on the fire before the Lord, so that the cloud from the incense screens the cover that is over [the Ark of] the Pact. . . ." In this case the cloud of incense functions to screen off the Divine Presence, but by virtue of this very role it necessarily serves as a constant reminder of the Presence. Again, when the Temple was dedicated by Solomon, we are told that "the cloud filled the House of the Lord, and the priests were not able to remain and perform the service because of the cloud, for the Presence of the Lord filled the House of the Lord."[32] The appearance of the cloud signifies that the Divine Presence, as it were, takes up residence in the House built for God. Once again, the "cloud" must refer to the smoke of the incense, as is shown by a comparison with the heavenly temple scene that Isaiah saw in his vision. He too says that the "House kept filling with smoke."[33] He can only, in context, be referring to the smoke of the burning incense. In light of the above, it can readily be understood how the cultic role and meaning of the cloud of incense could have functioned as the prototype for the wilderness symbol of the Divine Presence.

The miracle at the sea

Whatever body of water is to be identified with the "Sea of Reeds," it was there that a spectacular victory of Israel, or rather of the God of Israel, over Egypt took place. A fierce wind parted the sea, sweeping back the waters and piling them up like a wall on either side, thus allowing the Israelites to traverse the seabed onto the opposite shore. The pursuing Egyptians came after them into the sea, but God threw them into a panic. Their chariots became immobilized and the Egyptians tried to retreat in flight, but to no avail. God abruptly caused the sea to return to its normal state, so that the watery walls came crashing down, engulfing the Egyptians and drowning the entire host. The waves cast up the corpses onto the shore for all to see.

Such, in outline, is the prose account of the miracle at sea as described in Exodus 13:5–14:30. With this event, the fear and the threat of Egypt is finally removed. Thereafter, Egypt is no longer a factor in biblical history until the period of the Israelite monarchy.

The narrative prose account of the crossing of the sea is followed by a poetic composition that is a hymn of triumph.[34] It commences with the phrase "Then Moses and the Israelites sang this song to the Lord," and closes with another prose statement summarizing the victory: "For the horses of Pharaoh, with his chariots and horsemen, went into the sea; and the Lord turned back on them the waters of the sea; but the Israelites marched on dry ground in the midst of the sea." Encased within this prose framework is the hymn that opens with,

> I will sing to the Lord, for He has triumphed gloriously;
> Horse and driver He has hurled into the sea

and that concludes with the exultant affirmation of God's sovereignty: "The Lord will reign for ever and ever!"

This genre of literature, the combination of prose narration with a laudatory hymn extolling the victory, is found here in the Bible for the first time. Another outstanding example is the fateful battle of Israel against the Canaanite king, Jabin of Hazor, in the days of Deborah. The narrative prose account of the Book of Judges Chapter 4 is followed by the "Song of Deborah." Actually, the genre is the Hebrew counterpart of a literary phenomenon that appears in Egypt in the period of the New Kingdom.[35] It first emerges in mature form in the Kadesh Battle inscriptions of Rameses II, who is the most likely candidate for the pharaoh of the oppression, and it is again featured in the Stele of Merneptah, the so-called Israel Stele. A crucial difference, however, is that whereas the Egyptian models concentrate on panegyrizing the fantastic heroic exploits of the pharaoh, in the "Song of Moses" it is not man but God who is the focus of praise. That is why the great event is celebrated again and again in the biblical texts and serves as the paradigm of God's salvation of His people. In the several so-called historical psalms, that is, those psalms that refer to historical events recorded elsewhere in the Bible, it is the splitting of the sea that is highlighted most frequently in dealing with the Exodus.[36] What is of particular interest is that often the drowning of the Egyptians is either secondary or ignored altogether. Thus the psalmist calls upon all the earth to hymn the praise of the Lord, and he invokes all people to come and see the works of God,

> who is held in awe by men for His acts.
> He turned the sea into dry land;
> we therefore rejoice in Him.[37]

Another psalm celebrates the event in these words:

You are the God who works wonders;
You have manifested Your strength among the peoples.
By Your arm You redeemed Your people,
    the children of Jacob and Joseph.
The waters saw You, O God,
    the waters saw You and were convulsed;
    the very deep quaked as well.
Clouds streamed water;
    the heavens rumbled;
    Your arrows flew about;
    Your thunder rumbled like wheels;
    lightning lit up the world;
    the earth quaked and trembled.
Your way was through the sea;
    Your path, through the mighty waters;
    Your tracks could not be seen;
You led your people like a flock in the care of Moses and Aaron. [38]

In these passages, and in several more, the triumph is the sovereignty of God over nature and over history in the rescue of His people, but not a word is said about the drowning of the Egyptians. This new perspective is evident not only in the psalms, but is already present in the Book of Joshua. Following the crossing of the Jordan into the Promised Land, Joshua charged the people to set up a memorial to the event so that future generations may be moved to reflect on the history of the nation. He tells them:

For the Lord your God dried up the waters of the Jordan before you until you crossed, just as the Lord your God did to the Sea of Reeds, which He dried up before us until we crossed. Thus all the peoples of the earth shall know how mighty is the hand of the Lord, and you shall fear the Lord your God always. [39]

The prophet Isaiah too echoes this same theme:

> Awake, awake, clothe yourself with splendor
> O arm of the Lord!
> Awake as in days of old,
> As in former ages!
> It was you that dried up the Sea,
> The waters of the great deep;
> That made the abysses of the Sea
> A road the redeemed might walk.[40]

Isaiah again returns to this theme:

> Where is He who brought them up from the Sea
> Along with the shepherd of His flock?
> Where is He who put
> In their midst His holy spirit,
> Who made his glorious arm
> March at the right hand of Moses,
> Who divided the waters before them
> To make Himself a name for all time,
> Who led them through the deeps
> So that they did not stumble. . . .[41]

In all these texts the focus is on the celebration of God's mighty deeds and on the redemption of Israel. There is no thought of relishing revenge upon the national enemy or any notion of rejoicing at his downfall.[42] The entire emphasis falls on God's care for His people, His absolute sovereignty over nature, and His control of history.

Manna and quails[43]

By exactly one month after leaving Egypt, the euphoria attendant on the miraculous escape at the Sea of Reeds had given way to the harsh realities of life in the wilderness as the people trekked from one oasis to another. Food was now in short supply, and public dissatisfaction soon surfaced and broke into a clamorous outcry against the leadership of Moses and Aaron. In response, the people were promised provisions of "bread from heaven" in the morning and "flesh" in the evening. This cryptic and hardly credible assurance actually translated itself into a fine, flaky substance that settled on the ground, and the arrival of quails. The former became known as "manna," and is poetically described as being "bread from heaven,"[44] "heavenly grain," in order to distinguish it from the usual "bread from the earth."[45]

According to the narrative, the substance received its name from the fact that the strangeness of the phenomenon naturally elicited the question "What is it?"—in Hebrew, *man hu*.[46] The normal form of the interrogative pronoun for things ("what?") is *mah*, not *man*, which occurs nowhere else in biblical Hebrew. However, a study of Semitic languages shows the form with -*n* to be very ancient and widespread. Ugaritic has *mn*, although its pronunciation is uncertain;[47] the old Canaanite dialect that is reflected in the El Amarna texts reveals *manna* and *mannu* for "what?";[48] biblical Aramaic has *man*;[49] Jewish Aramaic has *mena'*;[50] and Syriac, *mana'*. The Hebrew *man*, therefore, could preserve an ancient dialectic form. Still, since explanations of names in the Bible rarely provide exact philological equivalence but are often based on similarity of sound, for example, in the case of the name Moses, it is quite likely that *man* was the original designation for the substance among the denizens of the wilderness.

This food is said to have been the staple diet of the Israelites throughout their forty years' wanderings until they crossed the Jordan into Canaan.[51] The varied references to it yield the description that the manna fell during the night, was flaky, as fine as frost, resembled coriander seed, was white in appearance, but also had the color of bdellium, and tasted like wafers in honey, and like rich cream. The manna would be collected, ground between millstones or pounded in a mortar, boiled in a pot, and made into cakes. Any of it not eaten the day it was collected became infested with maggots and stank.[52]

There is no known substance that corresponds to this description in all details. There is, however, a biological phenomenon attested to this day in the Sinai Peninsula that is sufficiently close as to make it all but certain that it is this that lies behind the biblical manna tradition. The hardy tamarisk bush grows in semi-arid localities in the Mediterranean region. Two types of homopterans, or sucking insects, infest this plant, the *Trabutina mannipara E.* in the mountainous areas of the Sinai Peninsula, and the *Najacoccus serpentinus G.* in the lowlands. These scale insects suck the sap of the tamarisk, which is rich in carbohydrates, and excrete the surplus onto the twigs in the form of tiny globules that soon crystallize due to rapid evaporation and fall to the ground. They are very sweet and sticky, and are edible. They have to be collected before the heat rises, for then the ants get to them. Chemical analysis of these granular excretions reveals a combination of three basic sugars with pectin. The quantity of this manna is conditioned by the winter rainfall. There would be very little available in a year of drought. The phenomenon usually commences in early June and lasts no more than six weeks. It is estimated that the average annual yield of this kind of manna in the entire Sinai Peninsula is between five and six hundred pounds (two hundred twenty-five to two hundred seventy kilograms).[53]

The foregoing examination of the possible natural background to the biblical manna tradition is useful in illustrating and perhaps clarifying some salient features of the story, but it does not do justice to the purposes of the narrator. The several references to the manna in diverse genres of biblical literature, and particularly the injunction of Moses to preserve in a jar a measure of the substance as a kind of permanent exhibit,[54] indicate that the episode assumes considerable importance in scriptural historiosophy, that is, in the didactic use of historical data.[55]

First of all, there is the context in which the provision of manna is introduced. It belongs to a series of stories about the carpings and grumblings on the part of the people at the miserable conditions of wilderness survival. Furthermore, the discontent and fault-finding follow soon after the great events at the Sea of Reeds. The dating of the episode—just one month to the day after the Exodus—emphasizes this point. The extreme language of the complaints betrays profound lack of faith in God and base ingratitude. This understanding is explicit in Psalm 78:17–25. After detailing the marvels and benefactions that God performed for Israel, the psalmist says:

> But they went on sinning against Him
> > defying the Most High in the parched land.
> To test God was in their mind
> > when they demanded food for themselves.
> They spoke against God, saying,
> > "Can God spread a feast in the wilderness?
> True, He struck the rock and waters flowed,
> > streams gushed forth;
> > but can He provide bread?

Can He supply His people with meat?"
The Lord heard and He raged;
    fire broke out against Jacob,
    anger flared up at Israel,
    because they did not put their trust in God,
    did not rely on His deliverance.
So He commanded the skies above,
    He opened the doors of heaven
    and rained manna upon them for food,
    giving them heavenly grain.
Each man ate a hero's meal;
    He sent them provision in plenty.

The second point to be noted is that regardless of the people's in-gratitude and lack of faith, God still showed His concern for the hungry, and in His compassion provided for their needs. This is significant because one of the cardinal principles of biblical theology is *imitatio dei*, "the imitation of God," the obligation of humankind to emulate, where possible, divine attributes—in the present instance, forbearance under provocation, empathy, magnanimity, and caring for the needy and the hungry.

Then there is the peculiar interplay of the natural and the super-natural. The quails that descended in the evening, like the manna the people found in the morning, may have a natural explanation. The narrative says little about them, and there is certainly no suggestion that they were available every day. It is well known that the quail, known to ornithologists as *Coturnix coturnix*, migrates in huge flocks from Europe to central Africa in the autumn and returns in the spring. A short-tailed game bird of the pheasant family, it flies rapidly at very low altitudes. Due to the long distance involved, the migration is carried out in stages. The small quails twice each year land exhausted on the Mediterranean shore, where they can be easily captured by hand and by nets in great quantities. Their flesh and eggs are said to be delicious, and to this day they are prized food among the local population and are exported as a delicacy to Europe.[56] The season of the year in which the Israelites encountered the quails fits in precisely with the bird's migratory pattern. The natural background for the story is thus well established. In the same way, the manna, as a material substance, may be reasonably accounted for as a recognizable phenomenon of nature that is susceptible of scientific analysis. It is the opportune arrival of these realities that imparts to them a supernatural quality. They providentially appear just when they are sorely needed. In order to emphasize that the manna, in particular, is the product of divine intelligence and will, the narrative records several singularities that are designed to take these events of the Exodus outside the realm of the mundane and the secular. Thus, whereas the natural manna only appears for about six weeks, in limited quantities and in select areas of the Sinai Peninsula, the biblical substance is available in sufficient measure to feed the entire population and is present throughout the wilderness wanderings, a geographic distribution and a continuity that cannot be explained on rational grounds. Moreover, irrespective of the amount of manna gathered by each individual, the allotted ration of one *omer* per person per diem resulted. On Fridays, each received twice that amount without even realizing it. No manna fell on the Sabbath, and even though what was left over until the next morning normally became rancid, this deterioration did not happen to the collected manna that remained from Friday to Saturday. All this is consistent with the main thrust of the Exodus narrative that makes God, not man, the prime actor.

The battle with the Amalekites

Another event that occurred in the wilderness, and that left a deep impression on the national historical consciousness, was a battle against a people called Amalek.[57] Our narrative simply tells us that "Amalek came and fought with Israel at Rephidim." However, a fuller account appears in Deuteronomy 25:17–19. There it is related that, "undeterred by fear of God, he surprised you on the march, when you were famished and weary, and cut down all stragglers in your rear."

The reference to the "fear of God" is highly significant, for as we explained in Chapter One, it often appears in connection with situations that invoke norms of moral and ethical conduct. "Fear of God" in the biblical concept thus decisively affects human conduct. It acts as the ultimate restraint upon perfidy and inhumanity, particularly in situations in which self-interest might tempt one to exploit the weak and the disadvantaged, and where the threat of legal sanctions does not exist. Conversely, it also functions positively as the motivating force for decent behavior, and it imposes obligations and duties. A brief selection of prescriptions from the Book of Leviticus well illustrates these observations:

> You shall not insult the deaf, or place a stumbling block before the blind. You shall fear your God. . . .[58]

> You shall rise before the aged and show deference to the old. You shall fear your God. . . .[59]

> Do not wrong one another, but fear your God. . . .[60]

> If your brother, being in straits, comes under your authority. . . do not exact from him advanced or accrued interest, but fear your God.[61]

> If your brother under you continues in straits and must give himself over to you, do not subject him to the treatment of a slave. . . . You shall not rule over him ruthlessly; you shall fear your God.[62]

In the case of the Amalekites, what occurred was treacherous, brutal, unprovoked aggression against an unsuspecting and largely defenseless Israel at the moment of its national liberation. The Amalekites attacked from the rear so that it was the infirm, the weak, and the weary who bore the brunt of the merciless and indiscriminate assault. The Amalekite aggressors were not "God-fearing"; they were impervious to any considerations of morality.

In response to the attack of the Amalekites, Moses instructed Joshua to select men and go out and do battle with the adversary the next day. He himself, accompanied by Aaron and Hur, went up to the top of the nearby hill, a vantage point from which he could survey the scene. The narrative says that whenever Moses held up his hand, Israel prevailed; but whenever he let down his hand, Amalek prevailed. Being but human, Moses could not keep his hands raised indefinitely, so his two aides sat him on a stone and supported his hands on either side: "thus his hands remained steady until the sun set." The result was that "Joshua overwhelmed the people of Amalek with the sword."

This story contains several puzzling features. Joshua and Hur are introduced without prior identification. They must already have been recognized and important personages, although earlier traditions about them are lost. Later on, Joshua is revealed to be the son of Nun and a grandson of Elishama, who was a chieftain of the tribe of Ephraim. [63] He is Moses' faithful attendant and a young man at this time. [64] He succeeded Moses to the leadership of the people, and as commander-in-chief of the army of Israel he conducted the wars of conquest against the Canaanites. Hur too was surely a public figure even though no more information about his origins is forthcoming, for he is once again associated with Aaron when he judges the people during the absence of Moses on Mount Sinai. [65] Josephus, the Jewish historian of the Second Temple period, preserved a tradition that Hur was the husband of Miriam, sister of Moses. [66] He may be identical with the grandfather of Bezalel of the tribe of Judah, the master craftsman who built the Tabernacle in the wilderness. [67]

What can be the meaning of the influence of the state of Moses' hands on the fortunes of the battle? This is not easy to recover, given the absence of any parallel or analog. At first glance, a gesture of prayer and supplication comes to mind. To appeal to the deity in time of military crisis would be the most natural thing to do. [68] Indeed, the idiom "to raise the hands," that is, in an attitude of prayer or as a synonym of the verb "to pray," is well documented and is widespread in several Semitic languages. The difficulty is that the verbal stem r-w-m, "to be high, exalted," which is used in the present context, is never employed in that sense. Moreover, we can hardly assume that Moses ceased to pray when his hands flagged, and that, as a consequence, Amalek obtained an advantage.

Some interpreters have pointed out that the hand, according to the notions current in the ancient Near East, generally connoted strength and power, so that by raising his hands Moses, in some mysterious manner, was mediating divine power to the Israelite warriors. [69] If such be the case, it is significant that the action has been refined and separated from the mode of pagan magic in that there is neither magical ritual nor magical formula involved, and there is no notion of an appeal to meta-divine forces, or powers that are supposed to be able to control the divine realm itself.

Another, quite persuasive suggestion is that Moses held up an ensign that served to rally the Israelite forces and to bolster morale.[70] Ensigns with religious symbols on them were widely used in the ancient world.[71] The term for an ensign in Hebrew is *nes*, and it can hardly be coincidental that after the battle Moses named the altar he built *YHVH-nissi*, which means "The Lord is my ensign"—around whom Israel rallied. The ensign that Moses upheld would thus have signified to the warriors the presence and support of God in the camp of Israel, and its lowering, therefore, could well have had an adverse effect upon morale. This interpretation comes close to that of the early rabbis as expressed in Mishnah Rosh Ha-Shanah 3:8: "Did Moses' hands really control the course of battle? No! The text indicates that so long as the Israelites set their sights on High and subjected themselves to their Father in heaven, they prevailed; otherwise they fell."

The account of the war with Amalek closes with another puzzling detail. We are told that God instructed Moses as follows: "Inscribe this in a document as a reminder, and read it aloud to Joshua: I will utterly blot out the memory of Amalek from under heaven!" This declaration is reiterated by Moses in more explicit terms: "The Lord will be at war with Amalek throughout the ages."

This passage, which incidentally contains the first mention of writing in the Bible, envisages a long cycle of wars between Israel and Amalek. Having beaten off the first savage attack from that people, Israel is not to delude itself, but must expect Amalek to strike again and again. Accordingly, the Scriptural passage alerts Israel to the grim reality of life for weak peoples in the Near East, while at the same time it promises God's support and His assurance of the ultimate extirpation of this ruthless enemy. The importance of this theme may be measured by the fact of its repetition in Moses' farewell addresses in the Book of Deuteronomy. In Deuteronomy 25:17, 19, the leader exhorts Israel: "Remember what Amalek did to you on your journey, after you left Egypt. . . . Therefore, when the Lord your God grants you safety from all your enemies around you, in the land that the Lord your God is giving you as a hereditary portion, you shall blot out the memory of Amalek from under heaven. Do not forget!"

The intense and implacable hostility toward Amalek manifested in these statements must be understood against the long and bitter history of the interactions of this people with Israel. In the absence of any mention of Amalek in external sources, we must fall back on the only documentation available—the several notices preserved in the Hebrew Scriptures.

We first encounter Amalek in the genealogies of Genesis 36:12, 16. There he is the eponymous, or name-giving, ancestor of the people so called. He is the son of Eliphaz and therefore a grandson of Esau, twin brother of Jacob. The data given in that passage are quite revealing. Of all the descendants of Esau there listed, only he is described as being born of a concubine rather than of one of the wives. This alone implies a low status. Then the lists enumerate twelve descendants of Esau apart from Amalek. This means that the Esau/Edomite tribal confederation consisted of twelve entities.[72] Twelve-tribe confederations are also encountered in respect of the Arabs—sons of Ishmael, and the Arameans, not to mention the Israelites. The same tradition is to be found among the Greeks. The Ionian, Achaean, and Aeolian Leagues each comprised twelve neighboring city-states. The most famous league of this kind was the twelve-tribe "Amphictyonic League" centered on Delphi. The Etruscans in Italy were similarly organized on the basis of twelve city-states centered on the Fanum Voltumnae, a sanctuary near Volsinii.

The relevance of all this is to show that the twelve-tribe confederation of the Esau/Edomite tribes given in Genesis Chapter 36 constitutes the original organization, and that the listing of Amalek as the thirteenth son and as born of a concubine is a sure indication that the Amalekites were latecomers to the league and had a subordinate status. Furthermore, the note that Timna, mother of Amalek, was a Horite, that is to say, one of the aboriginal inhabitants of Mount Seir who were displaced and largely extirpated by the Edomites, is additional proof that Amalek was not originally within the legitimate Edomite line.[73] This fits in with the absence of any Semitic etymology for the name Amalek. The tribe had apparently been forced out of its original homeland and pursued a nomadic existence deep in the Negev of Judah and in the Sinai Peninsula, at first in subservience to the Edomites, but then independently of them.[74] The seer Balaam was able to observe the Amalekite camp from his vantage point in Moab, and then described them as "a leading nation," thus testifying to their hegemony in the region.[75] This helps to uncover the motive for the surprise attack of Amalek on Israel. The sudden Israelite appearance in the region must have been viewed as a possible threat to its traditional hegemony and as menacing its control of the oases and pasturelands, and Amalek decided on a preemptive strike without bothering to elicit the facts. Later on, Israel experienced a second clash with the Amalekites in the course of the wilderness wanderings. Apparently there was an attempt on the part of some Israelites to penetrate Canaan from the Negev and hill country via Arad and Hormah. The Amalekites joined forces with the Canaanites in repulsing it and compelled the Israelites to make a wide detour. Numbers 14:45 records that Israel suffered "a shattering blow" on that occasion. Subsequently, throughout the period of the judges, Amalek proved to be a constant thorn in the side of Israel.[76] It was not until the founding of the monarchy that relief came. Saul, first king of Israel, successfully engaged the tribe in combat, and in the climactic battle described in 1 Samuel 15, the Amalekites suffered wholesale slaughter.[77] Nevertheless, they were still capable of making nuisance raids into Israelite territory in the Negev in David's day.[78]

Before leaving the Amalekite episode, one further observation is called for. The exhortation to have a written "reminder," to "remember" and "not forget" what that people did, deserves further elaboration.[79] It draws attention to a unique and extraordinary phenomenon: the study of history is made into a religious obligation in Israel. This intense preoccupation with the past, so frequently enjoined in the Bible, is not to be misunderstood as backward looking, as a morbid fascination with what once was; it does not suggest a view of the past as a haunting specter that impedes progress and bedevils the conception of the future. After all, it was this same Israel that equally uniquely produced the glorious vision of Messianism. Rather, a clarification and closer definition of the Hebrew terminology rendered in English by "remember" is needed. The stem *z-k-r* does not connote mere intellectual activity, a simple recall or retrieval of information stored away somewhere in the cells of the brain, and the power to reproduce images of what no longer exists. It is that and much more. Hebrew *z-k-r* is better rendered "to be mindful," and this includes awareness and paying heed. "To be mindful" implies involvement. The attitude is subjective and relational. There is concern, engagement, and responsibility. That is why the stem *z-k-r* is frequently accompanied by a verb of action, and may in fact interchange with or parallel the verb *sh-m-r*, "to observe, practice."[80]

In the present context, the injunction to remember calls for a realistic appraisal of Israel's situation as a weak nation in a hostile world. It is a summons always to be prepared for self-defense.

The organization of the judiciary

The action thus far has proceeded at a frenetic pace with momentous and stirring events following one another in rapid succession. The breathless tempo now slows down to permit a calming pause in preparation for the dramatic climax, the revelation at Sinai. Between the war with the Amalekites and the great national theophany at Sinai, a personal note about Moses' domestic life is injected into the narrative.[81] We are treated to a description of a visit by Jethro to his son-in-law, now the shepherd of God's flock in place of his father-in-law's. Apparently, for safety's sake, Moses had left his wife and sons in Midian in the care of their family during the critical and dangerous times preceding and following the departure from Egypt. Jethro brings Zipporah, his daughter and the wife of Moses, together with their two sons, Gershom and Eliezer, to be reunited with Moses. He sends word ahead of time, and Moses goes out to greet Jethro and pays him much respect. Moses then conducts Jethro to his tent and gives him an account of all that has happened. Jethro is delighted at what he hears, and blesses the Lord for delivering Moses and the people from the Egyptians. He then brings a burnt offering and sacrifices to God. He, Aaron, and the elders of Israel all partake of a meal "before God."

The next day, Jethro observes Moses acting in the capacity of sole magistrate while the people stand around from morning until evening awaiting their turn for adjudication. Jethro is appalled at the inefficiency of the system of justice, with its inevitably debilitating effects on Moses himself and the hardships it imposes on the public. Thereupon, he privately recommends practical measures for the reform of the judicial administration, but does not concern himself with the content of the legislation. First, it is necessary to have an informed citizenry knowledgeable in the law, and Moses is to act as teacher to the people. Jethro believes, perhaps, that this kind of popular instruction might diminish the volume of litigation. Next, he advises on the appointment of subordinate judges to deal with ordinary, uncomplicated cases, and he specifies the social, spiritual, and moral qualifications of such appointees. They must come from "all the people," they must be "capable men who fear God, trustworthy men who spurn ill-gotten gain." These men are to be empowered to administer the law as "chiefs of thousands, hundreds, fifties, and tens." This ranking by population division is unclear and better fits a military rather than civil administration. Moses himself is to act as the court of last resort for difficult cases. Moses accepts and implements these recommendations. He then bids his father-in-law farewell and Jethro returns to his own land. [82]

It is most extraordinary that Scripture freely attributes the establishment of Israel's judicial system to the advice of a foreign priest, particularly in light of the later history of hostility between Israel and Midian. Yet there is a pattern of such openness in the Bible. When King David organized the administration of his realm, he took full advantage of the non-Israelite talent that was available, and he had no hesitation about making use of foreign technical and professional assistance. The report in 1 Chronicles Chapter 27 well illustrates this situation. The king's counsellors, Ahitophel and Hushai the Archite, almost certainly belonged to the pre-Israelite population of Jerusalem and its environs; the custodian of the royal camel herds was Obil the Ishmaelite; Jaziz the Hagrite was in charge of the royal flocks; Baal-hanan, the Gederite, supervised the olive and sycamore trees; Cherethites and Pelethites composed the king's bodyguard. It will be remembered that when King Solomon set about building the holy Temple in Jerusalem, he enlisted the help of skilled artisans from the Phoenician city-state of Tyre. [83] It is also noteworthy that early Jewish biblical exegesis, reflected in both Josephus[84] and rabbinic sources, [85] praises Moses for giving proper credit to Jethro, the non-Israelite, for devising the new system of justice.

The chronology of the events just described became a subject of critical examination very early in the history of biblical exegesis, and some medieval Jewish commentators noted that there are several aspects of the narrative that place Jethro's visit after, not before, the revelation at Sinai even though the story precedes that event. [86] Thus the Israelites are already "encamped at the mountain of God"[87] at this time, whereas the report of their arrival at that site is not given until Exodus 19:1–2. Indeed, the parallel account of the establishment of the judiciary given in Deuteronomy Chapter 1 specifies that the reorganization took place at the close of their stay at Horeb, which is Sinai. In addition, references to "the laws and teachings of God"[88] are certainly more appropriate after the giving of the law on Mount Sinai than before. Finally, the departure of Jethro and his return to his own land, reported here in Exodus 18:27, is said in another source to have occurred in the second year after the Exodus and after the erection of the Tabernacle.[89] This makes it all the more likely that the burnt offering and sacrifices that Jethro brought were offered on the altar in the Tabernacle, and that the sacral meal that followed also took place there "before God."

The question now poses itself: Why are the events of this chapter placed where they are—out of chronological sequence, and wedged between the war with Amalek and the revelation at Sinai? For one thing, the episode does provide the much-needed relaxation of tension that we mentioned above, and it may well have been inserted here to function as just such a literary retardation device. For another, the two parts into which the narrative naturally divides—verses 1–12 and 13–27—form a most appropriate bridge between the foregoing and the following sections, as we shall soon see.

A story in 1 Samuel Chapter 15 sheds some light on this subject. There we are told that when King Saul undertook his campaign against the Amalekites in order to exact "the penalty for what Amalek did to Israel, for the assault he made upon them on the road on their way up from Egypt," he first approached the Kenite clan with this message: "Come, withdraw at once from among the Amalekites that I may not destroy you along with them; for you showed kindness to all the Israelites when they left Egypt." That the Kenites lived in close proximity to the Amalekites is also the impression one gains from Numbers 24:20–21, where we are told that from his hilltop vantage point, the seer Balaam is able to observe both Amalekites and Kenites almost simultaneously. Now as we noted in Chapter Two, Moses' father-in-law is designated a "Kenite" even though he is also a Midianite. It is instructive that the phrase King Saul uses to describe the friendship of the Kenites for Israel includes the Hebrew word *hesed*, a term that frequently connotes a special relationship sealed by treaty and involving loyalty and obligation.[90] It is quite feasible that behind Jethro's visit is a now-lost narrative about a covenant between the Kenites and the Israelites.[91] The sacrificial meal that Aaron and the elders shared with Jethro would then have been the kind that is well documented in the ancient Near Eastern world as an essential concluding element in the transacting of treaties.[92]

Seen in this light, the story of the visit of Moses' father-in-law affords a striking contrast between the relationship and behavior toward Israel of the two neighbors, Amalek and the Kenites. The one was viciously hostile and treacherous, the other friendly and helpful. The contrast is heightened by the literary juxtaposition.

The second part of the chapter, the establishment of Israel's system of judicial administration, acts, of course, to focus attention upon "God's laws and teachings." In this way, the narrative serves as a kind of prologue to the ensuing revelation of the Torah, preparing the reader for that climactic event.

CHAPTER VII

The Ten Commandments; Moses and Monotheism

EXODUS 19–20

Preparations for the theophany

It was in the third month following the Exodus that the Israelites arrived at the wilderness of Sinai, and encamped before the mountain where Moses had first experienced the call to leadership.[1] Thus far the relationship between God and Israel had been wholly one-sided, with Israel being the passive beneficiary of God's active role in history. It was God who took the initiative in sending Moses to the pharaoh, who coerced the tyrant by way of the plagues to liberate Israel, who performed the wonders at the sea, and who supplied the Israelites' physical needs in the wilderness. Now a new phase in Israel's history is about to commence. God's redemptive acts on Israel's behalf require a reciprocal response on the part of Israel. The liberated multitude of erstwhile slaves must be united not only by a vital sense of a shared tragedy and a common experience of emancipation, but even more by bonds of perceived ideals —a vision of a new order of life, namely, the establishment of an essentially different kind of society from what had hitherto existed.

The precondition for the fulfillment of this goal, indeed its instrumentality, is to be the forging of a special relationship between God and Israel. This relationship is to be sealed by a covenant, which would establish Israel as God's "treasured possession," as "a kingdom of priests and a holy nation."[2]

130

The full range of meaning of the first designation, "a treasured possession" (in Hebrew, *segullah*),[3] has been illuminated by epigraphic
finds from the ancient Near East. From the city of Alalakh on the River
Orontes in Turkey comes a royal seal of King Abban that cannot be
later than the fifteenth century B.C.E. The term *sikiltum*,[4] the Akkadian
equivalent of *segullah*, is used in the titles of the monarch in parallel
with "servant" and "beloved" of a god.[5] Another text derives from the
city of Ugarit. At the moment when the royal palace was being destroyed
soon after the year 1200 B.C.E.,[6] scribes were baking some inscribed
clay tablets in the kiln. The fate of the royal officials is unknown, but
the abandoned tablets remained in place for the next three thousand
years until discovered by modern excavators. One of the documents in
question is a translation into Ugaritic of an Akkadian letter sent by the
Hittite suzerain to his vassal Ammurapi, the last known king of Ugarit.
Here the Hittite overlord characterizes the latter as "his servant" and
"his special possession" (*sglth*).[7] Clearly, the biblical designation of Israel
as God's "treasured possession" is used in a special sense that has political
and legal implications.

The second description of Israel as "a kingdom of priests and a holy
nation"[8] alludes to the consequences that flow or should flow from that
special relationship with God. The priests are set apart from the rest of
the people by dedication to the service of God, by their consecration to a
distinctive way of life that gives expression to this intimate involvement
with the divine through special duties and restrictions, and by the obligation to serve the people. This concept of priesthood provides the model
for Israel's self-image and for its role among the nations of the world.

The narrative tells us that Moses transmitted to the people God's
vision of their future destiny, and "All the people answered as one,
saying, 'All that the Lord has spoken we will do!' "[9] God's election of
Israel is matched by a corresponding response and commitment on the
part of the people. The mood has been set for the solemn, formal
enactment of a covenant between God and Israel, which would seal
for all time this reciprocal relationship. For three days the people prepared themselves to participate in this awesome experience. They had
to maintain a state of purity, abstain from sexual relations, launder their
clothes, and treat the mountain as strictly off-limits, under penalty of
death, until a long blast of the ram's horn would signal the termination
of the theophany.[10]

The atmospheric disturbances

We are told that with the morning dawn on the third day came resounding peals of thunder that shattered the solitude of the wilderness. Flashes of lightning illumined the desolate, wild landscape, and a dense cloud enveloped the mountain from which smoke billowed up and obscured it. The mount itself trembled violently. The blare of the horn grew ever louder, as the entire people assembled at the foot of Sinai. Then the Lord descended upon the mount "in fire."[11] In Exodus 24:17 we read: "Now the Presence of the Lord appeared in the sight of the Israelites as a consuming fire on the top of the mountain," and this image is further elaborated in Deuteronomy 4:11: "The mountain was ablaze with flames to the very skies, dark with densest clouds." The fire, of course, recalls the picture of the Burning Bush in Exodus Chapter 3.

This vivid, majestic, and terrifying imagery cannot be interpreted literally as proof of volcanic eruption behind the description, as some commentators would have it. For one thing, there is no evidence of active volcanoes in the Sinai Peninsula in historic times. For another, the description in the present context cannot be treated in isolation from several similar representations of theophanies found elsewhere in the Bible. In fact, in the preceding chapter we drew attention to the conventional use of highly figurative, poetic language in the Scriptural portrayals of God's self-manifestation, and we looked at a few examples from the literature. Those, and a host of others, when carefully examined and compared, demonstrate that once again we are dealing with standard poetic imagery to describe the awe-inspiring impact of the event upon those who experienced it. The psalmist may similarly portray in concrete terms the abstract idea of the sovereignty of God. In Psalm 97:1-5, for instance, he joyously proclaims:

> The Lord is king!
> Let the earth exult,
>   the many islands rejoice!
> Dense clouds are around Him,
>   righteousness and justice are the base of His throne.
> Fire is His vanguard,
>   burning His foes on every side.

His lightnings light up the world;
    the earth is convulsed at the sight;
    mountains melt like wax at the Lord's presence,
    at the presence of the Lord of all the earth.

It is instructive to compare Isaiah's prediction of a future divine judgment on Babylon with Joel's description of a plague of locusts:

Therefore I will make the heavens tremble,
And the earth will be shaken out of its place.[12]

The earth trembles before them;
The heavens shake.[13]

The conventionality of the language is readily apparent. Moreover, these poetic figures of speech are not restricted to the Bible but are common in Akkadian literature as well. Frequently used epithets of the Mesopotamian gods are "shakers of mountains," "shaker of the earth," "at whose thunder the heavens trembled, the earth shook, the mountains quaked," "the one at whose thundering people were benumbed, the steppes trembled, the field writhed." Similar language was employed by the great warrior kings of Assyria in describing their devastatingly victorious onslaught against their enemies.

It would seem that the ultimate source of this widespread literary pattern is to be sought in descriptions of storms and earthquakes.[14] In the pagan religions, where the gods inhere in nature and are not outside it and independent of it, upheavals of nature, violent and turbulent atmospheric disturbances, are literally taken to be aspects of the lives of the gods themselves. In the Bible, however, they are nothing of the kind. They are simply powerful poetic images that register the consciousness of the intensified Presence of God at a particular moment in time.

The striking contrast between Near Eastern paganism and Israelite monotheism in just this respect is emphasized with crystal clarity in the extraordinary story of Elijah's theophany at this same wilderness of Horeb, as told in 1 Kings 19:11–12:

And lo, the Lord passed by. There was a great and mighty wind,
splitting mountains and shattering rocks by the power of the Lord;

but the Lord was not in the wind. After the wind—an earthquake, but the Lord was not in the earthquake. After the earthquake—fire, but the Lord was not in the fire. And after the fire—a soft murmuring sound.

The phenomena of nature constitute, as it were, the background music, the orchestral harbinger of and accompaniment to the momentous divine activity, but they are essentially unrelated to it. The function of the detailed, elaborate, and animated descriptions of the upheavals of nature is to convey in human terms something of the ultimately inexpressible, ineffable impact of the awesome and mysterious manifestation of the Divine Presence.

The covenant concept

One of the most significant, consequential, and seminal terms to be found in the Hebrew Bible is b'rit, "covenant."[15] And no wonder, for the establishment of the most desirable behavior of human beings toward one another and the ordering of the proper relationships between humankind and God are the dominant concern of the Scriptures. The Hebrew b'rit, usually translated "covenant," embraces a treaty as an instrument of international diplomacy, a compact between a king and his subjects, a pact that defines mutual understanding and responsibilities between two individuals, and is even used of matrimony.

Without doubt, the overwhelming usage of the "covenant" is to designate the function and effect of the great national experience at Sinai. By so doing, the Bible describes a living reality, an actual legal circumstance, nothing less than the assertion of the conclusion of an eternally binding pact between God and His people. Thereafter, the entire history of Israel, as portrayed in the Bible, is governed by this outstanding reality. Covenant consciousness suffuses all subsequent developments.

The fortuitous recovery of a considerable number of international treaties from the region of the Fertile Crescent has helped to place both the Sinaitic revelation itself and the literary expression it finds in the Bible in sharper focus and in more meaningful perspective. We do not know when and where the treaty form originated. The extant documentation takes us back some forty-five hundred years to ancient Mesopotamia. The fact that a non-Semitic people like the Hittites of Asia Minor would use Akkadian technical terminology like *riksu*, "covenant," and *mamitu*, "oath," suggests that the civilization between the Euphrates and Tigris Rivers first produced the treaty form.[16] As a matter of fact, the two earliest preserved treaties come from this region. The first is contained in the "Stele of the Vultures" (before 2500 B.C.E.), which commemorates the victory of Eannatum, ruler of the Sumerian city-state of Lagash in southern Mesopotamia, over the people of the neighboring state of Umma, thirty miles (forty-eight kilometers) to the west.[17] The name of the stele derives from the depiction of the birds of prey devouring the corpses of the enemy. Its occasion was the sacking of Umma for the latter's violation of an earlier boundary treaty regulating the use of land and water resources. The other third-millennium treaty is that of Naram-Sin (ca. 2280 B.C.E.), king of the city-states of Kish and Akkad, with Elam.[18] This one is a treaty of alliance between the two signatories. Both these documents testify to the existence already this early of a long legal tradition in that part of the world.

Apart from these documents that demonstrate the great antiquity of the covenant form, the preserved treaties divide themselves into three general groupings: the examples recovered from the royal archives of the Hittite Empire (ca. 1450–ca. 1200 B.C.E.) found at Hattusas, present-day Boghazköy in modern Turkey, about a hundred twenty-five miles (two hundred kilometers) east of Anakara;[19] the Aramaic treaties from Syria (ninth century B.C.E.);[20] and those from the Assyrian Empire that date between the ninth and seventh centuries B.C.E.[21] Within this total corpus of ancient Near Eastern treaties, two basic types can be differentiated. Where the contracting parties are on equal terms, we may speak of "parity treaties"; where the initiative for the agreement comes from an unquestionably superior power, the resultant treaty regulates a suzerain–vassal relationship. The outstanding example of the international parity treaty is that concluded between the Hittite king, Hattusilis III, and Rameses II of Egypt (ca. 1280 B.C.E.) that ended the rivalry between the two great powers.[22] The contracting parties entered, on equal terms, into a pact of nonaggression, mutual assistance, and careful delineation of their respective spheres of influence in Syria. However, given the role of imperial powers in the history of the Near East, it occasions no surprise to learn that the bulk of the surviving treaty documentation belongs to the second type.

The Israelite covenant concept of the forging of a formal, legal, binding relationship between God and a people is so extraordinary that to have been intelligible, it would have had to be expressed in terms of its contemporary, universally recognized, legal instruments. By the very nature of the situation, such a relationship between God and Israel would find its closest analogy in the suzerain–vassal treaties. It would be expected, therefore, that an analysis of the form, structure, and terminology used in the biblical texts to describe the Sinaitic revelation and the covenant between the two contracting parties would disclose many affinities with the ancient Near Eastern treaty procedures and texts. This is indeed the case, and there can be no doubt of the patterning of the *b'rit* after them.

When we state that the national covenant between God and Israel, the *b'rit* at Sinai, is inspired by the ancient Near Eastern suzerain–vassal treaties, we refer to the concept and the outward form. That is to say, this kind of solemn treaty as the accepted instrument by which desired relationships were effectuated and regulated served as the conceptual model; and the conventional, formal, written expression of these arrangements influenced the biblical narration. We do not mean to suggest, however, that the biblical *b'rit* is a slavish imitation of contemporary Near Eastern norms. On the contrary, it displays an originality and independence that transforms it into a wholly new creation, the innovative nature of which can only be adequately appreciated against the background of the classical model.

It is to be noted that throughout the millennia-long recorded history of the ancient Near East, the fundamental constituents of treaties, their legal terminology, and their literary pattern exhibited a remarkable continuity, consistency, and tenacity. Scribal training had a lot to do with it, as is proven by extant Mesopotamian formularies and vocabulary lists intended for scribes who specialized in legal phraseology.[23] Scribes and diplomats who drafted treaties then, as today, generally hewed closely to standard prototypal structures, although variation in detail, and often in order, of the essential elements took place. The oldest of the three groups of treaties described above—the Hittite collection—does, however, possess a number of distinctive features that mark it off from the other two. Intriguingly, it is this collection with which the closest affinities with the Scriptural material are displayed.[24]

The Hittite treaties more or less conform to a six-part pattern. First comes the *preamble*, in which the initiator of the treaty is identified by name, and his titles, attributes, and genealogy are listed. Next comes the *historical review*, in which the past relationships between the contracting parties are set forth. In particular, and this is its main function, there is a reminder of the previous benefactions bestowed by the suzerain upon the vassal. These constitute the present claim of the suzerain on the gratitude and allegiance of the vassal. Then follow the *stipulations*, which are the core of the treaty; the call for the *deposition* of a copy of the document in the vassal's sanctuary, often with provision for its periodic public reading; a long list of gods who act as *witnesses* to the terms of the treaty; and finally, a statement of *curses and blessings*, the former describing the dire consequences in the event of the vassal's infraction of the treaty terms, and the latter pointing to the beneficial results of faithful adherence to them.

Near Eastern parallels

Turning now to the Covenant at Sinai, one can detect at once some striking similarities between it and the structure of the Hittite treaties as just described. The Ten Commandments open with a *preamble* identifying Him who initiates the covenant: "I am the Lord your God. . . ."[25] Then comes the *historical review*, a retrospect of the chief benefaction that God bestowed on Israel: ". . . who brought you out of the land of Egypt, the house of bondage." This is the overriding, pivotal event, the dominant theme in Israelite history that cemented the relations between God and Israel, and that remained the cause for Israel's eternal gratitude and the basis of the obligations it owed Him. The third section, the list of "you shall" and "you shall not," comprises the *stipulations*, the principles on which the future relations of Israel and God are to be grounded.

The other three basic elements of the Hittite treaties are not included in the Decalogue document, but are present elsewhere. Thus the *deposition* in the Sanctuary of a copy of the Covenant is required in Exodus 25:16: "Deposit in the Ark [the tablets of] the Pact which I will give you."[26] This is reminiscent of the clause in the treaty between the Hittite king Shuppiluliuma (ca. 1375–1335 B.C.E.) and Mattiwaza of the kingdom of Mitanni in Upper Mesopotamia: "A duplicate of this tablet has been deposited before the sun-goddess of Arinna. . . .In the

Mitanni land [a duplicate] has been deposited before Tessub, the lord of the *kurinnu* [sanctuary or shrine] of Kahat."[27] Similarly, just as this same treaty stipulates that "At regular *intervals* shall they read it in the presence of the king of the Mitanni land and in the presence of the sons of the Hurri country," so provision is made in the Torah for the periodic public reading of the text of the Covenant: "Every seventh year, the year set for remission, at the Feast of Booths, when all Israel comes to appear before the Lord your God in the place which He will choose, you shall read this Teaching aloud in the presence of all Israel."[28] Of course, there is no room for gods in Israel's monotheistic religion, but their place as *witnesses* is taken by "heaven and earth": "I call heaven and earth this day to witness against you. . . ."[29] Finally, *the curses and the blessings*, though in reverse sequence, are very much present in the great admonitions of Leviticus Chapter 26 and Deuteronomy Chapter 28.[30]

It is taken for granted that the Ten Commandments comprise the minimal moral imperatives essential to the maintenance of an ordered and wholesome society; but here again, is there anything uncommon about their contents? What was the state of the world prior to the revelation at Sinai? Was it steeped in savagery and barbarism? The Bible itself assumes the existence of a moral code of universal application from the beginning of the appearance of civilized life on this planet.[31] Otherwise, how could Cain's slaughter of his brother have been a culpable offense? For what "lawlessness" could God have brought the great Flood, and for what "evil" would the inhabitants of Sodom and Gomorrah and their allied cities have been brought to account? The people of Israel arrived very late on the world scene. By then, the great civilizations of the Fertile Crescent had all passed their prime and were already heirs to ancient traditions and cultures. Obviously, these great civilizations could not have come about or functioned without a "social contract," without a commitment to enforceable criteria of right and wrong that covered most of the principles enshrined in the Ten Commandments.

The factuality of this elementary presupposition is well illustrated by the discovery of several collections of laws from the ancient Near East, stemming from the third millennium down. We shall discuss these in some detail later on. Suffice it to point out here that all these collections rest upon foundations of ethical and political principles of justice and morality. In addition to them, we have the wisdom and didactic compositions of Egypt[32] and Mesopotamia,[33] which are replete with the majority of the injunctions found in the Decalogue. Most pertinent to the issue are the lists of moral and ethical violations found in various ancient compilations. Thus there is a series of magical texts from Mesopotamia called *Shurpu*, many of which derive from the old Babylonian period (ca. 1800 B.C.E.).[34] The term means "burning," and refers to the magical act that was performed simultaneously with the recitation of the incantation. Its purpose was to effect ritual purification. It is often assumed that sickness results from the violation of a taboo, so that a list of wrongs committed is included. In the second tablet of the *Shurpu* series, the gods are beseeched for forgiveness for such sins of an ethical and moral nature as, among others, false witness, estranging children and parents from one another, disrespect of parents, theft, adultery, and murder.

The most instructive text of this type comes from Egypt and is the "Declaration of Innocence," often called the "Negative Confession," located in the 125th chapter of the Egyptian collection of spells popularly known as the Book of the Dead.[35] The original title was "Going Forth by Day," which expressed the yearnings of the Egyptian to transcend death through attaining life in the hereafter, and being able to return therefrom by day. The magical formulae to be uttered in order to achieve this goal include a list of offenses that the deceased declared he had not committed. In the presence of the god Osiris and his court, convened in the "Hall of Two Truths," the dead man professed, among other items: "I have not committed evil. . . . I have not stolen. . . . I have not been covetous. . . . I have not robbed. . . . I have not killed men. . . . I have not told lies. . . . I have not committed adultery. . . . I have not blasphemed against my local god."[36] This negative formulation testifies to the reality of positive moral ideals, widely accepted. It is obvious beyond cavil that the prohibitions of theft, murder, adultery, false witness, and so forth, were hardly novel at the time of the Exodus. Rather, they had long been accepted as the elementary standards of civilized, organized life. The fundamental question therefore arises: Wherein lay the uniqueness of the Ten Commandments?

Israelite innovations

The parallels we have listed above are sufficient to demonstrate that the Covenant at Sinai falls within the scope of the ancient Near Eastern treaty-making tradition. It is in the dissimilarities, however, that the significance of the biblical institution becomes evident.

First and foremost is the revolutionary expansion of the original treaty concept in that God and an entire people become parties to the Covenant. There is no known parallel in history for such a notion, no analogy to Israel's claim to have undergone such a national religious experience and no conceptual prototype of that claim.

This innovation is connected with another. Unlike all other treaties, which are individual, discrete documents of state, the Sinai covenant is embedded in a narrative context from which it cannot be separated and from which it derives its meaning and justification. It, in turn, affects decisively the entire subsequent course of the Scriptural narrative. The ensuing history of Israel is measured and determined by the extent of the people's fidelity to or infraction of the Covenant.

It will doubtless have been noted that while all six formal elements of the Hittite treaty type can be located in the Torah, three of them are detached from the account of the Sinaitic revelation and are diffused through the rest of the literature: the deposition, the witnesses, and the curses and blessings. This separation constitutes another major departure from the Hittite prototype. The deviation is conditioned by the biblical claim that not just the Ten Commandments but the entire corpus of laws included in the Torah also has its origin at Sinai and is equally constitutive of the Covenant between God and Israel.

This leads to still another distinctive feature of the Israelite Covenant. Near Eastern treaties, being political documents that order interstate relationships, are usually concerned solely with matters of external affairs and ignore internal affairs except insofar as these might impinge upon the interests of the suzerain state. At Sinai, however, every aspect of the internal life of the "vassal" Israel, particularly interpersonal relations, falls within the scope of the Covenant stipulations. Moreover, the terms of the Near Eastern treaties are invariably time-bound rules of mutual conduct pertinent to a specific historical situation. Although the treaties are always formulated as though they are eternally binding, their unlimited validity is, of course, a fiction. The chronic impermanence of political relationships assured this, and not all the guarantors of the treaties, the fearful curses, and the host of divine witnesses proved to be any protection against the enticements of expediency in abrogating the treaty. Furthermore, the great imperial powers, much less the petty vassal states, were not exempt from the iron law of history. The afore-mentioned parity treaty between Hattusilis III and Rameses II repeatedly emphasized that its provisions are enforceable "forever," "until all and everlasting time," yet within eighty years of its signing the mighty Hittite empire crumbled into the dust. The Ten Commandments, on the other hand, are general precepts of universal applicability unconditioned by temporal considerations and unaffected by shifting political conditions. They are of truly binding validity for the present and the future. This, of course, is so because the "suzerain" who dictates the terms of the covenant is none other than God Himself. The "vassal" may contravene them, but it is beyond his capacity to rescind them. God and Israel are henceforth inextricably bound to one another by a vital and indissoluble bond.

A further critical distinction between the Decalogue and other ancient Near Eastern texts lies in the source and sanction of law. No biblical law is ever attributed to Moses personally or to any prophet. The narratives know nothing of a lawgiver-sage or a lawgiver-king. The great empire builders and organizers, David and Solomon, have no connection with law codes. The great reformers Jehoshaphat,[37] Hezekiah,[38] and Josiah[39] reorganize the judiciary and the cult, but they do so only to implement the ancient law of God. They make no claim to innovation. The only name connected with law is that of Moses, and he is not its source but a prophet who mediates the divine communication to Israel.

This picture is in striking contrast to the situation in the ancient world, where the legislators are kings, princes, and sages. The king and the state constitute the source of law, its sanction, and the authority behind it.[40] It is true that the gods desired that mankind be in possession of just laws, even though they themselves were not thought of as needing to behave according to moral norms. They wanted the king to establish justice in the land. Some gods, such as Shamash the sun god, were looked upon as the custodians of justice and equity. Thus Hammurabi invokes the gods in the prologue to his laws, and the stele on which they are inscribed is decorated with a relief depicting the god presiding

over their promulgation.[41] The text, however, leaves no doubt that
Hammurabi ascribes the laws to himself: "I established law and justice
in the language of the land. . . . The laws of justice which Hammurabi,
the efficient king set up. . . . I am the king who is preeminent among
the kings; my words are choice; my ability has no equal. By the order
of Shamash, the great judge of heaven and earth, may my justice prevail
in the land; by the word of Marduk, my lord, may my statutes have no
one rescind them."[42] It is very much Hammurabi who is the author of
the laws, not the gods. The role of the god in law is to serve as the
source of wisdom, as the one who implants in man the faculty of the
discernment of truth and the perception of justice. This is what enables
kings to make just laws. But the actual origin and source of law lie in
human wisdom, not in the revealed will of the gods. In Israel, however,
the provisions of the Ten Commandments are not the fruit of prudential
wisdom or the product of reason, but are literally conceived to be the
revealed will of God.

This explains the total absence of specific penalties for the violation
of the individual injunctions and prohibitions in the Ten Commandments. We find only "You shall" or "You shall not"—unqualified,
absolute declarations without definitions, limitations, or threat of punishment. While this apodictic style, as it is called, is not original to the
Torah, its use in Near Eastern treaties is very rare, and the conditional
formulation is customary. The Decalogue's adoption of the apodictic
form is no coincidence. It goes to the heart of the meaning and significance of the document. The "You shall" prescription and the "You
shall not" prohibitive form express categorical imperatives that are of
eternally binding validity. They declare that there are certain God-given
values and behavioral norms that are absolute. Morality is the expression
of the divine will. The motivation for observing the law is not fear of
punishment but the desire to conform to the will of God. The Decalogue
thus becomes a self-enforcing code in that its appeal is to the conscience,
not to enlightened self-interest, and its enforcing mechanism is the
spiritual discipline and moral fiber of the individual, not the threat of
penalty that is imposed by the coercive power of the state.

No less revolutionary than the divine source and sanction of law are
the implications that flow from the very concept of a divine covenant
with the people of Israel. The entire nation is conceived as being a
corporate entity, a collectivity, a sort of "psychic totality." The obligation

to keep the law is national, societal, and communal, as well as individual. Evil is a breach of the Covenant and undermines society. The welfare of society, the integrity of its fabric, is contingent upon the observance of the law. No wonder, then, that the conventional treaty provision requiring periodic public reading of the treaty's stipulations was expanded in Israel and transformed into a wholly new category: the obligation, oft repeated, to disseminate the law among the masses; that is, the universal duty of continuous self-education.[43]

In the ancient Near East the opposite situation was the case. Hammurabi, it is true, wrote the laws (so he said) in order that a plaintiff or defendant might know what they were. But this was largely a fiction since mass illiteracy was the rule, and interest in the law was aroused only after the inception of a case, and was restricted to the details of the particular paragraph of the code that applied in the circumstances. More in common with the spirit of Mesopotamian society was the injunction forbidding the dissemination of the details of the temple service for the New Year festival.[44] One is reminded that until Draco (ca. 621 B.C.E.) codified the laws of Athens, these remained the exclusive knowledge of the nobility, and their publication among the masses was forbidden. Diametrically opposed to such a notion is the biblical outlook in which the mass dissemination and study of the law in all its details is a major priority and a religious duty. The reason is obvious: the study of the law is not simply an intellectual exercise but a spiritual and moral discipline through whose instrumentality the entire society is shaped.

One other important aspect of the Ten Commandments is the interweaving of what today would be called the "religious" and the "secular" or social demands. This is well illustrated by the opening and closing words of the document: "God" and "fellow-being." The first few commands relate to the divine-human sphere, and contain the phrase "the Lord your God"; the others govern interpersonal relationships and do not have that formula. The "religious" demands precede the sociomoral because only a sense of responsibility and accountability before God provides the ultimate guarantee of the observance of one's duties to one's fellow beings. Social concern is rooted in the religious conscience. Conversely, professed belief in God, and the observance of the outward forms of religious expression, are well-nigh worthless unless they profoundly affect human relationships. This interweaving of the spiritual, the cultic, the moral, and the legal, this lack of differentiation between "religious" matters, matters of interpersonal relationships, and matters of social and sexual morality—this is one of the quintessential, differentiating characteristics of biblical law. All other systems in the ancient world display an atomistic approach to life. Civil obligations belong to the domain of law, moral demands to the domain of wisdom literature, and cultic responsibilities to the domain of priestly manuals. Law is strictly secular in content. In Israel, however, life is treated holistically. It is not compartmentalized. Crime is therefore also sin. An offense against sexual morality, against business morality, against social morality, is simultaneously a "religious" offense because, one and all, they are infractions of the divine will.

There are other constituents of the Decalogue that are wholly without parallel in the biblical world, and that are unqualifiedly Israelite innovations. These are, of course, the demand for the exclusive worship of one God, the prohibition on idolatry in all its forms, and the institution of the sabbath.

The prohibition against idolatry

One of the major themes of biblical literature is the struggle against paganism. The Patriarchal narratives, as we noted in Chapter Four, give no inkling of this phenomenon. They do not feature any tension between the Patriarchs and their surroundings as far as religion is concerned. The matter is simply not an issue. It is the arrival of Moses on the scene of history that heralds the first appearance of the notion of a war on polytheism, expressed by the statement in Exodus 12:12: "I will mete out punishments to all the gods of Egypt, I the Lord." The Ten Commandments clearly and unambiguously mandate the absolute prohibition on polytheism and idolatry for the entire people of Israel:

You shall have no other gods besides Me. You shall not make for yourself a sculptured image, or any likeness of what is in the heavens above, or on the earth below, or in the waters under the earth. You shall not bow down to them or serve them. [45]

This strict and comprehensive formulation demands the exclusive recognition of and allegiance to one God, the One who showed Himself to be active in history and who is known to Israel by the name that is consonantally written in Hebrew *YHVH*. It prohibits any material representation of celestial, terrestrial, and subterranean objects. In order to understand this prohibition against the plastic arts it must be remembered that the essence of polytheism lies in the divinized personification of cosmic phenomena. Further, in the polytheistic system an image that depicts natural forces and objects is not simply symbolic in function. The image or statue inevitably becomes endowed with divinity. As such, it is automatically invested with influence, and the representation is somehow ultimately identified with the deity itself. It is looked upon as the place and presence of the deity, and becomes the focus of veneration and worship. The most glaring and notorious examples of this process come from Egypt in the period of the New Kingdom. The statues of the monarchs are elevated to the status of independent deities, and the ultimate absurdity is reached when the king is depicted worshipping his own statue![46]

All this constitutes the opposite of Israelite monotheism, the essence of which is that God is absolutely sovereign precisely because He is wholly independent of the world He created, and He does not inhere in it. To represent an invisible God in any material and tangible form whatsoever is by definition to distort the divine reality. It compromises God's absolute transcendence. If God is said to be also immanent in the world, that is to say, if God is not withdrawn from the human arena but is present in the life of the world, it means that His presence is attested to by the impact of His personality on the human scene, not by a visible material representation.

The Sabbath

The narrative about the creation of the world as set forth in the Book of Genesis closed with the statement that God

ceased on the seventh day from all the work which He had done. And God blessed the seventh day and declared it holy, because on it God ceased from all the work of creation which He had done.[47]

This passage contains no mention of the sabbath as a fixed, weekly institution. It refers only to the seventh day of Creation, to the divine cessation from creativity, and to the blessing and sanctification of that day. But the term "sabbath" is not to be found, only the cognate verbal form. Nevertheless, the Decalogue features the explicit connection between the weekly sabbath day and creation:

> Remember the sabbath day and keep it holy. Six days you shall labor and do all your work, but the seventh day is a sabbath of the Lord your God: you shall not do any work—you, your son or daughter, your male or female slave, or your cattle, or the stranger who is within your settlements. For in six days the Lord made heaven and earth and sea, and all that is in them, and He rested on the seventh day; therefore the Lord blessed the sabbath day and hallowed it.[48]

This same rationale of the sabbath day is presented once again in another Exodus passage that emphasizes that the institution is an external sign of the covenant between God and Israel:

> . . .you must keep My sabbaths, for this is a sign between Me and you throughout the ages, that you may know that I the Lord have consecrated you. You shall keep the sabbath, for it is holy for you. He who profanes it shall be put to death: whoever does work on it, that person shall be cut off from among his kin. Six days may work be done, but on the seventh day there shall be a sabbath of complete rest, holy to the Lord; whoever does work on the sabbath day shall be put to death. The Israelite people shall keep the sabbath, observing the sabbath throughout the ages as a covenant for all time: it shall be a sign for all time between Me and the people of Israel. For in six days the Lord made heaven and earth, and on the seventh day He ceased from work and was refreshed.[49]

These passages understand the seventh day to be an integral part of the divinely ordained cosmic order. It is infused with blessing and sanctity, not by any action on the part of man but by God Himself. Its cosmic reality is entirely independent of human effort, and it is beyond the power of human beings to abrogate or change it.

The antiquity of the existence of the sabbath day in Israel is presupposed in all the legislation and even in the narratives. Barely one month after the departure from Egypt, and prior to the revelation at Sinai, it is assumed to be in force. The Israelites were to receive a double portion of the manna on Fridays, and were told that " 'Tomorrow is a day of rest, a holy sabbath of the Lord. . . . Six days you shall gather it; on the seventh day, the sabbath, there will be none. . . . Mark that the Lord has given you the sabbath; therefore He gives you two days' food on the sixth day.' "[50] This text assumes the sabbath to have been an established institution before Sinai, and the same impression is conveyed by the wording of the Decalogue: "Remember the sabbath day." It has every appearance of referring to an observance already in practice.

The biblical sabbath has no known analogy in the ancient world. In fact, the very conception of a seven-day week is unique to Israel. This is surprising in view of the widespread use of a seven-day unit of time in the ancient Near East both as a literary convention and in cultic observance.[51]

The Sumerian Gudea, ruler of Lagash (twenty-second century B.C.E.), built or rebuilt the temple E-ninnu ("The House of the Fifty") of the god Ningirsu and celebrated its dedication for seven days.[52] The Atrahasis epic mentions a seven-day magical rite for pregnant women in confinement.[53] In the Old Babylonian version of the Gilgamesh epic, the hero mourns over the death of his friend, Enkidu, for seven days.[54] Utnapishtim, the Babylonian Noah, completes his shipbuilding in seven days, the rains last six days and subside on the seventh, and the hero sends out a dove on the seventh day after the ship rested on Mount Nisir.[55]

In the Ugaritic myths, the same convention is applied. Thus, in the course of the construction of a palace for the god Baal, fire purges the building for six days and is extinguished on the seventh when the work is completed.[56] In the Keret epic, the king's army reaches the town of Udm by a seven-day march.[57] In the legend of Aqht, Danel gives oblation to the gods for seven days and celebrates for seven days when it is announced that he would have a male heir.[58]

In the Mesopotamian lunar calendar, the seventh, fourteenth, twenty-first, and twenty-eighth days of certain months, corresponding to the four phases of the moon, were all regarded as unlucky days. The nineteenth day, being the forty-ninth day after the new moon of the previous month, was called a "day of wrath."[59] These times were thought of as being controlled by evil spirits, and special fasts were prescribed. One ritual text forbids the king to eat cooked flesh, to change his clothes, to offer sacrifice, to ride in a chariot, and to render legal decisions on these days. A seer may not give an oracle, nor may a physician attend to the sick. Curses uttered against enemies are ineffective.[60]

From all the foregoing, it is clear that each seventh day of the lunar month possessed a special, if baneful character, and it can have nothing to do with the biblical sabbath, which is a day suffused with blessing and sanctity. Furthermore, and this is truly astonishing, whereas all major units of time in the ancient Near East—the year, the month, the week—were uniformly based on the phases of the moon and the solar cycle, the Israelite seven-day week is wholly independent of either. It is completely disconnected from the movement of the celestial bodies.[61] This extraordinary fact, coupled with the grounding of the sabbath in creation, direct attention to the quintessential idea of Israelite mono-theism that God is entirely outside of and sovereign over nature. He is lord of time as well as of space. The seventh day each week is removed from the mundane sphere of secular time and is endowed with a divine dimension. In a very real sense, therefore, the institution of the sabbath day constitutes a suspension of time. By proscribing work and human creativity on that day, and by enjoining the inviolability of nature one day a week, the Torah delimits human autonomy while it restores to nature its pristine freedom. At the same time, human freedom is im-measurably enhanced, human equality is strengthened, and the cause of social justice is promoted by legislating, with divine sanction, the inalienable right of every human being, irrespective of social class, to a day of complete rest every seven days.[62]

Moses and monotheism

It can hardly be coincidental that several new and revolutionary fundamentals of the religion of Israel first appear with the advent of Moses. Two distinct phases in the history of the national religion are distinguishable in the biblical sources. The first begins with the divine call to Abraham. While, as we have noted, the narratives do not indicate the existence of any tension between the Patriarch and his contempo-raries in the sphere of religion, yet several discrete items of information point implicitly to the consciousness of a religious break between him and his forebears. Most telling is the fact that the formula "God of my/ your/his father," so frequent with Isaac and Jacob, is never used by, to,

or of Abraham. There is complete discontinuity with the past, a conclusion strengthened by the clear statement in Joshua 24:2 that Abraham's ancestors were idolaters. This situation is also subtly portrayed
in the story of the pact between Laban and Jacob at Gilead as told in
Genesis 31:53. Laban declares, "May the God of Abraham and the
God of Nahor judge between us." Significantly, the Hebrew verb is in
the plural form, indicating lack of identity between the two deities
mentioned, even though Nahor was the brother of Abraham.[63] At the
same time Jacob refrains from employing Laban's formula when it is
his turn to take the oath, not wishing to invoke the "God of Nahor."
Nevertheless, it remains a fact that the Patriarchal narratives contain
no inkling of any war against paganism. As we observed above, this
development is first registered in the Exodus texts.

We have also previously drawn attention to the testimony of such
passages as Exodus 3:13–16 and 6:2–3 that the predominance of the
Tetragrammaton, the Divine Name YHVH, as the name of the God
of Israel first occurs in this same Mosaic period, a conclusion that is
reinforced by a study of the Hebrew personal names. These do not
feature any compound of YHVH in its various forms until, most significantly, the appearance of Jochebed, the name of Moses' mother.[64]
Thereafter, the Israelite onomasticon, or thesaurus of names, is replete
with examples of this kind. In addition, the period of the oppression
and Exodus witnesses the discontinuance of the Patriarchal divine name
El Shaddai, except residually as a poetic device, as well as of the title
"God of the fathers."

All the foregoing constitutes mute but eloquent corroboration of the
assertion that the advent of Moses marks a radically new development
in the religion of Israel. If it be further remembered that the concept
of a national covenant between God and an entire people, the insistence
on the exclusive worship of one God, the thoroughgoing ban on representing God in any material or corporeal form, and the emergence
as a national institution of the messenger-prophet,[65] the *navi'* as he is
called in Hebrew, are all innovations of the same period, then the
conclusion becomes inescapable that we are faced with a revolutionary
religious phenomenon, a sudden and new monotheistic creation the
like of which had not hitherto existed and the characteristic ingredients
of which were not to be found on the contemporary religious scene.[66]

In the entire known history of the world's religions, revolutionary developments have always been the work of outstanding personalities, of creative geniuses, of inspired and skillful leaders. Wherever and whenever such transformations have occurred they have been dramatic, swift, and sudden. The gradual, evolutionary progression from polytheism to true ethical monotheism simply cannot be documented.[67] Accordingly, Moses must be seen as the towering figure behind the aforementioned religious developments that took place in Israel. Tradition has left us no other name but his, and his role as the first and greatest leader of Israel, as the spiritual titan, the dominating personality that powerfully informed for all time the collective mind and self-consciousness of the community, is unassailable.

As always, when dealing with singular phenomena in ancient Israel, the question inevitably arises as to whether external forces exerted any influence on Moses' religious outlook or contributed to the shaping of his thinking and to the crystallization of his thoughts and ideas. The question is legitimate in view of the late appearance of the people of Israel on the scene of history, when the great civilizations of the Nile and Tigris-Euphrates Valleys were already past their prime. This having been admitted, however, the answers sometimes offered by scholars more than justify a lurking suspicion that authentic scholarly concerns are occasionally beset with an ingrained prejudice that finds it all but impossible to credit the people of Israel with any originality. Since the developments described above cannot be matched in the well-documented related cultures of the ancient Near East, scholars with creative skill and luxuriant imagination will turn for enlightenment to those peoples about whom nothing is known.

An excellent case in point is the "Kenite hypothesis."[68] This maintains that Moses learned the Divine Name YHVH from the Kenites while he lived with Jethro in Midian, and that he took over into Israel the Kenite cult. It will be recalled that Moses' father-in-law is termed a "Kenite" in Judges 1:16 and 4:11. It is also related that when Jethro came to visit his son-in-law in the wilderness, he invoked the name YHVH in response to Moses' account of the great events of the Exodus, and he acknowledged the superiority of this God "over all gods." Further, he brought a burnt offering and sacrifices for God[69] (*'elohim*) and partook of a sacred meal together with Aaron and the elders of Israel. Apart from these bare facts and the little that can be gleaned from the biblical sources concerning the Kenites, we know nothing about this clan. Their language, culture, history, and religion are all shrouded in obscurity, except perhaps that they were wandering tinkers. Nevertheless, there are scholars who wish to make them the source and inspiration for Israel's religion!

On the surface, the theory suggesting some kind of connection between Mosaic monotheism and the revolutionary cult of the heretic pharaoh Akhenaten is more sophisticated and seemingly more plausible.[70] This king, Amenophis IV, or Akhenaten (ca. 1364–1347 B.C.E.), proclaimed the solar disk, called Aten in Egyptian, to be the supreme god. The exclusive worship of Aten became the official state religion, and the worship of other gods seems to have been outlawed. Extraordinarily, the god Aten was not allowed to be represented in either human or animal form. Whether or not the new religion was truly monotheistic is still a matter of scholarly dispute among Egyptologists.

While the religion of Aten gives the appearance of being a new and sudden manifestation, in actuality the basic idea had long been germinating.[71] Its history stretches far back in Egyptian records. We noted earlier on, when dealing with the plagues, that the sun was one of the pivotal fundamentals of Egyptian life and was personified as a deity. It was looked upon as the founder of kingship in Egypt from whom the pharaohs claimed biological descent. The prominence of the cult of the sun god, his universal sovereignty, the notion that other gods of the pantheon were but variant forms and manifestations of him, were all well rooted in Egyptian culture. Hymns to the sun god date back to the Pyramid Age, from as early as the Fifth and Sixth Dynasties (twenty-fifth to twenty-first centuries B.C.E.). It was in this period that Heliopolis, which means "sun-city," situated in Lower Egypt, became very influential. (It was called Iunu or Onu in Egyptian, which is the biblical On mentioned in Genesis 41:45.) The great temples of the sun god Re, Re-Atum, or Re-Harakhty, in this city achieved enormous power, second only to those of Amun at Thebes in Upper Egypt. The word Aten, in the sense of "sun disk," was already in use during the Middle Kingdom (twenty-first to eighteenth centuries B.C.E.). However, it was in the course of the XVIIIth Dynasty (ca. 1552–1306 B.C.E.) that it really came into prominence, not simply as the physical disk of the sun, but as the name of the god himself. Amenophis (Amenhotep) I (ca. 1527–1507 B.C.E.) was described at his death as having ascended to the sky to "become one with the Disk . . . blended with him out of whom he came." His successor, Thutmosis I (ca. 1507–1494 B.C.E.), adopted among his royal titulary the epithet "The One who comes out of the Disk." More than any other single factor, it was the imperial expansion of Egypt under Thutmosis III (ca. 1490–1436 B.C.E.) and his son, Amenophis (Amenhotep) II (ca. 1438–1412 B.C.E.), that gave the impetus to the promotion of the sun cult. By their conquests in Africa and Asia, these kings turned Egypt into a world power. The result was a marked expansion of cultural and religious horizons. The considerable volume of international trade, the confrontation and intermingling with other cultures, and the cross-fertilization of ideas that ensued, all served to encourage a universalistic outlook that expressed itself in syncretistic trends and in the introduction into Egypt of Asiatic influences. Thus was stimulated the development of the concept of cosmic deities, the increased solarization of the gods, and the tendency toward universalizing the sun god. Aten was elevated to membership in the pantheon, and in the days of Amenophis II we already find the symbol of the sun disk equipped with a pair of embracing arms. A scarab from the reign of Thutmosis IV (ca. 1412–1403 B.C.E.) features the Aten as a universal deity.

With the reign of Amenophis (Amenhotep) III (ca. 1403–1364 B.C.E.), father of Akhenaten, comes a considerable increase in the inscriptional use of the term Aten treated as deity. The king himself named a newly built palace on the west bank of the Nile in the vicinity of Thebes, "Splendor of the Aten" (or "The Aten Gleams"), and he gave the same name to the royal barge that he installed for the queen on the manmade lake in the palace grounds. His own royal titulary incorporated the phrase "Heat which is in Aten," and the name of this god was also attached to one of his children. Further evidence for the spread of the cult of Aten in the days of Amenophis III comes from a hymn to the sun god that is inscribed on a stele erected by two brothers, Suti (Seth) and Hor (Horus), architects at Thebes. In it they hail the "Aten of the daytime" as the creator and maker of all things.

The impact of imperial conquest certainly created a favorable climate for the growing ascendancy, acceptance, and diffusion of the concept of a universal, cosmic, solar deity in this period, but it cannot explain the fact that this movement found specific expression through the elevation of Atenism. To account for this particular development, attention must be paid to internal Egyptian affairs, which takes us back to the rise in importance of Thebes in Upper Egypt. This city is commonly referred to in Egyptian texts as *níwt*, "The City," or Níwt 'Imn, "The city of Amun," a name that appears in the Bible as No' 'Amon in Nahum 3:8, and more usually, simply as No'.[72] Situated along the banks of the Nile in the area of modern Luxor, it was one of the most famous of Egyptian cities. The pharaohs of the XIth Dynasty (twenty-first to eighteenth centuries B.C.E.) turned it into the administrative capital, thereby enhancing the prestige of its god, Amun. It was in the sixteenth century B.C.E., however, that Thebes and Amun were set on the path of ever-increasing power and prosperity. It was here that the resistance to the Hyksos invaders was organized. Its royal house—King Kamose and his successor, Amose I (1552–1527 B.C.E.)—succeeded in ridding Egypt of the hated foreigners, founded the XVIIIth Dynasty, and inaugurated the New Kingdom. Amun now became the national god, and his temple establishment grew in wealth and influence. As Egypt embarked upon its course of energetic empire building to become the paramount military power in the Near East, so the god Amun became an imperial divinity. Immense wealth flowed into the coffers of the priesthood, sustained by the spoils of foreign conquests and by lavish royal endowments of land, personnel, and livestock from within Egypt itself, not to mention the special privileges accorded the temple. Ecclesiastical titles included those of "High Priest of Re" and "High Priest of Ptah," and the Theban priesthood asserted supremacy over all other priesthoods and temples.

Some idea of the tremendous economic, and hence political, power that the Theban clergy could wield may be gained from the data given in an Egyptian papyrus that details the resources at the disposal of the temple of Atum at Thebes.[73] It possessed 924 square miles of arable land, 433 gardens, 65 market towns, 46 work-yards, and 83 boats. In addition, it engaged a work force of 81,322 men and owned 421,362 beasts. All this immeasurably exceeded the holdings of the other two great temples at Heliopolis and Memphis. While these figures come from the reign of Rameses III (ca. 1183–1152 B.C.E.), they may be safely taken to reflect the state of affairs in the period of Thutmosis III (ca. 1490–1436 B.C.E.) and Amenophis II (ca. 1438–1412 B.C.E.) as well, when the Theban priesthood had reached the pinnacle of its power.

It is obvious that the priestly class constituted a threat to the pharaonic seat of power itself. This potential danger was aggravated by the emergence of two other foci of power that were the inevitable by-products of Egyptian imperial expansion. One was an entrenched, virtually hereditary, bureaucracy with which the priesthood was closely involved. The other was the standing army with its elite corps of professional officers. It interlocked with the royal line, and some of the high positions in the civil administration were manned by military men.

In this complicated situation the pharaohs began to take steps to neutralize the threats to royal power. Trusted individuals were appointed to the high priesthoods of the gods of Ptah of Memphis and Re of Heliopolis, and the smoldering rivalry between these and the priesthood of Thebes was carefully stoked. The offices of "High Priest of Amun" in Thebes and of the "Supreme Priest of all Priests," that had formerly been united in the person of one individual, were uncoupled and held by two separate appointees. Amenophis III (ca. 1403–1364 B.C.E.) saw to it that the position of "Chief of the Prophets of the South and of the North" was no longer held by the clergy of Amun. Furthermore, he discontinued the practice of filling secular offices with members of the Theban hierarchy. Above all, the city of Memphis assumed ever-greater importance as the administrative center of the country. Strategically positioned just south of the economically important Nile Delta on the border between Lower and Upper Egypt, this city was a far more convenient site than Thebes from which to conduct affairs of state in the period of the empire. Amenophis II had been born in Memphis and had occupied the office of high priest of the god Ptah there. His grandson, Amenophis III, made another break with tradition by marrying a commoner, the daughter of a commander of the chariotry. This queen, Tiy by name, became the "Great Royal Wife." Possessed of considerable ambition and ability, she became highly influential in the affairs of state, particularly in the struggle against the Theban hierarchy.

From all the above, it is clear beyond doubt that the new religion of Akhenaten was not a sudden revelation. Whatever it owed to the personal theology and inspiration of its founder, it also had roots in Egyptian history and culture. In the final analysis, it was influenced by a complex of converging factors. These included traditional Egyptian religious concepts, mundane political considerations, and the increasing cosmopolitanism of Egyptian society that came with imperial expansion.

In addition, it is not unlikely that the impact of Aryan cults, imported from Asia, was also present.

The new religion of Aten was a short-lived phenomenon, and lasted about fifteen years. Nothing is known of the birth and youth of Amenophis IV, who succeeded his father, Amenophis III, ca. 1364 B.C.E. He changed his name to Akhenaten, which means something like "He-Who-is-serviceable-to-Aten," thereby demonstratively abandoning the religion of Amun and elevating Aten to the official state god. He abandoned Thebes and built himself a new royal city on virgin soil, which he called Akhetaten, "The Horizon of the Sun Disk." It was situated on the eastern bank of the Nile about midway between Memphis and Thebes and roughly corresponds to the present-day Tell el-Amarna. Akhenaten systematically expunged the name Amun from the monuments, and also effaced the names of other gods. He even, on occasion, changed the plural form "gods" to "god." The old mortuary cult of Osiris was suppressed, and the mortuary prayers were addressed to Aten directly or through the intermediacy of Akhenaten.

Was the new religion truly monotheistic? As we previously noted, this is still a debatable point. The king's great hymn to Aten, probably his own composition, refers to that deity as the sole god, apart from whom none other exists.[74] The difficulty is that similar phraseology is used of various gods in a much earlier phase of Egyptian religion when it implies not exclusivity of existence but the concentration upon a specific god. Furthermore, Akhenaten continued to call himself "son of Re," which god he identified with Aten, and Re remained a component of the names he gave to members of his family. In the earlier part of his residence at Akhetaten he seems to have found no contradiction between his conception of Aten and the notion that the sacred Mnevis-bull of Heliopolis was an incarnation of the sun god, for he made special provision for its ceremonial burial in the new city. Particularly serious is the question of the status of the king himself. He claimed to have issued from the body of Aten, and while, as far as is known, he did not explicitly refer to himself as a god, but as the son of the god, he nevertheless did not deny his own divine role. He was certainly worshipped as a god by his followers. He claimed to be the one in whom Aten manifested and revealed himself, and his cartouche and that of Aten appeared side by side, thus implying a shared divinity.

He even appointed a high priest to himself in the same way as he functioned as Aten's high priest. It is highly significant that the mayor of his new capital city bore a name that meant "Akhenaten created me." It is beyond doubt that, whereas the king and his family communed with Aten directly, the members of his court could have no access to the god except through the intermediacy of the king.

A striking feature of the new religion, insofar as the celebrated "Hymn of Aten" is concerned, is the complete absence of any ethical or moral content. That composition expresses no ethical values or moral imperatives, and makes no demands on the believer in terms of human behavior.[75] It calls for no ethical discipline in the formation of character and evinces no interest in social justice or the welfare of society. Akhenaten's own sexual morality as exhibited in his marriages is repugnant to biblical standards. He married his twelve-year-old daughter in order to obtain a male heir, and later took to wife another daughter as well. Certainly, the religious revolution of Akhenaten in no wise constituted any advance upon traditional Egyptian values in the sphere of ethics and morality.

We now return to the issue of the possible influence of Akhenaten's movement upon Mosaic monotheism.[76] If Moses' career is to be dated in the fifteenth century B.C.E., as some scholars believe, then the question is invalid, of course, and it might be wondered whether Akhenaten's theological thinking might not have been influenced by the teachings of Moses. Since, however, the weight of the evidence now at hand favors locating the Exodus in the thirteenth century B.C.E., it means that Moses grew to maturity not very long after the death of Akhenaten ca. 1347. Whether or not he knew of that king's religious reform is a moot point that can never be known. The new religion lasted no more than about fifteen years, and disappeared as suddenly as it arose. The city of Akhetaten was completely abandoned soon after the king's death. His successor, Tutankhaten ("The Living Image of Aten"), changed his name to Tutankhamen ("The Living Image of Amun") in capitulation to the Theban hierarchy, reinstated the old gods, and restored the special privileges of their priesthoods. He moved his administrative capital to Memphis.

The religion of Akhenaten had been confined to members of the royal family and the new aristocracy that he created and had no impact on the Egyptian people. It is not impossible that its revolutionary ideas lingered on for a while, and enjoyed an underground existence among small groups. However, they did not advance the religion of Egypt in the direction of monotheism. True, Aten was not represented in material form, whether human or animal, but he was not an invisible god, being very much visible in his daily shining circuit across the sky. This religion showed no concern for the common man, and its ethical content was ambiguous at best. Its emergence was rooted in Egyptian political and religious history, and without the person of the pharaoh as the sole and indispensable intermediary between the god and the people, it was meaningless. There is no basis for a conclusion that Akhenaten's Atenism was the inspiration for Mosaic monotheism.

CHAPTER VIII

The Laws

EXODUS 21–24

The administration of justice is indispensable for the orderly and continuing functioning of any civilized society. No organized community can exist without the apparatus of law. We have already seen how, at the suggestion of Jethro, Moses established the judiciary system. But what about the content of the law? The Ten Commandments do not constitute a legal system. They express general principles of right and wrong, but they contain no provisions for their enforcement. There are no humanly imposed penalties for their violation. No court of law could possibly adjudicate specific cases on the basis of the Ten Commandments alone. Accordingly, the legal code necessary for everyday application in a social context is now set forth in the Torah in some detail.

The Book of the Covenant

The collection of laws that is found in Exodus 21:1–23:19 is conventionally referred to in scholarly literature as the "Book of the Covenant" or the "Covenant Code."[1] These titles derive from the narrative in Chapter 24 that describes the ceremonies and rituals attendant upon the ratification of the covenant between God and Israel. There it is related that "Moses then wrote down all the commands of the Lord," and that he "took the record [Hebrew: *sefer*] of the covenant and read it aloud to the people" (Exodus 24:4, 7). It is inferred by scholars that what Moses recorded was the corpus of legislation laid out in the preceding chapters of Exodus. Certainly, the section expresses the fundamental biblical teaching that the context of Israel's relationship to God is obedience to His laws.

Apart from the Book of the Covenant, the Torah literature also contains two other collections of legal material. One comprises Leviticus Chapters 17–26, and has been designated the "Holiness Code" by modern scholars because it is characterized by the recurrent theme[2] that Israel must strive for holiness in imitation of God's holiness, which expresses itself in moral actions. The other appears in Deuteronomy Chapters 12–28. All three corpora of Torah legislation share much in common by way of content, stylistic formulation, and treatment. Nevertheless, each possesses features peculiar to itself, particularly in regard to its respective concerns and ideological thrust. As we shall see, the first corpus, the Book of the Covenant, is exceedingly ancient and has numerous points of contact with the documents of law recovered in the course of excavations in the lands of the Near East, particularly Mesopotamia.[3]

The composition opens in Exodus 21:1 with the statement: "These are the rules [Hebrew: *mishpatim*] that you shall set before them." It closes in Exodus 24:3 with the report that "Moses went and repeated to the people all the commands of the Lord and all the rules. . . ." These two terms, *mishpatim* ("rules") and *devarim* ("commands"), distinguish the two different sections into which the corpus is divided: Chapters 21:2–22:16 and 22:17–23:19. The first encompasses a variety of disparate topics, as the following summary of its contents demonstrates:

1. Chapter 21:2–11 deals with laws relating to the institution of slavery, specifically the imposition of legal restraints on the power of a master over his Hebrew male and female slaves, and the establishment of the legal rights of slaves.
2. Chapter 21:12–17 lists four offenses that incur the death penalty: premeditated murder (as distinct from accidental homicide), an assault on either of one's parents, cursing either one of them, and the crime of kidnapping.
3. Chapter 21:18–27 relates to the infliction of physical injury by one person on another, be the victim one of the combatants in an altercation or a slave at the hands of his master or a pregnant woman innocently caught in a fight between men. This subsection includes the *lex talionis*, or law of retributive justice.

4. Chapter 21:28–36 pertains to the infliction of physical injury on living creatures, whether it be a case of an ox's goring human beings or of a human being's causing injury to an ox or an ass through negligence or of an ox's goring another ox.
5. Chapters 21:37–22:3 have to do with laws of theft of livestock, and with burglary.
6. Chapter 22:4–5 deals with compensation to be paid for causing damage to another's crops either by grazing livestock or by fire.
7. Chapter 22:6–14 concerns the loss or damage of personal property entrusted to another for safekeeping or on loan. These laws touch on matters of restitution and on the procedure to be followed in case of suspected misappropriation.
8. Chapter 22:15–16 covers the liability of one who seduces a virgin not yet betrothed.

The casuistic formulation

A glance at the Scriptural texts cited above shows at once that the entire collection of laws is formulated in terms of specific concrete situations in life that are presented hypothetically and from which the legal consequences are drawn. This is what is called casuistically formulated law. By way of illustration we may point to the case set forth in Exodus 21:18–19:

When men quarrel and one strikes the other with stone or fist, and he does not die but has to take to bed—if he then gets up and walks outdoors upon his staff, the assailant shall go unpunished, except that he must pay for his idleness and his cure.

It is obvious that no legal concept or theory of justice is here advanced, although the fact that such is not made explicit does not mean that the laws lack underlying philosophical postulates or are not rooted in ideas or goals that express values that the particular law seeks to realize. It is simply that biblical law in its earliest stage, like Semitic law in general, preferred the "casuistic" legal style. This form almost certainly developed naturally out of the practice of arbitration. The judgment, accepted in the community as having binding validity, served as a precedent and would be extended into general application beyond the specific case that precipitated the ruling. An excellent example of this process in action is provided by the story told in Leviticus 24:10–14. The son of an Israelite mother and an Egyptian father got involved in a fight with another Israelite, in the course of which he uttered the Divine Name in blasphemy. He was brought before Moses who had him held in custody pending the receipt of a divinely revealed decision. The death penalty by stoning is prescribed. This episode and the judgment then give the opportunity for the formulation of a generalized rule of law (verses 15–16).

Another instance is furnished by the story of the daughters of a certain Zelophehad of the tribe of Manasseh, as detailed in Numbers 27:1–11. This man had died in the course of the wilderness wanderings leaving no sons, but five daughters. These demanded for themselves the right of hereditary succession. "Moses brought their case before the Lord" and the verdict was: "The plea of Zelophehad's daughters is just: you should give them a hereditary holding among their father's kinsmen; transfer their father's share to them." This decision is now accorded the status of a legal precedent, and a general principle is derived from it and is formulated in casuistic terms:

> If a man dies without a son, you shall transfer his property to his daughter. . . . This shall be the law of procedure for the Israelites, in accordance with the Lord's command to Moses.

It should be emphasized that the authority and sanction of the law is the divine command, and this is so throughout the entire corpus of biblical law. All aspects of life are deemed to be regulated by God's will as it expressed itself in law.

The antiquity of the Book of the Covenant is apparent from an examination of the social and cultural milieu it projects.[4] It is presupposed that people live in houses and not in tents, but while they live in settled communities, there are none of the signs of urbanization, none of the institutions of the city-state system or of the monarchy. In fact, in Exodus 22:27 the leader of the people is called a "chieftain" (Hebrew: *nasi'*), not a "king." The atmosphere is rural and the way of life uncomplicated. There is no mention of artisans, craftsmen, merchants, and commerce. The ox, the ass, and the sheep are vital commodities, and figure prominently in the collection. The legislation has every appearance of serving a settled community, the economic basis of which is agriculture on a small scale, and cattle raising.

The ancient Near Eastern laws[5]

We have previously drawn attention to the fact that these laws that are set forth in Exodus 21:2–22:16 under the rubric of *mishpatim* possess numerous affinities with the ancient legal collections uncovered at various sites in the Near East. More specifically, it is Mesopotamia that supplies the necessary materials for comparative studies, and it does so with a superabundance and a variety that practically defies the efforts of any one scholar to master the entire available corpus within the span of a single lifetime. The history of cuneiform law takes us back at least to the middle of the third millennium B.C.E. For the next two thousand years and more, Mesopotamia exercised a dominating influence upon legal developments throughout the Near East and was a center of diffusion in much the same way as the great body of Roman law left its indelible mark on Byzantine civilization and on the West. Accordingly, it is not inaccurate to speak of a common cuneiform legal culture in the area, even though local, ethnic, linguistic, social, and political variables may be present.

Each of the three cultures of Mesopotamia—Sumerian, Babylonian, and Assyrian—contributed collections of cuneiform laws, all of them employing the casuistic style of formulation. The earliest extant compilation, though by no means the first to be made, is that of Ur-Nammu,[6] founder of the Sumerian Third Dynasty at the city of Ur, situated west of the Euphrates River in southern Iraq. This city was the capital of the Mesopotamian Valley ca. 2060–1950 B.C.E. Unfortunately, the original document, which was probably incised on stone, has not been recovered. What has come to light are copies made on clay tablets hundreds of years after its promulgation. One such, found at Nippur, is poorly preserved, and the prologue it contains is only partially legible. Another, found at Ur, consists of two disconnected fragments of what were once a single document. The long prologue to the laws extolls the virtues and achievements of King Ur-Nammu, "the mighty warrior." In issuing his laws, the monarch claims to be actuated by "principles of equity and truth," inspired to "establish equity in the land" and to "banish malediction, violence, and strife." During his reign, he says, "the orphan was not delivered up to the rich man; the widow was not delivered up to the mighty man; the man of one shekel was not delivered up to the man of one mina [equals 60 shekels]."

Of the laws themselves, only a few are in sufficiently good state of preservation to be read with certainty. These deal with sexual offenses, false accusations, bodily injuries, the punishment of a slave woman who puts herself on a level with her mistress, witnesses in lawsuits, and damage to another's land. Without future recovery of more of Ur-Nammu's compilation, the full range of legal topics that the original encompassed must remain unknown. It may be safely assumed that the laws originally closed with an epilogue. What is of major importance is that the legislation is drafted in the casuistic style that is characteristic of all subsequent collections of cuneiform laws, as well as of the biblical *mishpatim*. The following paragraph is a typical example:

If a man's slave-woman, comparing herself to her mistress, speaks insolently to her . . . her mouth shall be scoured with one quart of salt.

We are more fortunate in the case of King Lipit-Ishtar[7] (ca. 1870 B.C.E.) of the city of Isin in central Lower Mesopotamia, successor to the empire of Ur III. While his collection of laws is also fragmentary, much more of it has survived. Written in the Sumerian language, it may also have been promulgated in an Akkadian version since the dynasty to which the king belonged was Amorite. The document has been reconstructed from several clay tablets, all but one found at Nippur. It contains a prologue from which the end portion is missing, about thirty-eight laws in part or whole, and an epilogue with several gaps in it. The prologue is self-adulatory. Lipit-Ishtar calls himself "the wise shepherd" who was called to rule "in order to establish justice in the land, to banish complaints, to turn back enmity and rebellion by force of arms, [and] to bring well-being to the Sumerians and Akkadians." "The humble shepherd," he "established justice in Sumer and Akkad," and inaugurated certain social reforms. The legal enactments deal with matters relating to the hiring of boats, the care of orchards and gardens, slavery, estate taxes, inheritance, marriage, and injuries to a hired ox. A strange feature of the compilation is the haphazard arrangement of the laws. No organizing principle is apparent. It is uncertain whether this is original and reflective of a totally different concept of order from that of moderns or whether it results from the available copies' being actually scribal exercises drawn at random from a more systematically arranged archetype. The king's epilogue, like the prologue, is self-approbatory but contains an interesting ingredient. It invokes blessings on him who will not interfere with the text of the stele, and heaps curses on the one who does.

An important stage in the development of the Babylonian legal system is represented by the laws of Eshnunna,[8] an Amorite city-state, now the ruined site of Tell Asmar, east of the middle Tigris, lying on its tributary, the Diyala River. The laws have survived in two tablets found at Tell Harmal on the outskirts of Baghdad. Both were copied from the same original and they overlap in content, although there are some minor differences between the two. Regrettably, neither tablet yields a complete copy of the laws. One is almost complete, but its surface has been badly eroded in places; the other is preserved only in its lower half. The king who promulgated the collection is unknown. He obviously antedated the extant copies, the second of which is tentatively dated ca. 1850 B.C.E. As of now, the approximately sixty legible laws are the oldest such collection written in the Akkadian language. Apart from their intrinsic interest, they assume historic importance in light of the fact that they bear marked resemblance in substance, form, and phraseology to the later laws of Hammurabi, even to the extent of distinguishing the threefold stratification of society that is characteristic of these latter. The surviving secondary copies have neither prologue nor epilogue, both of which almost certainly were originally present. As is the case with Lipit-Ishtar's collection, Eshnunna's is chaotically arranged, and the same alternative explanations for this phenomenon suggested above apply here too. As to the contents of the laws, much attention is devoted to economic matters, such as the regulation of prices of commodities, the hire of wagons and boats, and the wages of laborers. Other topics are marriage and divorce, assault and battery, the goring ox, a mad dog, and criminal negligence.

The longest, most comprehensive, best arranged, most sophisticated, and best preserved of the cuneiform law collections is that of Hammurabi[9] (ca. 1728–1686 B.C.E.), the great empire builder of Babylon. Inscribed on a black diorite stele about eight feet high, it is the crowning glory of Mesopotamian jurisprudence. It long stood in the temple of Esagila in Babylon. About 1160 B.C.E. the stele was carried off to Susa (biblical Shushan), capital of Elam (southwestern Iran), probably by King Shutruk-Nahhunte, as part of the booty from his invasion of Mesopotamia. It was unearthed at that site by a French expedition in the winter of 1901–1902, and has since been housed in the Louvre in Paris. Subsequent to its modern discovery, other copies of the laws have been found, thus enabling scholars to restore most of the paragraphs between numbers 65 and 100, which the Elamites had chiseled off, apparently in preparation for a commemorative inscription of their own that was never written. A bas-relief decorates the upper part of the front of the stele and shows a god, Shamash or Marduk, investing the king with the symbols of sovereignty, that is, authorizing him to issue his laws. A long prologue and even longer epilogue frame the collection, which comprises 282 paragraphs arranged in fifty-one columns.

The poetic framework is replete with expressions of Hammurabi's self-aggrandizement, but he defines his idealized concept of kingship as being "to promote the welfare of the people," "to cause justice to prevail in the land, to destroy the wicked and the evil, that the strong might not oppress the weak." It is Hammurabi who "makes law prevail, who guides the people aright." He says, "I established law and justice in the language of the land, thereby promoting the welfare of the people." In the epilogue he describes his compilation as "The laws of justice . . . by which he caused the land to take the right way and have good government," and he states that he set up the stele "in order that the strong might not oppress the weak, that justice might be dealt the orphan [and] the widow." He goes on to declare:

> I wrote my precious words on a stele, and in the presence of the statue of me, the king of justice, I set [it] up in order to administer the law of the land, to prescribe the ordinances of the land, to give justice to the oppressed. . . . Let any oppressed man who has a cause come into the presence of me, the king of justice, and then read carefully my inscribed steles and give heed to my precious words, and may my stele make the case clear to him; may he understand his cause; may he set his mind at ease!

Finally, the king commends his laws to his successors, and heaps curses upon him who would abolish, distort, or otherwise tamper with them.

The topics with which Hammurabi's collection deal may be broadly subsumed under a limited number of headings. The first forty-one laws are basically concerned with matters of public order: the subversion of the judicial system through unsubstantiated accusations, false evidence, and a judge's wrongful judgment (§§1–5); the violation of property rights through theft, misappropriation, kidnapping, harboring fugitive slaves, robbery, and looting (§§6–25); and in connection with the duties of tenants of the crown (§§26–41). The rest of the collection mainly features matters of private law: the regulation of relations between the landowner and the farmer (§§42–52), responsibility with respect to the irrigation of land (§§53–56), shepherds and grazing (§§59–65). Then follow laws governing economic transactions (§§67–126), marriage, the family, the devolution of property, and wet-nursing (§§127–194). Next come laws concerning the redress of injuries to persons in cases of assault (§§195–214), and damages awarded against professional men and against people in skilled trades (§§215–240). The last sections deal with problems arising out of the practice of agriculture (§§241–267); tariffs for hiring boats, wagons, and laborers (§§268–277); and finally, laws concerning slaves (§§278–282).

One characteristic feature of Hammurabi's compilation has already been met with in the laws of Eshnunna, and that is the threefold stratification of society. Everyone seems to be typed as an *awilum*, a *mushkenum*, or a *wardum*.[10] The last term unambiguously refers to the slave population, but the first two have as yet not been defined with precision. The first term literally means "a man," and specifically here a member of the upper class of freeborn citizens. The *mushkenum* belongs to a class of lower social prestige; "a commoner" seems to be the best translation. The law was not applied impartially and uniformly to all persons, but could vary according to social class. Another feature of the collection is the *lex talionis*, or law of exact equivalence. This will be treated at length later in this chapter.

It is generally agreed that the king issued his law collection toward the end of his forty-three-year reign, but there is no unanimity as to his motivation in doing so. One theory has it that Hammurabi wanted to impose some kind of unity upon the diverse political entities that made up his far-flung empire. Far more likely, as we shall see, theoretical rather than practical considerations guided his action. We shall have occasion to return to this theme later on. In the meantime, one other cuneiform legal collection must engage our attention.

The ancient city of Asshur, modern Qal'at Sharqat, located on the west bank of the Tigris River in northern Iraq, has yielded a number of clay tablets that seem to belong to the twelfth century B.C.E. but which probably go back to a prototype three centuries older. They contain, in all, about one hundred ten legal paragraphs, several being no longer legible. Coming from the ancient religious center of Assyria, these Middle Assyrian Laws,[11] as they are called, reflect societal conditions and legal concepts that are quite different from those behind Hammurabi's compilation. Its formulations are far more complicated than those of the other "codes," a phenomenon that raises questions as to its exact nature. A goodly section relates to women, and constitutes the largest and most ancient such collection. Other matters included in the tablets concern the holding of land, the devolution of property by inheritance and sale, and irrigation rights. A particularly repulsive aspect of the Assyrian laws is the savagery of their penal provisions.

Aside from these Mesopotamian cuneiform collections, and a few very small compilations not here reviewed, mention must also be made of the Hittite[12] laws discovered at Boghazköy in Asia Minor, which was the capital of the Hittites from ca. 1800 to ca. 1200 B.C.E. The two hundred laws surviving from a larger corpus of legislation are written in Old Hittite (ca. 1650–1595 B.C.E.) on several tablets, most of which are late copies. They were apparently never inscribed on a stele and were not accessible to the common people but remained exclusively available to professional scribes. The several recensions are particularly valuable for tracing a process of periodic reform. The formulas "formerly" and its contrasting "now" are often employed in repeating a law in which the penalty has been revised. The instances of capital punishment have been progressively reduced and replaced by restitution. In fact, the increasing emphasis on the latter rather than on retribution as a guiding principle is an unusual feature of the laws. There is evidence of Babylonian influence on the Hittite legal scholars who drafted the collection. The social background is patriarchal and feudal.

Finally, a note about Egypt.[13] Although that civilization, by virtue of its antiquity, must have had a history of lawmaking older than any other in the Near East, it has not bequeathed to posterity anything of detailed written law. Nothing resembling the Mesopotamian or Hittite collections has survived despite the discovery of hundreds of legal documents. Nor is there any reliable tradition about royal or official activity in this connection except for an extremely late Greek report that Pharaoh Bocchoris (ca. 718–712 B.C.E.) instituted legal reforms.[14] How this situation is to be explained is not clear, but a plausible suggestion is that the customary law was understood to be the word of the pharaoh and that the concept of the king's divinity was not compatible with the existence of the independent authority of a written codified law.

The nature of the law collections

The term "law code" has been studiously avoided in the foregoing survey of ancient Near Eastern law, the reason being that none of the collections that have come down to us merits such a description.[15] By definition, codification implies an attempt to produce a comprehensive, systematic compilation of authoritative law, private and public, civil and criminal. There is no evidence that such was the intent of those who made the ancient collections. Even the most extensive exemplars contain large gaps and serious omissions. Furthermore, all indications point to the conclusion that the collections were not regarded by contemporaries and by succeeding generations as sacrosanct authoritative legislation that served as a source for judicial decisions, as we shall see.

First of all, it is to be noted that in those instances in which the prologues to the collections have been preserved, the royal author never declares the preceding laws to be null and void, and never decrees that henceforth the judges and magistrates within his realm must operate according to his new code. Although they bear no prologue, the Hittite laws may constitute something of an exception in that there is explicit substitution of new rules for old.

Another, and more serious, point is that even the fullest collections maintain extraordinary silence on important spheres of legal practice. That of the city of Eshnunna has nothing to say about the laws of partnership, adoption, and inheritance. Admittedly, though, something about them may have been included in the missing portions.

It is the laws of Hammurabi that are most revealing in their omissions, precisely because they are otherwise so extensive and so well preserved.

Surprisingly, they have little to say about murder or, for that matter, about criminal law in general. Attempted murder is not mentioned, and only one law deals with actual murder. It concerns the special case of a wife who has arranged to have her husband killed for the sake of a lover (§153). Another law deals with a false charge of murder (§1), and that is all. There also is nothing about rustling cattle even though the theft of agricultural implements is a legal topic (§§259–260). Arson is ignored, and so also is looting in general, but what is specified is the punishment for looting a burning house while trying to extinguish the fire (§25). In the area of civil law, no heed is paid to partnerships and the regulation of sales. The laws deal in some detail with special cases of marriage (§§133–136, 159–161, 175–177), and we learn incidentally that a written contract was required (§128), and that the groom paid a marriage price to his prospective father-in-law (§159), but the everyday rules of procedure for marriage are not given. The ordinary citizen who had to rely solely on the "code" would not know how to get married!

The same limitation applies to the Hittite laws, which also deal only with exceptional cases of marriage. Adoption, inheritance, and contracts are also omitted.

Another powerful argument against regarding the ancient Near Eastern law collections as codes, apart from their incompleteness, is provided by the following facts: scores of thousands of private and court documents deriving from the actual living practice of law are available. Many of them deal with topics omitted from the written compilations. Frequently, legal decisions given do not conform to what the "codes" prescribe. Most decisive is the fact that not a single extant court record ever cites or refers to the royal collections by name in any manner or form.

The conclusion is inescapable that there existed in the ancient Near East a huge body of unwritten customary and common law that regulated day-to-day living and that treated of a very wide range of legal issues. The written collections dealt with exceptions, amendments, and reforms relating to the customary law. This would explain the highly selective contents of the various collections. The individual written laws may well have stemmed from the king, while acting in his judicial capacity. The assembling of such legal decisions into large compilations would have been useful in offering guidance to judges. It now seems more and more likely, however, that the incentive for the royal collections came less from the field of jurisprudence than from the realm of religion.[16]

The compilations were actually written in the first place for the god. The prologue and epilogue and laws were directed to the deity first and to human posterity second. That is why Hammurabi, for example, set up his law stele in the Esagila, the temple of Marduk. The king demonstrates to the god that he has faithfully carried out the social responsibilities with which the god has charged him when he installed him on the throne. He has truly turned out to be a "just king." Looked at from this point of view, the provisions of the written collections may frequently be idealized or utopian rather than actual normative practice.

The nature of the Torah's collections of laws

Even a cursory examination of the Book of the Covenant is persuasive that it is highly selective in its contents and exceedingly limited in its scope.[17] This verdict, in fact, also applies to the other two legal corpora of the Torah, and to all three collections even in combination. For example, the laws of inheritance are ignored except for the restriction of Deuteronomy 21:15–17 establishing the primacy and privileges of the firstborn son. This clearly modifies an earlier practice which itself finds no expression in any collection, but which is attested to in the narratives about the Patriarchs.[18] The degrees of hereditary succession are only formulated coincidentally as an appendix to a narrative about the claims of Zelophehad's five daughters on their father's estate,[19] but they do not appear in the legal compilations. We do not know from the texts what ceremony legalized marriage in ancient Israel, but the law governing seduction formulated in Exodus 22:15–16 treats certain aspects of the law of matrimony, such as the "bride price," as commonplace. Similarly, the slave law of Exodus 21:9 assumes that everyone is familiar with "the practice with free maidens" who enter into wedlock, an item not spelled out. That the custom of hiring wet nurses was current in Israel is beyond doubt,[20] but it is not regulated in the written laws. The entire field of commercial law is for all intents and purposes nonexistent. There is all but total silence surrounding such matters as merchants, sales, contracts, pawns, pledges, sureties, and partnerships. Yet several passages in the Book of Proverbs, for example, clearly presuppose well-rooted practices in many of these areas.[21] Not a word is said about land rentals or sales, yet with regard to the latter item we do have independent information. The account of the purchase of a plot of land by the prophet Jeremiah shows that in transactions of this nature "the rule and law" required "a sealed deed of purchase" and "an open one."[22] In Exodus 21:12–14, the murderer with malice aforethought is denied the privilege of asylum. That means that he cannot enjoy the protection from forcible removal that is normally afforded by a sanctuary or altar. This exclusion implies the prior existence of a well-entrenched custom in Israel of the altar's affording refuge for criminals indiscriminately. Indeed some still regarded the earlier practice to be in vogue even in the time of Solomon; witness the narratives of 1 Kings 1:50–51 and 1 Kings 2:28–34.

Admittedly, some of the lacunae, especially in the realm of commercial law, may be due to the great antiquity of the Book of the Covenant in that it legislates for a society far less developed than that of Babylon, one in which the transfer of goods from one person to another was a fairly simple procedure and no elaborate provisions were required to govern the transaction. But this explanation has only limited force, and cannot hold for most of the above-cited examples. Indubitably, an unwritten, orally transmitted body of customary law or ancestral traditions circulated in ancient Israel, and it regulated vast areas of human relationships. The legal collections found in the Torah are no more codes than are their Mesopotamian counterparts. Rather, they are to be looked upon as records of amendments, supplements, or annulments of an already-existing body of practice that had long governed the lives of the Israelite tribes.

The distinctive features of Israelite law[23]

It would not be a difficult exercise to isolate numerous parallels between the laws of the Torah and those of one or another of the law collections of Mesopotamia and Anatolia. The affinities in literary form, in technical terminology, in legal formulation and techniques, as well as contextually, are too numerous and too close to allow of any other explanation than that Israel shared in the common legal culture of the ancient Near East, which is hardly a startling or unexpected conclusion, but certainly is one that has nothing to do with imitation or borrowing.

To use these latter terms would be to ignore the nature of the phenomena of cultural diffusion and continuity. On the other hand, to speak of rootedness in an ancient tradition that is shared by many peoples is really to reveal very little about the nature of the culture under study. After all, to document in precise detail the debt of much of Western law to the law of the Roman Empire would not tell us a great deal about the distinctive values, postulates, and internal development of the former. Accordingly, for the sake of scholarly integrity we must direct our attention to an examination of the distinguishing features and singularities of the laws of the Torah. There is no better way of starting our investigation than by returning to the Book of the Covenant. The nature of the material inevitably entails a measure of repetition of many of the points made in the preceding chapter in connection with the Ten Commandments, but a restatement of fundamentals is unavoidable if justice is to be done to biblical law as a self-contained and independent subject of study.

We must begin our inquiry with a rather prosaic comment that all the *mishpatim*, the rules and the provisions of the legislation contained within the first section of the Book of the Covenant, Exodus 21:2–22:16, fall within the scope of the coercive power of the state and come within the jurisdiction of the law courts. The second part of the collection, however, is quite different. Exodus 22:17–23:19 consists of a miscellany of social, ethical, moral, and religious prescriptions that are predominantly couched in the concise, apodictic style of the Ten Commandments with their magisterial, authoritative tone. They come under the rubric of *devarim*, "the commands," mentioned in Exodus 24:3, and they constitute normative standards for controlling human conduct, standards imposed by a transcendent divine will. Apart from the first three prohibitions outlawing sorcery, bestiality, and sacrificing to other gods, their enforcement is left to the individual conscience, not to political institutions.

In these laws, heavy emphasis is placed on the concern for the unfortunates of society. The stranger must not be wronged; the widow and orphan may not be abused:

> If you do mistreat them, I will heed their outcry to Me, and My anger shall blaze forth and I will put you to the sword, and your own wives shall become widows and your children orphans. [24]

Particular sensitivity to the needs of the poor is enjoined:

> If you lend money to My people, to the poor among you, do not
> act toward them as a creditor: exact no interest from them. If you
> take your neighbor's garment in pledge, you must return it to him
> before the sun sets. . . . In what else shall he sleep? Therefore, if
> he cries out to Me, I will pay heed, for I am compassionate.[25]

These admonitions are followed by injunctions against reviling God
and cursing one's rulers, by the requirements to set aside the first-fruits
offerings, to dedicate to God the firstborn male and the firstlings of
cattle and flocks, and to promote holy living by eschewing unlawful
meat.[26] Next comes a series of prohibitions designed to maintain the
integrity of the judicial system and to preserve the impartiality of justice.[27] Another precept that intersects the preceding forbids indifference
to the plight of one's enemy:

> When you encounter your enemy's ox or ass wandering, you must
> take it back to him. When you see the ass of your enemy lying
> under its burden and would refrain from raising it, you must
> nevertheless raise it with him.[28]

The idea is that one must not allow feelings of personal antipathy to
overcome one's humanity. Behind this law is most likely also the psy-
chological truth that such civilized conduct must inevitably disarm
mutual hostility.

The list of obligations and duties continues with still another prohibition against oppressing the stranger (Exodus 23:9), with the institutions of the sabbath of the land every seventh year during which it
lies fallow and its yield is free for the needy and the beasts of the field,
and with a reiteration of the law of the weekly sabbath which is to be
enjoyed equally by the Israelite, the bondman, and the stranger, as well
as by the beasts of burden (verses 10–12). The collection closes with
an exhortation not to give recognition to other gods by mentioning their
names (verse 13), and with laws relating to the three annual pilgrimage
festivals (verses 14–17), to the preservation of sacrifices from corruption
(verse 18), to the need to bring the first fruits to the house of the Lord,
and to the prohibition of boiling a kid in its mother's milk (verse 19).

As we noted above, the apodictic-style rules and regulations that are found in the second part of the Book of the Covenant are overwhelmingly of the kind that make compliance or noncompliance not easily detectable, and they are hardly enforceable in the courts. They are, in the main, matters of private conscience. It may well be that their observance runs counter to self-interest, defies utilitarian considerations, and is seemingly contrary to the dictates of prudence or the call of expediency. Nevertheless, precisely for the reason that these precepts are not presented as salutary maxims but as the imperatives of divine will, they become self-imposed and self-enforcing duties. The sole motive power for moral rectitude lies in the conviction that divine sanction authorizes these demands.

Now nothing of the kind is to be found in the extrabiblical legal collections. These concern themselves entirely with issues of secular law. Ethical precepts, religious exhortations, and cultic prescriptions belong respectively to other, separate, genres of literature. There is absolutely no analogy to the Torah's indiscriminate commingling and interweaving of matters "secular" and "religious," of cultic topics and moral imperatives. All alike are taken as varied expressions of divine will. The Torah treats life holistically. The law is a single, organic whole which cannot be reduced to discrete elements. The constitutive units retain an organic relationship to one another and to the whole.

Another fundamental and distinguishing characteristic of the Torah is that its legislation is embedded in a narrative matrix of which it is an inseparable component and from which it draws its meaning and significance. Separate the laws from their accompanying narrative, and their sum and substance are seriously impaired. As a result, the law is seen to be an indispensable ingredient of the divine-human relationship. The context of Israel's history is determined by obedience or disobedience to God's laws. It is the law that constitutes the instrumentality for the realization of the ideal that Israel be "a kingdom of priests and a holy nation."[29] By way of contrast, each law collection outside the Bible is a discrete entity. Each possesses its own intrinsic integrity as a legal document unconnected with anything else.

This difference leads to yet another. The other Near Eastern laws are unilaterally imposed by the king upon his people. In Israel, the body of legislation is envisaged as comprising the stipulations of the covenant made between God and the entire people. A covenant or contract entails mutuality, so that the narrative has Israel being first informed of the content of the laws and then freely accepting them.[30]

Furthermore, in the case of all other Near Eastern collections the written form is primary. In fact, as we have already noted, the laws are not really normative codifications to which jurists had recourse, but rather formulations of idealized situations that display the king's sense of social responsibility and concern for the welfare of his people. The compilation is a sort of pious accounting on the part of the monarch to his god who had charged him with the duties of kingship. The written document is the essential witness to the king's faithful and exemplary execution of the charge he had received. In the Torah, however, the oral promulgation precedes the written form. Like the Ten Commandments, the laws are first orally communicated, and only then reduced to writing. The sequence is of paramount importance. The laws must be heard by all the people, for the people constitute a corporate personality answerable to God for the fulfillment or infraction of the law. That is why the legislation is prefaced by the divine statement to Moses, "These are the rules that you shall set before them," and closes with confirmation of the fact that Moses indeed read aloud all the laws and that they received popular and unanimous assent.[31] Only thereafter did he commit them to written form. In addition, Moses took the precaution of also reading the written document to the assembled populace, which once more ratified its acceptance of the covenant terms. The written text becomes henceforth the permanent embodiment of the covenant and its stipulations for future generations.

This public nature of the law is still another distinguishing feature of the Torah, for it generates the obligation on each person to be informed of its contents. Education thereby becomes a religious duty incumbent upon each and every individual member of the House of Israel. The study of the law develops into a spiritual and moral discipline.[32] It is not an intellectual exercise or a matter of professional training or vocational expertise in order to master the art of litigation.

Another outstanding feature of the biblical legal texts is the "motive clause."[33] Appended to a specific law will often be found an observation that furnishes its own rationale or provides a motivation for obedience to it. These explanatory clauses may cite a reference to the Exodus, issue a warning of dire consequences in case of infraction, convey an assurance of the benefits of implementation; or they may ground compliance in purely humanitarian considerations. While motive clauses do appear, with rarity, in the laws of Hammurabi and in the Middle Assyrian Laws, they are decidedly not characteristic of either. Where they exist, they invariably deal with civil matters and do not appeal, as in the Bible, to the historical, religious, or ethical sense of the individual.

Typical of the laws of Eshnunna,[34] and especially of Hammurabi, are graduated penalties according to the social status of the victim. For instance, if a man strikes a pregnant woman of the *awilum*, or upper class, and causes her to miscarry, he pays ten shekels of silver as compensation for the loss of the fetus. If, however, the victim belonged to the *mushkenum*, or class of commoners, then he pays only five shekels of silver.[35] The Torah, on the other hand, knows nothing of social stratification in matters of adjudication. It dispenses equal justice for all, irrespective of class distinction. The sole exception is the slave, whose status will be discussed presently.

A very strange aspect of some of the laws is vicarious punishment. In several cases, the offender does not pay the penalty but someone else who stands in relation to him. For example, in the Middle Assyrian Laws,[36] the rape of an unbetrothed virgin who lives in her father's house is punished by the ravishing of the rapist's wife, who also remains thereafter with the father of the victim. Hammurabi decrees that if a man struck a pregnant woman, thereby causing her to miscarry and die, it is the assailant's daughter who is put to death.[37] If a builder erected a house which collapsed, killing the owner's son, then the builder's son, not the builder, is put to death.[38] Judicial vicarious punishment is unthinkable in the Torah. In fact, it is explicitly outlawed in Deuteronomy 24:16:

> Parents shall not be put to death for children, nor children be put to death for parents: a person shall be put to death only for his own crime.

Biblical legislation, with rare exception,[39] eschews brutal punishments of the kinds found elsewhere in the Near Eastern world. Ur-Nammu, for instance, punishes a slave woman who is insolent to her mistress by having her mouth scoured with a quart of salt.[40] Hammurabi prescribes sixty blows with a scourge of oxhide for the one who strikes a superior,[41] and the amputation of the hand of a son who strikes his father.[42] The same penalty awaits a surgeon whose patient dies under the operation or who loses an eye in the case of eye surgery.[43] A slave who strikes the cheek of a member of the upper class[44] or who wrongfully challenges his master's title to him has his ear cut off.[45] The tongue of an adopted son who formally repudiates his foster parents is cut out, and he loses an eye if he discovers his natural parents and goes to live with them.[46] If an infant in the care of a wet nurse dies, and the nurse accepts another infant without revealing the fact to the next set of parents, her breasts are removed.[47]

Instances of the mutilation of the body in the Middle Assyrian Laws are too numerous to list, but the following examples of their barbarities are typical. The cutting off of the nose and ears of a slave is prescribed for receiving stolen goods from the mistress of the house.[48] Her ears may also be cut off by her husband, if he so chooses.[49] A man who kisses the wife of another has his lower lip excised with a blade.[50] Castration is the punishment for sodomy and for other sexual offenses.[51] Flogging for both men and women is especially frequent, usually comprising fifty stripes, but one crime incurs one hundred.[52]

Another characteristic of this collection of laws is multiple punishments, something generally avoided in the Torah. Thus a man who accuses his neighbor's wife of promiscuity but does not initiate judicial proceedings against her is flogged with staves forty times; he must also do a month's hard labor, be castrated, and pay a talent of lead.[53] A harlot who is seen on the street wearing a veil loses her clothing, is flogged fifty times, and has pitch poured on her head.[54] He who steals a sheep and replaces its ownership mark (brand) suffers one hundred stripes, the tearing out of his hair, and a month's hard labor, and also has to make restitution to the owner of the sheep.[55]

Biblical law further separates itself from its Near Eastern counterparts in another very striking way. Notwithstanding Hammurabi's pious sentiments in his prologue and epilogue that his aim was to promote the welfare of his people and to take care of the weak and in order that the orphan and the widow might be dealt justice, the fact is that his laws exhibit almost no concern for the disadvantaged of society. The general tendency of his collection is to safeguard the interests of the upper class, and to preserve and promote its rights. The landowner and slavemaster are the principal beneficiaries of his legislation. The same is true of all the other "codes." Human life is cheap, but property is highly valued. This appraisal is revealed through the large number of laws that impose capital punishment, particularly in cases of offenses involving property.[56]

Thus Hammurabi imposes the death penalty for the theft of the property of "god or palace," for receiving stolen goods of any kind and not being able to produce a contract proving ownership, for assisting in the escape of a slave, and for harboring a fugitive slave.[57] Death by drowning is punishment for an ale-wife (barmaid) who cheats her customers on the price of a drink.[58] If someone is hired by a landowner to cultivate his field, but instead rents out the oxen to a third person or steals the seed corn, he must make restitution of a specified quantity of grain. Failure to meet this obligation incurs being dragged to and fro across the field while tied to the oxen.[59]

The death penalty faithfully reflects conceptions of what threatens the social structure of a society, of what is regarded as essential for the stability, vitality, and continuity of an ordered society.[60] In the case of the Mesopotamian laws, it is quite clear that the protection of property occupied a very exalted position in its hierarchy of values. In polar contrast, the legislation of the Torah deals with crimes of theft and never imposes the death penalty for the violation of property rights, although it is more severe than its compares in matters of sexual offenses and in certain violations of religious norms. The sacredness of human life is paramount in its value system; the sanctity of private property is unquestionably inferior to it. That is why the Torah places so much emphasis on the plight of the poor and on the condition of the disadvantaged of society, and why it exhibits so much concern for the slave and the alien.

These values find legal expression in the Torah in various ways. Take, for instance, the matter of debts. In biblical times, loans would partake of the nature of philanthropy and not be categorized as a commercial transaction. The borrower would overwhelmingly belong to the poverty-stricken class. He would generally be a peasant who desperately needed the loan to tide him over until the next harvest. The taking of interest, therefore, would be the exploitation of another Israelite's misfortune, and is accordingly prohibited in all three Pentateuchal law collections.[61] The provisions of the Book of the Covenant on this matter have been cited earlier in this chapter. The "Holiness Code" reads as follows:

> If your brother, being in straits, comes under your authority . . . do not exact from him advance or accrued interest, but fear your God. Let him live by your side as your brother. Do not lend him money at advance interest, or give him your food at accrued interest. I the Lord am your God, who brought you out of the land of Egypt, to give you the land of Canaan, to be your God.[62]

The law of Deuteronomy is equally emphatic on the subject:

> You shall not deduct interest from loans to your countrymen, whether in money or food or anything else that can be deducted as interest.[63]

Not only, uniquely, are the rights of the creditor not given preference over the borrower's, but the Torah is particularly sensitive to the preservation of the dignity of the borrower and to his basic needs. The above-cited text of Exodus 22:25–26 abundantly illustrates this religious, humanitarian approach. Deuteronomy 24:10–13 is even more explicit:

> When you make a loan of any sort to your neighbor, you must not enter his house to seize his pledge. You must remain outside, while the man to whom you made the loan brings the pledge out to you. If he is a needy man, you shall not go to sleep in his pledge; you must return the pledge to him at sundown, that he may sleep in his cloth and bless you; and it will be to your merit before the Lord your God.

The economic rights of the creditor are restricted in favor of human dignity and basic human needs. In such matters, the rights of the borrower decidedly take precedence.

Another aspect of the Torah's exceptional concern for the sacredness of human life is demonstrated in the case of the goring ox.[64] This example is especially important because it occurs in almost identical form in the laws of Eshnunna (§§54–55), in those of Hammurabi

(§§250–252), and in Exodus 21:28–32. All three sources treat of the same problem. The owner of an ox that is known to be a habitual gorer has ignored due forewarning of the fact, and has not taken proper precautions; the ox gores a man to death. The Mesopotamian laws solely concern themselves with the economic side of the affair, namely, the amount of compensation to be paid to the family of the victim. There is no sensibility of the loss of a life. Nothing at all is stated about the fate of the ox and the status of its negligently culpable owner. The Book of the Covenant, however, operates in accordance with the rule laid down in Genesis 9:5:

> But for your own life-blood I will require a reckoning: I will require
> it of every beast; of man, too, will I require a reckoning for human
> life. . . .

The sanctity of human life is such as to make bloodshed the consummate offense, one viewed with unspeakable horror. Neither man nor beast that destroys a life can remain thereafter untainted. Hence, unlike the laws of Eshnunna and Hammurabi, the Torah decrees the death of the ox and prohibits its use for food. The flesh of a beast that has taken a human life cannot be fit for human consumption. The owner of the ox also deserves to die, but in the absence of malicious intent and direct involvement in the fatality he may redeem his life. It is this profound conviction of the incomparable sanctity of human life that explains another biblical command outlawing the acceptance of monetary payment in satisfaction of murder, a restriction unexampled in the ancient law collections.[65]

The rules governing slavery afford another opportunity for comparison and contrast between Israel and its neighbors.[66] This infamous institution existed throughout the ancient Near East from earliest recorded times. It was an accepted strand within the social fabric, although its importance as a factor in the economies of the various states in the area was not really great, and certainly never reached the proportions it did in Rome in imperial times. All the law collections regulate the status of the slave, and the Torah is no exception in this regard.[67]

In Mesopotamia, and in Israel too, slavery was largely of the domestic type. The slave was a member of the household and as such was inescapably recognized to be a human being. On the other hand, insofar as the master had a pecuniary investment in the slave whom he acquired by purchase or because of a borrower's default on debt, the slave was a chattel, a piece of movable property. The tension inherent in this paradoxical situation is reflected in the slave's social and legal status. He was not entirely without rights anywhere in the Near East and he was often even able to enter into business arrangements to earn a livelihood from outsiders so long as his master received regular revenue therefrom, and to own property, sometimes even other slaves. At the same time, the slave in Mesopotamia was branded;[68] his father's name was never recorded; injury to him was recompensed to his master,[69] not to him; he could be given as a pledge on a loan,[70] and could be sold or exchanged.

In the legislation of Israel that pertains to slaves there are many points of contact with Mesopotamian laws. But there is also a pronounced tendency to resolve the ambiguity inherent in the condition of slavery in a humanitarian spirit. The result is that the laws mitigate the harshness that accompanies the status of chattel, and they enhance the recognition of the slave as a human being. This characteristic of the Torah starkly contrasts with the otherwise complete absence of laws in the Near East that are designed to protect the slave against flagrant maltreatment by his master.[71] Exodus 21:20 uniquely specifies that if a slave is beaten to death by his master, the master is culpable.[72] Similarly unparalleled in the various "codes" is the remarkable provision that the slave automatically gains his freedom if he loses an eye or even a tooth at his master's hand.[73] Incidentally, the gender of the slave in respect of these two laws is quite immaterial. The fugitive slave law provides another example. According to Hammurabi (§§15–16), connivance at the escape of a slave, not to mention harboring a runaway slave, incurs the death penalty.[74] Diametrically opposed to this is the law of Deuteronomy 23:16–17:

> You shall not turn over to his master a slave who seeks refuge with you from his master. He shall live with you in any place he may choose among the settlements in your midst, wherever he pleases; you must not ill-treat him.

The partiality of the Torah for safeguarding the rights of the slave as a human being again expresses itself by according him the inalienable prerogative of enjoying the sabbath rest. One day in seven the authority of master over slave is severely curtailed. The Ten Commandments underscore this point. The version of Exodus 20:8–11 recalls that the seventh day of the week is sacred time that is incorporated into the very structure of creation. Because it is God Himself who integrated it into the cosmic order, the right of the slave to exercise his God-given privilege of resting on the sabbath overrides the master's right to profit from his "investment." This metaphysical rationale is reinforced by a historico-ethical motivation. The sabbath law as it appears in Deuteronomy 5:12–15, in prescribing the desisting from work by all living creatures, "so that your male and female slave may rest as you do," adds: "Remember that you were a slave in the land of Egypt and the Lord your God freed you from there with a mighty hand and an outstretched arm; therefore the Lord your God has commanded you to observe the sabbath day." In the same spirit, the slave, once he has been circumcised, thereby identifying with the covenant between God and His people, is entitled to partake of the passover offering—the ceremony that celebrates the liberation from slavery. [75]

Before leaving this topic, perhaps it is not inappropriate to cite the impassioned plaint of Job that, more than any other biblical passage, earnestly and luminously captures the singular essence of the biblical attitude to the slave:

> Did I ever brush aside the case of my slaves, male or female,
> When they made a complaint against me?
> What then should I do when God arises;
> When he calls me to account, what should I answer him?
> Did not He who made me in my mother's belly make him?
> Did not One form us both in the womb? [76]

Lex talionis, *or "an eye for an eye"* [77]

One of the most misunderstood legal principles in the Torah is the *lex talionis*, the law of retaliation, commonly known as "an eye for an eye." Few other sections of the Bible have suffered as much distortion. The phrase "an eye for an eye" at once evokes in the popular mind notions of primitive vengeance. Worse, it is then ignorantly portrayed as epitomizing the dominant principle of law in the Hebrew Bible, and this misrepresentation is exacerbated by projecting it into the realm of theology, with prejudicial effect.

It is taken for granted that the substitution of monetary compensation for physical injury in place of retaliation in kind constitutes a major advance away from barbarism and toward humanization of the judicial system. It may come as a surprise to learn, therefore, that the early law collections of Mesopotamia already prescribed pecuniary satisfaction for bodily injury, and not physical punishment. Thus the compendium of Ur-Nammu decrees that "If a man, in the course of a scuffle, smashed the limb of another man with a club, he shall pay one mina of silver. If someone severed the nose of another man with a *copper knife*, he must pay two-thirds of a mina of silver."[78] The laws of the city of Eshnunna similarly impose fines for the same class of offenses: "If a man bites the nose of another man and severs it, he shall pay one mina of silver. [For] an eye [he shall pay] one mina of silver; [for] a tooth one-half mina; [for] an ear one-half mina; [for] a slap in the face ten shekels of silver. If a man severs a[nother] man's finger he shall pay two-thirds of a mina of silver. . . ."[79]

The Hittite laws have similar provisions: "If anyone blinds a free man or knocks out his teeth, they would formerly give one mina of silver, now he shall give twenty shekels of silver and pledge his estate as security."[80] Several other laws in this connection continue in the same vein.

It was Hammurabi who first introduced physical punishment for physical injury. The texts are clear enough: "If a seignior has destroyed the eye of a member of the aristocracy, they shall destroy his eye. If he has broken a[nother] seignior's bone, they shall break his bone. If a seignior has knocked out a tooth of a seignior of his own rank, they shall knock out his tooth."[81]

At first glance it would appear that Hammurabi's innovation was retrogressive, a step backward in the humanizing process. However, it is now recognized that this judgment is inaccurate and that in fact his innovative measure actually constituted in conception a significant landmark not only in the development of Mesopotamian law but also in legal history. This reevaluation results from a revised understanding of the role and function of compensation and of physical retaliation, respectively, in different societies. Anthropological studies have shown that these sociocultural phenomena cannot be properly assessed without reference to social, political, and historical context. The finding is that the direction of the evolutionary process is not from "an eye for an eye" to pecuniary compensation, but the opposite, strange as it may seem.[82]

In primitive and in less-developed societies, an assault by one individual upon the person of another is a matter of private wrong that is to be settled between the parties involved. While the natural instinct of the victims and their families might propel them in the direction of violent retaliation or blood revenge as the proper response, experience teaches that such reaction in kind begets further violence, and that the private feud that is aroused is destructive of the social fabric. Hence, there is a coincidence of mutual and wider community interests in discouraging the cycle of vengeance and counter-vengeance. Ruptured social relationships are therefore repaired by the preferred substitution of pecuniary compensation for physical punishment. The amount is arranged by means of negotiations between the families of the assailant and the victim. With the development of centralized political and judicial authority, and increasingly with the emergence and growth of the city-state, the need to maintain social harmony becomes ever more imperative. The state gradually encroaches upon the private domain, so that what was hitherto a private matter between the feuding parties tends to become an issue of public welfare. In the interest of equity, the state now begins to regulate the payments for various physical injuries. This is the situation that prevails in the above-cited Mesopotamian and Hittite laws. However, there is a built-in inequality in the system, for it is easier for the rich than for the poor to make pecuniary restitution. Moreover, the operating legal concept is still that assault is a private affair, to be resolved between the parties, though in accordance with the guidelines set down by the state.

The innovation of Hammurabi in his "eye for an eye" legislation can now be seen in its proper perspective. This remarkable king succeeded, by conquest and by diplomacy, in unifying Mesopotamia. A natural concomitant of his empire-building was the increasing centralization of government with its deepening intrusion into the private domain. Perhaps it is no coincidence, therefore, that this highly capable administrator should have been the one to turn what had previously been a matter of private law into public law. An assault on the human person that entailed the infliction of actual physical harm was no longer simply a matter of civil proceedings, but was, in effect, redefined as criminal conduct. It was now recognized to be a crime against society. Private vengeance and the demand for compensation, to be negotiated by the families of the victim and the assailant, were replaced by public criminal law with its imposition of punishment by the state authority. Hammurabi's new law spoke to a realization that violence in interpersonal relationships undermines the order and stability of society, and that, as a consequence, the state assumes an obligation to promote domestic tranquility in order to protect the public and to preserve the security of its citizens. Furthermore, the new legal concept underlying the *lex talionis* gave expression to the striving for the achievement of exact justice. The nature and degree of punishment was made exactly proportionate to the injury inflicted: only one life for one life, only one tooth for one tooth, and so on.

It need hardly be mentioned that the foregoing discussion should not be construed to imply approval of the literal implementation of the "eye for an eye" rule or any connotation of a judgment that it is other than barbaric. What is to be understood, emphasized, and reiterated, however, is that Hammurabi's innovation, far from being primitive or retrogressive, was, in conception, revolutionary and progressive in its contemporary setting, if it is analyzed from the point of view of the legal philosophy behind it, the ideals and goals that it postulated, and its central thesis and concern.

Lex talionis *in the Torah*

The *lex talionis* principle appears three times in the Torah. It is variously featured in each of its three collections of law. The discovery of Hammurabi's "code" at once led to the assumption that this was the direct inspiration for the Mosaic law. Such a conclusion is now recognized to be unwarranted. Rather, the talionic principle that the punishment must exactly fit the crime is better explained as originating among the western Semites, who introduced it into Mesopotamia in the wake of their migrations to that region.[83] In other words, it was already a part of Israel's cultural heritage in pre-Exodus times. A close examination of the context in which it is placed within the Torah, of its literary legal formulation, and of its application reveals a distinctive development of the *lex talionis* in Israelite penal law.

The first reference to this legal principle appears in Exodus 21:22–25:

When men fight, and one of them pushes a pregnant woman and parturition results, but no *'ason* ensues, the one responsible shall be fined according as the woman's husband may exact from him, the payment to be based on reckoning. But if *'ason* ensues, the penalty shall be life for life, eye for eye, tooth for tooth, hand for hand, foot for foot, burn for burn, wound for wound, bruise for bruise.

The Hebrew text is replete with difficulties, not all of which need engage us here. The major problem is the lack of clarity in the description of the unfortunate circumstances. Did the blow received by the pregnant woman result in premature delivery or in the loss of the fetus? What is the precise definition of *'ason* here? Is it bodily injury or death? If the latter, does it refer to the subsequent demise of the newborn, premature infant or of the mother? The Hebrew *'ason* occurs only thrice elsewhere in the Bible, and if it cannot be proven to mean death, it certainly signifies a major disaster.[84] Whatever be the answers to these questions, one conclusion is beyond cavil: the list of injuries in the above-cited passage is entirely inappropriate to any possible context in which the legal issue can be placed. Loss of a tooth, a burn, or a bruise can by no stretch of the imagination be subsumed under the heading of *'ason*. If the mother dies, then the list of the other injuries she may have sustained is irrelevant. Furthermore, why is the list at all connected with the issue of the pregnant woman? If it be a general statement about the literal application of the *lex talionis*, one would expect it to be independently presented and not tied to an exceptional case to which it can hardly apply as a whole.

In short, the list of talionic provisions must be understood as a general statement of legal policy. It is a rhetorical formulation in concrete terms of an abstract principle—the law of equivalence. On the operational level this is possible only in respect of the death penalty. "A life for a life" can be implemented because all human beings are created equal. Exact equivalence in respect of bodily injury is literally unenforceable. In such cases, pecuniary compensation would be the logical procedure.

This conclusion finds further support through the next citation of the talion formula, which occurs in Leviticus 24:17–22, cited earlier in this chapter. Most remarkably, it too is inserted into a context to which it has no obvious relevant application. It is related that a person made blasphemous use of the Divine Name in the course of a brawl. In Israel, the cursing and reviling of God was an intolerable outrage that was regarded as striking at society's most fundamental concerns and as repudiating the transcendent values of the community, thereby imperiling its spiritual well-being. For this reason it was a capital offense. In the present instance, the blasphemer was the son of a mixed marriage, and it was not certain that the same law applied to the non-Israelite as to the native-born. The verdict was handed down that, stranger or citizen, one law applied to all. The narrative closes with the report that "they took the blasphemer outside the camp and pelted him with stones. The Israelites did as the Lord had commanded Moses"(verse 23).

This account is straightforward enough, except that between verses 16 and 23 the following passage is interpolated:

If a man kills any human being, he shall be put to death. One who kills a beast shall make restitution for it: life for life. If anyone maims his fellow, as he has done so shall it be done to him: fracture for fracture, eye for eye, tooth for tooth. The injury he inflicted on another shall be inflicted on him. He who kills a beast shall make restitution for it; but he who kills a human being shall be put to death. You shall have one standard for stranger and citizen alike: for I the Lord am your God.

Clearly, these regulations governing assault and battery are wholly alien to the topic of the narrative, which is the law of blasphemy. The present location of these verses is determined by the fact that the law of talion presented here provides another example, in addition to that of the blasphemer, of the equality of all, stranger and citizen alike, before the law. Another reason for their inclusion here may have been the circumstances of the blaspheming, namely, the brawl, which could well be expected to result in physical injury to at least one of the parties. The point is, however, that the irrelevant placing of the talionic list within the episode narrated in Leviticus 24:10–23 proves once again that we are dealing with a standardized formula. It is a discrete legal unit that expresses the abstract talionic principle just as we saw in Exodus 21:23–25, and it does not itself necessarily imply a literal interpretation. That the phrase "as he has done so shall it be done to him" need not mean exact equivalence is conclusively proven by the use of the identical phraseology in the mouth of Samson in Judges 15:11. The Philistines had burnt alive his wife and her father, whereupon Samson massacred them wholesale in revenge. In justification of his act, he says, "As they did to me, so I did to them." He did not burn alive the wives and fathers of the perpetrators. What he meant by his statement was that they had received their deserts.

One further clue to the interpretation of the formula is afforded by the above-cited passage, Leviticus 24:18: "One who kills a beast shall make restitution for it: life for life." Monetary compensation is called for, and a literal meaning is ruled out. This is the only possible understanding of "life for life." Hence, the argument against a necessary literal understanding of "an eye for an eye" is immeasurably strengthened.

The third instance of the talionic formula appears in Deuteronomy 19:18–19, 21. Here the context is the law of witnesses. One proven to be a false witness is subject to the same penalty that his perfidy would have inflicted on the defendant had it gone undetected. The text reads:

> If the man who testified is a false witness, if he has testified falsely against his fellow man, you shall do to him as he schemed to do to his fellow. . . . life for life, eye for eye, tooth for tooth, hand for hand, foot for foot.

The transparency of the stereotyped nature of the formula is crystal clear. The generalized talionic principle is precisely stated: "You shall do to him as he schemed to do to his fellow." The detailed specification is once again entirely inappropriate to the case in question, if taken literally. The simple fact is that bodily mutilation is not a punishment in biblical law.[85] No witness, truthful or lying, could by his testimony in court have caused the defendant to receive any of the mutilations listed. Hence the witness could never himself have lost an eye or a limb. The "eye for an eye" formula manifestly reiterates the generalized principle in concrete form for the sake of emphasis. It cannot possibly be interpreted here literally.

One final, inferential bit of evidence may be additionally adduced in support of the nonliteral application of the *lex talionis*. Summing up a discussion of the distinction between murder and manslaughter, and the legal procedure to be followed in the latter case, Numbers 35:31

solemnly warns that a willful murderer cannot elect to evade the death penalty by making a monetary payment:

> You may not accept a ransom for the life of a murderer who is guilty of a capital crime; he must be put to death.

Underlying this proscription is the obvious implication that in cases of physical assault other than murder, compensation was practiced and sanctioned. This, indeed, is the traditional rabbinic interpretation of the *lex talionis*.[86]

Thus in Israelite law, as in Hammurabi's legislation, it was accepted that causing injury to the person of another was not a matter of private wrong, but was prosecutable in a criminal proceeding. However, unlike its Near Eastern predecessors, the "eye for an eye" formula was stripped of its literal meaning and became fossilized as the way in which the abstract legal formula of equivalent restitution was expressed. The thrust of the talionic principle was not vengeful or penal but compensatory. Furthermore, whereas Hammurabi gave legal sanction to inequality, in that talion applied only where the victim was a member of the upper class (*awilum*) but otherwise pecuniary compensation was the rule,[87] the Torah applied talion equally, irrespective of economic and social distinction. Israel also rejected Hammurabi's vicarious punishment system. Talion was restricted to the person of the assailant.

CHAPTER IX

The Tabernacle and the Golden Calf

EXODUS 25–40

The national-religious experience has terminated. The very site at Sinai no longer possesses the sanctity that adhered to it throughout the duration of the theophany. The covenant between God and Israel has been consummated. The social and legal spheres of life have been regulated. The judicial system, with its institutions and laws, has been established. Still outstanding is the organization of the national cult. What is intended by this term is the entire complex of rites, ceremonies, practices, paraphernalia, symbols, institutions, and personnel that make up the formal, externalized aspects of religious life. These give outward expression to the transcendent concepts that underlie Israel's understanding of God. They enable man's quest for intimacy with the divine to find legitimate, normative means of realization. This sphere of life, the cult, still remained unsettled, and the lack generated tension and anxiety because the people are soon to move away from Mount Sinai in the course of their wearing journey through the difficult and dangerous wilderness to the Promised Land.

As assurance of the continued existence of an avenue of communication with God—some visible, tangible symbol that He remained always present in their midst, irrespective of the ever-increasing distance between themselves and the mount of revelation—became a pressing imperative. The erection of the Tabernacle, which is the term by which the wilderness sanctuary has traditionally come to be known in English, was a logical development. Through its instrumentality, the experience with the Divine Presence that occurred at Sinai could be extended as a living reality.

We are told that, at divine behest, Moses ascended the cloud-covered mount alone and remained there in prolonged communion with God. During this period he received elaborately detailed and lengthy instructions for undertaking the enterprise, and was also shown a vision of the completed edifice.

Obviously, the peculiar circumstances of being a people on the move dictated a mobile, portable sanctuary that could be assembled, dismantled, and reassembled without great complication in the advance from station to station in the wilderness. Unfortunately, notwithstanding the wealth of particulars recorded in the Torah, the Tabernacle cannot with confidence be reconstructed solely on the basis of the biblical data. The reasons for this are that many essential items are omitted from the prescriptions; several technical terms are still imperfectly understood; there are a number of other obscurities; and the account of the actual execution of the work sometimes differs in detail from the original directive.

The story of the construction of the wilderness sanctuary is contained in Chapters 25–31 and 35–40. The first section features the account of God's careful, theoretical instructions to Moses; the second reports on the actual realization of the plan. In between is inserted the narrative about the Golden Calf and its aftermath. As we shall see, this seemingly abrupt interruption of the sanctuary theme is deliberate and purposeful. The conjoining of the two topics indicates that the one illuminates the other.

The plan of the Tabernacle[1]

A peculiarity of the account is that the theoretical prescriptions of Exodus 25:10–27:19 commence with the details of the cultic vessels— the Ark, the Table for the bread of display, and the Lampstand—and only after that do they proceed to describe the Tabernacle structure. The organizing principle is movement from the interior outward, from the most important elements to the least important, so that the enclosure of the Tabernacle is the last item to be described. However, the narrative of 36:8–38:31 relating to the actual fulfillment of God's instructions reverses the order. It realistically first deals with the exterior structure

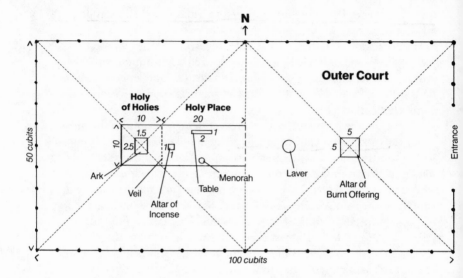

Ground Plan of the Tabernacle

and then continues inward, detailing the fabrication of the furnishings. This second section bears resemblance to the account of the building of Solomon's Temple in 1 Kings Chapters 6–7, and, like it, has been shown to possess an authentic archival character. Moreover, the entire narrative belongs to a common Near Eastern genre of temple-building reports.[2]

The materials to be assembled for the construction of the portable sanctuary and for its furnishings are carefully listed in Exodus 25:3–7. These comprise the three basic metals of antiquity (gold, silver, and bronze), fabrics of various kinds and colors, hides, acacia wood, oil, spices, and precious stones. The measurements are given in terms of the "cubit." This unit of linear measure, as the Hebrew *'ammah* indicates, means the distance from the extended tip of the middle finger to the point of the elbow of an average man. The value of the cubit differed from culture to culture. In fact, more than one value could be assigned to it even within a single culture. In Israel it could vary between

17.5 and 20.4 inches,[3] so that exactitude in recovering the dimensions of the Tabernacle and its contents is ruled out.

The Tabernacle itself was divided into three zones:[4] the Court, the Holy Place, the Holy of Holies. The Court was really the enclosure of the structure, three hundred cubits in perimeter.[5] It comprised a rectangle, the dimensions of which were one hundred cubits on the north and south sides and fifty cubits on the east and west sides. It will be noted at once that this constitutes two equal and adjacent squares of fifty cubits on the sides. The entrance to the Tabernacle lay on the east side[6] so that its axis was east-west, with the worshipper facing west. Along the twenty-cubits-wide entrance was a multicolored, embroidered, woven screen.[7] Within the square farthest from the entrance was another rectangle measuring thirty by ten cubits, and ten cubits in height.[8] This too was partitioned by means of an embroidered curtain, called in Hebrew *parokhet*.[9] The larger compartment was the Holy Place which covered an area of twenty by ten cubits. The smaller one was the Holy of Holies, and it formed a perfect cube measuring ten cubits on each side.

All around the perimeter of the outer enclosure, or Court, were hangings of fine twisted linen attached to upright posts of acacia wood five cubits high placed at intervals of five cubits. Each of the sixty posts was inserted into a socket of bronze. The posts were banded with silver and supplied with hooks.[10]

The Tabernacle proper, in the more restricted sense, the inner rectangle, was constructed of three walls made up of forty-eight *qerashim* of acacia wood, each being 10 by 1.5 cubits. This difficult Hebrew word has generally been rendered "planks," although some modern scholars prefer to understand the term as "frames."[11] The distribution of the *qerashim* was as follows: on the north and south sides there were twenty such, respectively; on the west side there were six, with an additional one at either corner. These forty-eight uprights were fixed in silver sockets, two to each, by means of tenons. Five wooden crossbars on each wall held them together. The east side remained open.[12]

This entire wooden structure was enclosed by a fabric which fitted over it. The covering was composed of ten sheets of fine twisted linen cloth fashioned of blue, purple, and crimson yarn into which was worked a design of cherubim. There were ten such sheets, each mea-

suring twenty-eight by four cubits. These were sewn together lengthwise
in two sets of five, thus yielding two sets of curtains each measuring
twenty-eight by twenty cubits. Fifty blue woolen loops were attached
along a twenty-eight-cubit edge of each. The two sets were coupled
together by means of fifty gold clasps. These latter, together with the
cherubim design, appear to have been visible to one looking up at the
ceiling from inside. All these constituted the lower or inner curtains.[13]

Another set of curtains, this one of goats' hair, was placed on top of
the linen ones.[14] In this case, there were eleven in all, each measuring
thirty by four cubits, and joined together, like the others, in two sets,
but this time of five and six curtains, respectively. The larger number
and size were to ensure that the structure would be completely covered.
The two sets were likewise coupled together by fifty loops and clasps,
but the latter were of bronze, not gold. Still another covering of red-
dyed rams' skins was placed over the preceding, and above that was one
of dolphin skins.[15]

As was noted earlier, a *parokhet*, or veil, separated the Holy of Holies
from the Holy Place. This hung from golden hooks on four wooden
posts overlaid with gold. The posts were set in four silver sockets.[16]

The furniture

Each of the three zones into which the Tabernacle was divided was
equipped with distinctive articles of furniture.

The outer Court contained two major items: the altar of burnt offering, and the laver on its stand. The first was made of acacia wood.
It measured five cubits square and three cubits high. Four horns pro-
truded from the corners, and were "of one piece" with it. The entire
altar was overlaid with bronze. It had a projecting ledge halfway up the
side, underneath which was fixed a grating of meshwork in bronze. The
altar's place was facing the entrance to the Holy Place.[17] Each day,
morning and evening, a lamb was offered upon it, together with a meal
offering and a libation of wine.[18]

Between the altar and the aforementioned entrance stood a laver, or
water basin, raised on a stand, both parts manufactured from bronze.[19]
Here the priests washed their hands and feet before entering the Holy
Place or before performing the sacrificial ritual. A peculiar feature of

the laver and its base is that they are said to have been fashioned from "the mirrors of the women who performed tasks at the entrance to the Tent of Meeting."[20] Polished bronze and mirrors were highly valued in the ancient Near East, and several have turned up in the course of excavations; but what is meant by the description of their original ownership is a puzzle.[21]

The Holy Place, or outer sanctum, had three articles of furniture. On the north side was the Table on which twelve fresh loaves were placed every sabbath day. This "bread of display" was arranged in two rows of six. The Table itself stood only 1.5 cubits high; its top dimensions were two cubits by one cubit. Constructed of acacia wood, it was overlaid with "pure gold."[22]

Facing the Table, on the south side, stood the Menorah, or Lampstand. Its measurements are not given; only its shape is described. Hammered out of a single ingot of "pure gold," its central shaft had a wide base. Extending from the shaft on either side were three branches, making six in all, each one ornamented after the flower of the almond tree. The lamps of the Menorah were lit at dusk each day by the high priest, and they burned until morning.[23]

The third article of furniture in the Holy Place was the "altar of incense," also called "the golden altar." This was positioned between the Table and the Menorah, directly in front of the veil that separated the Holy of Holies. The top of the altar measured one cubit square, and it stood two cubits high. Made of acacia wood, it too was overlaid with "pure gold." It also had a gold molding around it. Horns projected from each of the four corners. Every day at morning and at twilight Aaron would burn aromatic incense on this altar.[24]

The Holy of Holies, or inner sanctum, contained only the two tablets of stone reposing inside the Ark. The shape of this latter item was rectangular, 2.5 cubits long, and 1.5 cubits in width and in height. It was actually a wooden chest open at the top, which was entirely overlaid with "pure gold" inside and out, and it was surrounded by a gold molding. A plate of "pure gold," called in Hebrew *kapporet*, of the same size as the opening, provided the cover of the Ark. Golden cherubim of hammered work, "of one piece" with it, adorned this cover, one at either end. The cherubim had their wings spread out, touching overhead, shielding the cover. They were turned to one another, but they faced downward toward the Ark.[25] Although the *kapporet* was always attached to the Ark, several texts make clear that it possessed an identity of its own.[26]

The historical reality

Until fairly recently scholarly opinion held the account of the Tabernacle to be entirely unhistorical. It was claimed that it arose from a fictional retrojection of King Solomon's Temple into the narratives about the wilderness wanderings.[27] Questions were raised about procuring all the construction materials in Sinai, the wood, the precious metals, the costly fabrics, the expensive gems, and so forth. It was calculated, for example, that according to the summations of Exodus 38:24–31, the erection of the Tabernacle would have required about one ton of gold, over three tons of silver, and about two and one-half tons of bronze. The Ark together with its solid-gold cover have been estimated to have weighed at least five tons.[28] All these amounts, in turn, vastly complicate the problems of transportation, which are compounded by the issue of the *qerashim*. If these were really planks of acacia wood, and not frames, then each of the forty-eight such would have weighed at least half a ton. This raises the additional issue of their own height being out of proportion to the load they would have needed to bear. Other challenges to historicity concerned the ability of semi-nomads to recruit from their own ranks the needed skilled craftsmen and artisans. It was pointed out that hundreds of years later King Solomon had to hire Phoenicians in order to build his Temple. For all these reasons, critical scholars regarded the idea of a mobile Tabernacle in the wilderness as an idealized fabrication, unrelated to reality.

Of course, not all these problems are of equal gravity. The narratives themselves often tacitly exhibit sensitivity to them. The emphasis on the Israelites' bespoiling the Egyptians before they left the country may well be intended to explain in advance their ability to produce in the wilderness the raw materials for the erection of the Tabernacle.[29] The transportation of the various elements of the structure is explicitly said to have been facilitated by the use of wagons drawn by oxen.[30] Finally, there is no reason why, during their many years of forced labor in Egypt, the Israelites should not have acquired high proficiency in the many skills and techniques needed for the construction work. After all, they had experienced firsthand for a considerable period of time the most materially advanced civilization of antiquity.[31]

Irrespective of how convincing or otherwise may be these possible answers to the formidable problems raised by the narratives, it is quite fatuous, on other grounds, to deny the basic historic reality of a wilderness Tabernacle. First of all, the internal biblical evidence cannot be ignored. When David proposed the idea of a permanent Temple edifice to house the Ark, the divine response is given as follows:

> From the day that I brought the people of Israel out of Egypt to this day, I have not dwelt in a house, but have moved about in Tent and Tabernacle. As I moved about wherever the Israelites went, did I ever reproach any of the tribal leaders whom I appointed to care for My people Israel: Why have you not built Me a house of cedar?[32]

The obvious, irrefutable implication of this statement is reinforced by the terminology used in the various narratives to denote the wilderness sanctuary. The two basic Hebrew terms are *mishkan* and *'ohel*, both of which unmistakably point to the nomadic origins of the institutions. The first designation has traditionally come to be rendered into English by "tabernacle," while *'ohel* is translated "tent." In actuality the two words are synonymous and are used indiscriminately and interchangeably. They both go back to conditions that obtained prior to the Israelite settlement in Canaan.

The two stems *sh-k-n* and *'-h-l* are frequently paired and associated both in nominal and verbal forms in biblical Hebrew texts.[33] Moreover, *mishkan* is specifically employed in passages where it can only be taken in its literal meaning of "tent." Thus it is so used to describe the dwellings of the rebellious Korah, Dathan, and Abiram in the wilderness, of the Kedemite tribes who roamed the fringes of the Syro-Palestinian desert, and of shepherds in a pastoral setting.[34]

Further evidence of the original meaning of *mishkan* is provided by Ugaritic texts in which it is also paired synonymously with *'ahl*, "tent," to designate the abode of the gods.[35] In Akkadian, too, *maškanu* means "a tent, canopy,"[36] and in Targumic Aramaic *mashkana'* is the rendering for biblical Hebrew *'ohel*.[37]

All this leaves no doubt that the Hebrew designations for the sanctuary are terms that go back to nomadic origins. This explains why they could be employed poetically in archaizing reference to the fixed, monumental Temple in Jerusalem.[38] The usage is a carry-over from pre-settlement times. On philological grounds alone, therefore, there should never have been any reason to question the existence of a portable sanctuary in Israel in the course of the wilderness wanderings.

Archeological finds and literary sources from the ancient world have also had the effect in recent times of promoting a more positive evaluation of the story of the Israelite Tabernacle. Attention has been drawn to analogous Arab Bedouin practices. Two Islamic institutions, the 'utfah and the mahmal, are of special interest in this connection.[39]

The former is a tentlike structure made of thin wooden boards and having a domed top. It is fastened on the baggage saddle of a camel, and is in the custody of the Ruwala tribe. Allah is believed to reside in it, and supernatural properties are attributed to it. When the camel carrying it begins to move, the entire tribe follows suit, and where it kneels is where the camp is pitched. At critical moments in battle, the 'utfah is brought out to ensure victory.

The mahmal, known in various forms over a wide area of the Islamic Near East, is basically a pavilion made of a wooden framework covered with richly embroidered fabrics. It too was mounted on the saddle of a camel, and was believed to be able to select the route of the caravan on its way to Mecca.[40]

Even earlier, and still more pertinent to the subject, is the pre-Islamic qubbah, which was a small portable tent shrine constructed of red leather. The color is thought to be particularly significant because of the contrast with the usual black of Bedouin tents and because one of the coverings of the wilderness Tabernacle was made of rams' skins dyed red,[41] for which color no explanation is forthcoming in the text. The qubbah contained the idols and cult objects of the tribe, and was often mounted on the back of a camel. When the tribe pitched camp, the tent shrine was unloaded and set up beside the tent of the sheik. People would come to it seeing oracles. Given the innate and stubborn conservatism of nomadic traditions, the qubbah is likely to have represented a widespread custom of venerable antiquity among wandering tribes of the ancient Near East.

Evidence that such was indeed the case comes from material that harks back to pre-Christian times. Qubbahs are portrayed on two first-century B.C.E. images from Syria, and on a bas-relief from a temple of Bel at Palmyra, the oasis in the Syrian desert, which may derive from the fifth century B.C.E.[42] The Greco-Roman historian Diodorus Siculus (first century B.C.E.), in his *Bibliotheka Historica* (xx, 65),[43] mentions the sacred hut possessed by the Carthaginian armies, which was placed in their camp near the altar next to the hut of the general. This seems to be the descendant of Phoenicia's highly venerated wood statue and shrine, or portable temple, drawn by yokes of oxen, whose existence is reported by the sixth-century B.C.E. Phoenician writer Sanchuniathon. True, remnants of his work were preserved only in the translation made by Philo of Byblos four hundred years later, and were cited in the writings of the fourth-century C.E. church father Eusebius in his *Praeparatio Evangelica*. Yet, notwithstanding the late dates of transmission, Sanchuniathon's reputation for reliability has been repeatedly confirmed and enhanced ever since the discovery of the Ugaritic epics.[44]

Still more evidence for the antiquity of the use of portable shrines can be extracted from the Egyptian bas-relief of the battle scenes featuring Rameses II (ca. 1290–1224 B.C.E.), which portray the tent of the divine king and sacred objects of various kinds placed in the center of the oblong-shaped military camp. As a matter of fact, the construction technique employed for the Israelite Tabernacle can be traced back to at least the middle of the third millennium B.C.E. The tomb at Giza, Egypt, of Queen Hetepheres of the Fourth Dynasty, wife of King Sneferu and mother of the great pyramid builder Khufu (Cheops), yielded gilded wooden frames and beams equipped with hooks for the hanging of curtains to form a large canopy. Together with these was a wooden box overlaid with gold foil to house the draperies, as well as other gold-cased furniture such as the royal carrying chair and the queen's bed, to which was appended a detachable footboard and silver headrest. Other Egyptian finds exhibiting similar portable canopy-like structures testify to the prevalence of the basic construction technique of the Israelite Tabernacle long before Mosaic times. Closest to the period of the Exodus are the exemplars from the tomb of Tutankhamen (ca. 1350 B.C.E.), which consist of prefabricated oak shrines covered without and within with a thin layer of plaster to which thin leaves of gold foil adhere. In addition, a linen cloth hanging over a wood stand separated the two shrines.[45]

In light of all the foregoing variegated data, it is beyond cavil that

the Israelite wilderness Tabernacle, both as an institution and in its
mode of construction, was well rooted in the cultural and religious
traditions of the ancient Near East. Of course, what we are discussing
are the purely external and physical aspects. As we shall see, the essential
ideas that are enshrined in the Tabernacle and the religious concepts
that it expresses are wholly Israelite and radically different from its
compares.

The divine instructions and the celestial images

Two distinctive and dominating features of the account of the construction of the Tabernacle deserve further discussion. The first is that
the initiative for the enterprise and the detailed instructions for its
execution are said to have been manifested by God. The second, closely
related to the first, is the oft-repeated reference to celestial images of
the completed structure and of certain individual elements that Moses
is said to have been shown on Mount Sinai. He is told: "Exactly as I
show you—the pattern of the Tabernacle and the pattern of all its
furnishings—so shall you make it."[46] He is similarly instructed regarding
the Ark, its Cover, its Table, and its Lampstand: "Note well, and follow
the patterns for them that are being shown you on the mountain."[47]
The altar and its accessories come with the following instructions: "Make
it hollow, of boards. As you were shown on the mountain, so shall they
be made."[48] How indispensable to the Tabernacle narrative are these
twin features is further emphasized through the meticulously reiterated
fulfillment formula that all was indeed made as "the Lord commanded
Moses."[49]

Apart from these explicit statements, the conception of the Tabernacle
as the terrestrial objectification of a celestial image also finds implicit
expression in a manner that is not immediately apparent, but that
certainly underlies a detail of the narration. Two master craftsmen—
Bezalel and Oholiab—are appointed by Moses to execute and oversee
the construction work.[50] But the two personalities are not architects.
They possess the necessary skills to fashion the several individual items
in accordance with the instructions that they receive from Moses. However, when it comes to assembling the parts into an integrated whole,
it is Moses personally who performs the task, not they.[51] This really has
to be so, within the framework of the narrative, since only Moses carries

a mental picture of the Tabernacle in its completed, coherent form. No one else knows the disposition of the individual components and the harmonious interrelationships of the constituent elements.[52]

It remains uncertain as to what is intended to be conveyed precisely by Moses' being shown by God a "pattern" (Hebrew: *tavnit*) of the Tabernacle and its parts. It might imply belief in the existence of an actual, visible, celestial temple of which the earthly structure is to be a replica. This interpretation is favored by the famous vision of Isaiah, described in Chapter 6 of his book, in which he sees a vision of the ritual being enacted in the temple in heaven. Also, it can be shown that Hebrew *tavnit* usually refers to the imitative reproduction of a material entity that exists in reality.[53] On the other hand, it cannot be denied that *tavnit* might imply the conceptual form, the likeness and image of the ideal, invisible, archetypal form that is present in the mind of God, and that is made manifest to Moses, who alone is privileged to perceive it.

Before turning to a discussion of the meaning and significance of this phenomenon, it needs to be pointed out that analogies exist elsewhere in the Bible. The prophet Ezekiel, in a vision, is shown a model outline of the future Jerusalem with its renewed Temple, and is given detailed and elaborate verbal descriptions and specifications while he stands on "a very high mountain."[54] The same motif appears in the Chronicler's version of the original Temple project in Jerusalem. King David is said to have received the masterplan from God "by the spirit," as he says, a plan which "the Lord made me understand by His hand upon me."[55]

Attention has frequently been drawn by scholars to the fact that similar ideas about the origins and construction of sacred edifices were widespread in the ancient world.[56] The earliest analog is to be found in the inscription of King Gudea of Lagash (ca. 2200 B.C.E.), the Sumerian state that was located in southern Iraq at the present-day mound of Telloh between the Tigris and Euphrates Rivers. This king inscribed about three thousand lines on two clay cylinders (only one is extant). He recounted the initiation and execution of a temple-building (or rebuilding?) project. It is stated that the gods, in a dream-theophany, communicated to Gudea the need to build the temple of Ningirsu, god of fertility, thunderstorms, and the annual rise of the Tigris. Untrustful of his own interpretation of the dream, he went to great lengths to clarify and verify it. He sought the services of the divine dream interpreter, Nanshe, who advised him to seek a second message from Ningirsu. Gudea then performed the necessary incubatory cultic rituals and received details of the materials to be used. Of particular interest is the fact that the initiative, directives, and specifications all come from the god, and that Gudea is shown a prior vision of what the completed temple is to look like.[57]

The Babylonian creation epic known as *Enuma elish* basically expresses the same ideas when it ascribes the building of the Esagila, Marduk's temple in Babylon, to the gods themselves at the creation of the world, and when it has them intimately associated with all phases of the construction work.[58] The pervasiveness of the theme is demonstrated by Akkadian cylinder seals that pictorially represent the gods participating in all the manifold chores that the building of the great edifice entailed.[59]

A variant of the conception of the temple as the earthly reproduction of a celestial image is to be found in Egyptian religious thought in which historical temples are portrayed as having mythological origins that go back to the beginning of the world. That is to say, the actual physical sanctuary is conceived to be an extension and continuity of a mythical prototype on the same locality. Not only this, but the gods may specify the actual ground area of the sacred precinct and furnish the dimensions of the temple and its enclosure. For example, the temple of Re at Heliopolis was believed to have been planned by the god Thoth, the divine scribe and inventor of writing.[60]

What lies behind such widely diffused notions? In essence, they constitute a way of affirming the validity of the bold undertaking of the building of a sanctuary. They are necessary to the legitimacy of the sacred edifice, which thereby receives divine sanction. The temple is not considered to be a human institution, but a divine one, and because of that, the rituals performed therein are seen to be assured of divine acceptance. Doubtless, some or all of these beliefs were shared also by Israel. But there is more to it than this.

Paradoxically, by virtue of the very concept that Israel held in common with its neighbors, the wilderness Tabernacle takes on a wholly new dimension. The extra-biblical accounts arose out of a reality of existing temples. King Gudea, after experiencing his dream, paid visits to the other sanctuaries of his land. Our narrative, however, knows nothing of any prior history to the institution, which is presented as an innovation so unprecedented that without divine instructions, verbal and visual, it would be unintelligible. In other words, the narrative in this way deliberately disconnects and dissociates the Tabernacle from anything that is in Israel's world of experience. Ideologically, this approach conforms to the pattern of the Patriarchal narratives in the Book of Genesis. Abraham, Isaac, and Jacob erect altars and sacred pillars at various sites in Canaan in the course of their peregrinations. Never do they make use of an existing altar. Invariably, they build new ones. Nor are we told anything about Canaanite cult centers in that book. In other words, the narratives present the religion of the Patriarchs as a discontinuity and as innovative. The divinely given instructions and celestial images in connection with the Tabernacle here serve the same function.

The Tabernacle and Sinai

As we noted above, the Tabernacle was meant to be a living extension of Mount Sinai. The national experience with God that occurred there would be sustained and nourished through the presence of the sanctuary in the midst of the camp of Israel. This close association between the Tabernacle and Sinai is expressed in a number of ways.

During the theophany, the mount was separated into three distinct zones of increasing degrees of holiness and restriction of access. At the foot of the mount stood the people, and there the altar was set up; in like manner, the altar was placed in the Court of the Tabernacle to which the laity had access.[61] Higher up on the mount was the second zone of holiness, to which only the priests and elders were admitted. Corresponding to this in the Tabernacle was the Holy Place, which was restricted to the priesthood.[62] The summit of the mountain constituted the third zone, which was exclusively reserved for Moses. Its counterpart in the Tabernacle was the Holy of Holies.[63] Just as the Lord communicated with Moses on the mountaintop, so He does in the Holy of Holies; and in the same way that the cloud covered Mount Sinai after Moses had ascended, so the Tabernacle became enveloped in cloud on its completion, and the pillar of fire hovered over both Sinai and it.[64]

Finally, of course, the most powerful and most impressive reminder of
the experience at Sinai was provided by the two tablets of stone housed
in the Ark inside the Holy of Holies, which served as the focal point
of the entire edifice.

The all-Israelite emphasis

The Tabernacle, like the Sinaitic event, involved the people of Israel
in its entirety. It was meant to minister to the religious needs of the
whole of Israel, to be the cynosure of its spiritual yearnings and the
visible focus of the tribal unity. Hence, its creation must be a cooperative
enterprise. Therefore the narrative is punctuated with items that stress
the pan-Israelite nature of the institution. The first instruction that
Moses received was to issue a call to all Israel, to "every person whose
heart so moves him," to contribute the materials needed for its erection
and operation.[65] The response to this appeal on the part of the people
was overwhelming.[66] "And let them make Me a sanctuary," says God,
"that I may dwell among them"[67]—not inside the material structure,
be it noted, but "among them." Similarly, God declares, "I will abide
among the Israelites, and I will be their God. And they shall know that
I the Lord am their God, who brought them out of the land of Egypt
that I might abide among them. . . ."[68] When Moses is to commune
with God in the sanctuary, it will be "concerning the Israelite
people,"[69] not to serve his private needs. The names of the twelve tribes
of Israel are to be engraved on the stones that form an integral part of
the high priest's vestments. He is to "carry the names of the sons of
Israel on the breastpiece of decision over his heart, when he enters the
sanctuary, for remembrance before the Lord at all times."[70] The expense
of maintaining the daily services is to be defrayed by a poll-tax of one-
half silver shekel that is to be levied equally upon every adult male,
poor and rich alike.[71] When the work of construction is actually completed, it is said that "Just as the Lord had commanded Moses, so the
Israelites had done all the work."[72] In other words, the entire citizenry
was involved in the enterprise. Finally, as we are informed in the second
chapter of the Book of Numbers, the camp of the Israelites in the
wilderness was arranged in the form of an enormous square with the
Tabernacle in the center, and with the twelve tribes pitched around
it—three on each side.

Gradations of holiness[73]

The division of the sanctuary into three zones involved a progression from profane space outside of it into the sacred space inside in an ascending scale of holiness. As we mentioned above, access to the differentiated zones was permitted in accordance with the religious classification of the people. Laymen were restricted to the outer Court, priests and Levites ministered in the outer sanctum, the Holy Place, and admission to the Holy of Holies was barred to all except the high priest, and then he could enter it only once a year, on the Day of Atonement, to create a perfect and remarkable coalescense of the most sacred individual, the most sacred of space, the most sacred day of the year, and the most sacred rite.[74]

Another correlation obtains in respect of the relative value of the metals and the degree of sanctity of the zones in which they are utilized. The furniture and appurtenances of the outer Court were all bronzed; in the Holy Place, the outer plating was of "pure gold," that is, of gold that has been more thoroughly refined of impurities than is usually the case; while in the Holy of Holies, the Ark had the unique distinction of being overlaid with gold of that same superior quality inside as well as outside, and the *kapporet*, or Ark cover, was a solid slab of "pure gold." In like manner, the wooden posts that marked the perimeter of the Court were inserted into bronze sockets, whereas those that delimited the inner rectangle rested in silver sockets. The clasps of the outer, or upper, curtains were made of bronze; those of the inner, or lower, curtains were of gold.

In addition to these internal gradations, the entire area of the Tabernacle was walled off from the profane world outside by means of the protective screen that surrounded the Court, and furthermore, when the Israelites encamped in the wilderness, the tents of the priests and the Levites served as a cordon that separated the tents of the tribes from that outer perimeter.[75]

All these carefully contrived measures had as their purpose the protection of the holiness of the Tabernacle because it, in turn, gave expression to the presence within it of the ultimate Source of holiness. God's holiness is the very essence of His Being, and is intrinsic to Himself. The graduated sequences described above effectuate the gradual distancing from that ultimate Source of absolute holiness. Precisely

because the Tabernacle was constructed in the first place to give concrete, visual symbolization to the conception of God's indwelling in
the community of Israel, that is, to communicate the idea of God's
immanence, it was vitally important that His total independence of all
materiality, His transcendence, not be compromised. The gradations
of holiness are one way of articulating this, of giving voice to God's
unapproachable holiness, and of emphasizing His ineffable majesty and
the inscrutable mystery that He is.

God's omnipresence

The very existence of a Tabernacle carries with it the possibility of
engendering a false theology, for it might encourage an inferential
limitation of God's omnipresence. After all, throughout the Near East
the temple was commonly believed to be the dwelling place of the god.[76]
The dedicatory address of King Solomon at the opening of the Temple
in Jerusalem displays a keen awareness of the problem. It reads:

> But will God really dwell on earth? Even the heavens to their
> uttermost reaches cannot contain You, how much less this House
> that I have built![77]

Several aspects of the present narrative also exhibit sensitivity to the
issue, and seem to point to a conscious desire on the part of the narrator
to counteract mistaken notions of imparting a domestic connotation to
the sanctuary.

To begin with, there are the Hebrew designations for the institution:
mishkan, 'ohel. As we have earlier demonstrated, the former, although
traditionally rendered "Tabernacle," is in actuality a tent, just like *'ohel*,
and is a term that recalls the nomadic way of life. The verb *sh-k-n*,
derived from the noun, means primarily "to tent," that is, to reside
temporarily, moving from place to place.[78] The lack of fixity in a specific
locality negates the idea of a static God confined to a particular holy
space. Indeed, the original rationale of the sanctuary, as given in the
Torah, makes the point abundantly clear.

> Let them make me a sanctuary that I may dwell [*ve-shakhanti*]
> among them.[79]

I will abide [*ve-shakhanti*] among the Israelites, and I will be their God. And they shall know that I the Lord am their God, who brought them out of the land of Egypt that I might abide [*le-shokhni*] among them. . . .[80]

These primary texts leave no doubt that the sanctuary is constructed to answer human needs. God is not said to abide *in it* but *among* the Israelites. The Tabernacle is only the material, numinous symbol of God's immanence, of His Presence being felt in the community of Israel with particular intensification. It is this proper understanding of the stem *sh-k-n* that naturally led to postbiblical Hebrew *shekhinah* as the regular term for the Divine Presence.

Then there is the careful use of the verbs "to go down" (*y-r-d*) and "to go up" (*'-l-h*) in reference to the pillar of cloud in the Tabernacle.[81] It was this that communicated the presence of God and the termination of the people's perception of that condition. It is self-evident that the vocabulary nullifies the idea that God resides inside the Tabernacle or is confined by it. Rather, He is portrayed, just as at Sinai, as descending to it from on high.[82] We shall have more to say about this theme in dealing with the cherubim.

God's unity and perfection

The Tabernacle as a physical entity also enshrined other ideas about God that are at the very core of Israel's religion. Both in the instructions for its erection and in affirming their meticulous implementation, the text pointedly underscores the quality of structural unity and architectonic wholeness of the institution. Regardless of the variety of its component parts, its compositeness, and its internal gradations, the completed edifice was to constitute, and did so, an integrated sacred unity: ". . . so that the Tabernacle becomes one whole"; ". . . so that the Tabernacle became one whole."[83] It is difficult not to read into this emphasis an intent to produce a meaningful form that is expressive of the unity of the divine essence, and also, perhaps, of the unity of the people of Israel whose needs it was meant to serve. Furthermore, the fact that the Holy of Holies was a cube—the symbol of perfection—strengthens the compelling suggestion that God's unity and perfection were intended to be apprehended through the aesthetic form of the structure.

The tablets

A widespread practice in the ancient Near East was to record the texts of important public documents, especially treaty stipulations, on tablets of clay, stone, or metal. A celebrated example of the last-mentioned is the text of the treaty made between Rameses II and the Hittite king Hattusilis around the year 1269 B.C.E. According to the Egyptian version, the clauses of this treaty were inscribed on a tablet of silver.[84] The biblical tablets of stone, therefore, belong to a well-entrenched Near Eastern tradition.

At the close of the theophany at Sinai, it is related that God ordered Moses to ascend the mountain for the purpose of receiving "the stone tablets with the teachings and commandments. . . ."[85] It is then stated that "He gave Moses the two tablets of the Pact, stone tablets inscribed with the finger of God."[86] Later in the narrative it is told that the two tablets were inscribed with the text of the Decalogue.[87] Thereafter the phrase "the tablets of stone" invariably refers to these objects so engraved.[88]

Because the Decalogue comprises the terms of the covenant between God and Israel, the tablets are also called "the tablets of the Covenant" (in Hebrew, luhot ha-b'rit).[89] Another designation with the same denotation is "the tablets of the Pact" (in Hebrew, luhot ha-'edut).[90] This latter term is apparently much older than the preceding for it carries a special meaning for 'edut that is found in cognate Semitic languages but that became largely obsolete in Hebrew. Thus, Akkadian 'adû is used for the stipulations of vassal treaties,[91] as is 'dy' (= 'adaya'a, plural form) in Old Aramaic.[92] The same word is also found in a twelfth-century B.C.E. Egyptian text as a borrowing from Canaanite,[93] thus indicating a long pre-Israelite history for it as a legal term.[94]

The tablets are placed in a gold-plated wooden chest expressly made to contain them, and generally referred to in English as "the Ark." For this reason, the Ark is variously designated "the Ark of the Pact" (in Hebrew, 'aron ha-'edut)[95] and "the Ark of the Covenant" (in Hebrew, 'aron ha-b'rit).[96] It was deposited in the Holy of Holies, and was the only article of furniture that this most sacred domain contained.[97]

The importance of these facts cannot be overestimated. They bear witness to a radical break with all contemporary—indeed, with all— pagan concepts. Everywhere, and at all times, the most important feature of a temple was the cella, or innermost shrine that housed the image of the god. In Israel, with its uncompromising aniconic, imageless religion, in place of the representation of the deity came the tangible symbol of His Word—the stone tablets of the Covenant. The Ark and its contents became the focus of the collective consciousness of the community. It remained the symbol of the eternal covenant between God and the people, the record of His inescapable demands upon the individual and society in every sphere of life. It was this, not an image, that occupied the center of attention and that was at the core of the religion. This written reminder of God's revealed word constituted the sign of His presence and His indwelling in the midst of Israel. The "Ark of the Covenant," therefore, embodied one of the fundamental ideas of the religion: that it is only through His Word that true knowledge of God, the understanding of His essential nature, can be apprehended or at least pursued.

The Ark

What was the function of this Ark? Was it merely a receptacle for the tablets of the Decalogue and nothing more? The texts strongly suggest otherwise. We noted earlier that the tablets of stone form an analogy to the extrabiblical practice of recording the instrument of a treaty and other important documents on imperishable materials. The parallel takes on added interest if we also observe that it was customary to deposit such texts "before the god" or "at the feet" of the deity in a temple. A treaty of mutual assistance concluded between the Hittite king Suppiluliumas (ca. 1375–1335 B.C.E.) and Mattiwaza, king of Mitanni in Upper Mesopotamia, contains the notice that one "duplicate of the tablet" was deposited "before the sun-goddess" and another "before [the god] Teshub."[98] In general, the Hittite treaties make provision for the depositing of a copy in the temple.[99] A letter from Rameses II concerning the treaty he concluded with King Hattusilis explicitly mentions that a copy was placed "beneath the feet" of the god of the respective parties.[100] In Egypt, a rubric to a section of the Book of the Dead states that it was found in Hermopolis inscribed in genuine lapis lazuli on a block of iron(?) "under the feet of the majesty of the god."[101]

In light of these analogies to the depositing of the stone tablets in a chest inside the Holy of Holies, it is reasonable to suggest that in Israel the Ark was looked upon imaginatively as the equivalent of a footstool.[102] Definite evidence for such a conception is, in fact, to be found in 1 Chronicles 28:2: "King David rose to his feet and said, 'Hear me, my brothers, my people! I wanted to build a resting-place for the Ark of the Covenant of the Lord, for the footstool of our God.'" It is also certain that a phrase like "to bow down at His footstool," found in Psalms 99:5 and 132:7, has in mind the Holy of Holies. Finally, when Lamentations 2:1 uses "Footstool" in reference to the Temple, it is employing the figure of speech known as synecdoche, that is, mentioning the part when the whole is to be understood.

Now this well-attested conception of the Ark as a footstool clearly carries with it the implication that the divine throne was imagined to be situated above it inside the Holy of Holies. Here again, several texts leave no doubt that such was indeed the case. It will be remembered that the *kapporet*, or cover of the Ark, was adorned with two cherubim of gold, one at either end, and we are explicitly told that it was from this area that God would communicate with Moses, "from above the cover, from between the two cherubim that are on top of the Ark of the Pact. . . ."[103] Another passage informs us that "When Moses went into the Tent of Meeting to speak with Him, he would hear the Voice addressing him from above the cover that was on top of the Ark of the Pact between the two cherubim. . . ."[104] In other words, the Divine Presence was believed to settle, as it were, in the space between the two cherubim above the Ark.

The final and irrefutable proof that the poetic imagination pictured the divine throne as resting above the Ark is provided by the oft-repeated epithet of God as "Enthroned on the Cherubim." Reference is made to "the Ark of the Covenant of the Lord of Hosts Enthroned on the Cherubim," "the Ark of God to which the Name was attached, the Name Lord of Hosts Enthroned on the Cherubim."[105]

This conception of the sacred Ark of the Covenant as a footstool beneath the invisible throne of God in the Holy of Holies seems strange to the Western mind. It becomes intelligible, however, if it is viewed within the context of the thought world of the ancient Near East. There, the throne and the footstool go together so that often they may form a single article of furniture.[106] In many instances the footstool would be richly and symbolically decorated. So important were the two appurtenances of royalty that in Egypt throne and footstool were frequently entombed together with the mummy of the pharaoh. The reason for their extraordinary status is that they evoked notions of majesty, exaltation, preeminence, sovereignty, and power. In the Israelite Tabernacle there was no actual throne, only the boxlike Ark with its tablets of stone inside it and its cherubim on top of it—an abiding reminder both of the invisible presence of the sovereign God and of His inescapable demands upon His people.

All this explains why the Ark was thought to assume a numinous aspect and to possess a dangerous potency.[107] It constituted the understructure of the sacred space above it, space that was imbued with the extra-holiness radiated by the Divine Presence.[108] This also clarifies another detail. In order to facilitate the transportation of the Tabernacle, all major articles of furniture were equipped with rings. When camp was struck, the Levites responsible for the porterage would insert poles through the rings to carry the sacred object to the next station by means of these poles, and then remove them. The single exception to this procedure was the Ark. Its poles were never removed but remained permanently in the rings. The purpose of this was to avert the possibility that profane hands might come into direct contact with the Ark when it was being transported.[109]

The cherubim

One of the curious and intriguing features of the Tabernacle—and later of the Temple—was the pervasiveness of the cherubic motif.[110] The cover of the Ark was adorned with two golden cherubim,[111] and it was from the empty space between them that the divine Voice emanated.[112] The curtains of the structure had a design of cherubim worked into them.[113] The same motif was lavishly utilized for the decoration of Solomon's Temple,[114] and the prophet Ezekiel's visionary temple was likewise adorned with cherubim.[115]

This phenomenon, extraordinary in itself, assumes even greater significance if it is measured against the otherwise characteristically strict rejection of pictorial representations and of the plastic arts in Israel. The curiosity is further magnified by the oft-repeated epithet of God: "Enthroned on the Cherubim."

This last-mentioned phrase actually provides the key to understanding, for it clearly indicates a conception of the cherubim as bearers of

God's throne, and since they are invariably portrayed with wings, the intention is to express in art form, and poetically, God's mobility or, as we should say, His omnipresence, an attribute that, as we have seen, is also emphasized in the Tabernacle in other ways. Several biblical texts variously pictorialize this divine quality. One such is Psalm 18:11:

> He mounted a cherub and flew,
> gliding on the wings of the wind.

Another passage calls God the One "who rides the clouds."[116] Still other passages merge the cloud and chariot images:

> He . . . makes the clouds His chariot,
> moves on the wings of the wind.[117]

> The Lord is coming with fire,
> His chariots are like a whirlwind.[118]

The chariot motif is, of course, most expansively, elaborately, and imaginatively employed by Ezekiel in Chapters 1 and 10 of the biblical book that bears his name.[119] Neither his description nor the other biblical data permit the artist to reproduce a cherub, for the Scriptural texts are impenetrably vague and lack internal consistency. The creatures in the Tabernacle and the Temple possess two wings and one face,[120] while those depicted by Ezekiel now have four faces and four wings, now only two faces.[121]

The origin and meaning of the word *cherub*, a transliteration of the Hebrew *krub*, is uncertain. A fanciful rabbinic interpretation connected it with Aramaic *k-rabia*, "like a growing child."[122] This may well have been the inspiration for the conventional depiction of the cherub by Renaissance artists as a child with wings. A widely held modern scholarly view sees it as a borrowing from Akkadian *kurību*, which is the name given to the composite human–animal–bird figures placed at the entrances of the temples and palaces in Mesopotamia.[123] They were supposed to represent protective genii, and to act as intercessors to the gods on behalf of men. Similar symbolic, hybrid creatures, which bear close resemblance to those described by Ezekiel, have turned up over a wide area of the Near East, including Canaan.[124] In the Israelite version, their function is to guard over the tablets of the Covenant, to signify the presence of the sovereign God, and to act as the perfect embodiment of divine mobility.[125]

Needless to say, the cherubim do not exist in reality, which is why they could be employed in Israel without impinging upon the prohibitions of the Decalogue. They are the brilliant, if fantastic, fabrications of the fertile human imagination struggling to express symbolically profound and mystical abstractions—nothing less than the concepts of God's simultaneous immanence and His omnipresence, while preserving His absolute incorporeality and the aniconic nature of the national religion.

The Tabernacle, the Sabbath, and Creation

The section of the Torah that contains the instructions for the building of the Tabernacle—Exodus 25:1 to 31:11—comprises exactly six literary units each being readily distinguishable by its opening formula, "The Lord spoke/said to Moses."[126] Is this arrangement a deliberate device intended to recall the six days of creation? It surely can be no coincidence that the seventh, and concluding, unit deals with the sabbath. It stresses the paramount importance of its observance, and emphasizes the eternal validity of the institution as a symbol of the covenant bond that regulates the relationship between God and Israel: "For in six days the Lord made heaven and earth, and on the seventh day He ceased from work and was refreshed."[127]

As if to reinforce the correlation between the two themes, the account of the construction of the Tabernacle is also laced with phrases and expressions that unmistakably echo the Genesis creation story. Thus, on completion of the work of creation, it is said that God "saw all that He had made, and found it very good." That is to say, He inspected the finished product and found it to be precisely in accordance with His will. In the same way, it is related that "Moses saw that they had performed all of the tasks—as the Lord had commanded, so had they done. . . ."[128] The summarizing formula of Genesis 2:1, "The heaven and the earth were finished, and all their array," has its equivalent in Exodus 39:32, "Thus was completed all the work of the Tabernacle of the Tent of Meeting." Similarly, just as it goes on to state that "God finished the work," so it records that "Moses had finished the work,"[129] and even as God pronounced a blessing, so did Moses, who was also ordered to perform an act of consecration when the Tabernacle was completed, seemingly in emulation of God's culminating, sanctifying act after He finished His creative work.[130]

These resonances of Genesis in the account of the Tabernacle point to a perception and understanding of that institution as a symbol that is connected with, though not necessarily grounded in, cosmogony. This explains why the Tabernacle was finally erected "on the first day of the first month,"[131] which is New Year's day, a powerful symbol of the beginning of the creation of the world, the transformation of chaos into cosmos. The celebration of New Year's day annually inaugurates a new cycle in the life of humankind. That day was when "the waters [of the Flood] began to dry from the earth,"[132] when a new and purified world began to emerge, and the human race was given the opportunity to make a fresh start. In like manner, therefore, the Tabernacle was conceived to initiate a new era in the life of the community of Israel, and the rites that were performed in it thereafter afforded every Israelite the possibility of spiritual renewal and moral regeneration. The Tabernacle thus represented, as it were, a microcosm in which the macrocosmic universe was reflected.[133]

This cosmogonic association explains the otherwise curious juxtaposition of the Tabernacle and the sabbath to which we have previously drawn attention, a connective that is cemented by the reintroduction of the sabbath law to preface the account of the actual building of the Tabernacle after the interlude of the Golden Calf.[134] The same conjunction of the two themes is found twice more in the Torah: "You shall keep My sabbaths and venerate My Sanctuary: I am the Lord."[135] It would seem that the sequence here conveys a statement about a scale of values, a judgment about the relative importance of sacred time and sacred space. As we noted in connection with the Burning Bush, in the biblical value system the concept of the holiness of time takes precedence over that of the holiness of space. We pointed out that such a hierarchy of values is unique in the context of the ancient world, and is the polar opposite of its accepted standards. The Babylonian creation epic reaches its climax with the gods' building a temple to Marduk. There, sacred space is rooted in creation. The biblical version of cosmogony concludes with the sabbath. Only sacred time, not sacred space, partakes of the cosmic order.

The Israelite Tabernacle in the wilderness inherently exemplifies this principle, for by virtue of its mobility, the ground on which it is assembled can possess no intrinsic or permanent sanctity. Like the sites of the Burning Bush and Sinai, the locale of the sanctuary becomes sacred space only temporarily, and it loses that status the moment the Tabernacle moves to a fresh site. What the literary structure of Chapters 25–31 conveys is that the construction work on the Tabernacle is a kind of analogy on the human plane to God's cosmogonic acts, and, following divine precedent, must be suspended on the sabbath day. The sanctity of space must yield to the higher sanctity of time.

All this in no wise divests the Tabernacle of its preeminent, symbolic role or downgrades its functional significance and importance. It simply places it in its proper perspective within the biblical structure of values.

The Golden Calf[136]

The account of the instructions for building the Tabernacle closes, in Exodus 31:18, with the statement that God "gave Moses the two tablets of the Pact, stone tablets inscribed with the finger of God." This verse forms the connective with and the transition to the episode of the Golden Calf, which led Moses to smash the tablets in response to the apostasy of the people. It is important to note this because it demonstrates that the Book of Exodus has been deliberately structured so as to place that event between the two parts of the Tabernacle narrative—the instructions (Chapters 25–31) and their implementation (Chapters 35–40).[137]

The intrusion is thus seen to be purposeful, and as such it becomes a sort of commentary on the text, as we shall presently see. It is of no consequence whether or not the literary arrangement actually corresponds to the chronological sequence of the events which are related as follows:

Moses' prolonged stay on the mountain led to popular impatience and unrest. The absence of the great leader left a spiritual void. The people confronted Aaron and insisted that he fashion them a god who would lead them in place of Moses. Aaron thereupon demanded that they surrender to him the earrings of their wives, sons, and daughters. These were handed over and Aaron made of them a golden calf. At the sight of this image, the people responded with the cry, "This is

your god, O Israel, who brought you out of the land of Egypt!"[138]
Aaron then built an altar in front of the calf, and announced that "a
festival of the Lord" would be celebrated the following day. The people
rose early the next morning, offered up sacrifices, feasted, and made
merry.

At this point God apprised Moses of the situation in the Israelite
camp, threatened to wipe out the people, and promised to start afresh
by making Moses the father of a new nation. In other words, Moses
and his descendants would become the sole heirs to the promises made
to the Patriarchs. The great leader, however, nobly refused to accept
what God had proposed but instead earnestly entreated Him on behalf
of Israel. Moses' intercession succeeded in ameliorating the intended
punishment. Moses then descended the mountain bearing the tablets
of stone. As he personally witnessed the scene before him, he realized
the full extent of the degradation that had taken place and recognized
the enormity of the popular sin. Thereupon he shattered the tablets at
the foot of the mountain in the presence of the revelers, burnt the
image, pulverized it, strewed it upon the water, and made the Israelites
drink of the mixture. The people then went berserk, and Moses issued
a call for those who "are for the Lord." The Levites rallied to his side,
and a slaughter of three thousand persons ensued.

At this point it is necessary to pause and examine several details of
the narrative, which is replete with difficulties both of text and interpretation, not all of which need engage us here. The first question
relates to the popular perception of Moses. Why did his absence pre-
cipitate a crisis and a request for a "god"? The answer lies in the reaction
of the people to the theophany at Sinai, as recounted in Exodus 20:15–
18:

> . . . when the people saw it, they fell back and stood at a distance.
> "You speak to us," they said to Moses, "and we will obey; but let
> not God speak to us, lest we die." . . . So the people remained at
> a distance, while Moses approached the thick cloud where God
> was.

A report of a similar nature is given in Deuteronomy 5:20–24, where
Moses tells that all the tribal heads and elders had approached him at
Sinai in alarm:

When you heard the Voice out of the darkness, while the mountain was ablaze with fire, you came up to me, all your tribal heads and elders, and said, "The Lord our God has just shown us His majestic Presence. . . . Let us not die, then, for this fearsome fire will consume us; if we hear the voice of the Lord our God any longer, we shall die. . . . You go closer and hear all that the Lord our God says, and then you tell us everything that the Lord our God tells you, and we will willingly do it."

It is evident that Moses played the role of the exclusive mediator between Israel and God. He was the only recognized and acceptable channel through which the divine energy could flow to Israel, through which God's immanence could be perceived and His communication transmitted. No wonder, then, that Moses' protracted absence generated deep anxiety, a mood exacerbated by the people's consciousness of their impending departure from Sinai, the site of the national theophany. Their reaction was perfectly natural and understandable. What they demanded of Aaron was some material, visible entity that would fill the spiritual void created by Moses' absence, something that, by virtue of the symbolism invested in it, would extend the Sinaitic experience of closeness to God and the awareness of His ever-present providential care. It is all but certain that in demanding "a god," they intended nothing more than an appropriate object emblematic of the Divine Presence.[139] That is why Aaron could declare in all sincerity, after making the image, that the next day would be "a festival of the Lord." He uses the Tetragrammaton *YHVH*, the solemn, distinctive Israelite Name of God. There is no rejection of the national God. The people themselves associate the manufactured image with the God who brought them out of Egypt. It is the God who operates in history that they recognize, not a deity with mythological associations.[140]

By now, the parallel with the Tabernacle will surely have come to the reader's mind. Another glance at the opening section of this chapter will recall the similarities. What the people here demanded of Aaron, in order to counteract the pervasively oppressive feeling of hollowness that afflicted them, was precisely what the Tabernacle was meant to fulfill.

The question arises, of course, as to why a calf, specifically, was selected to signify the presence of God. It is tempting to point out the well-known phenomenon of bull gods[141] in ancient Egypt, and to attribute the choice to Egyptian influence. The cults of the Apis bull at Memphis and of the Mnevis bull at Heliopolis are the most famous examples, and even if these were too far from the Israelite area of settlement in Egypt to have been influential, bull worship can also be documented in the region of the Nile Delta.[142] Nevertheless, this would be far too facile a solution if only for the reason that it is inconceivable that Aaron and the people could, even for a moment, have identified the God who liberated Israel from Egyptian bondage with an Egyptian deity or have thought of representing Him in a manner characteristically Egyptian. Furthermore, the Egyptians did not worship images of the bull, but the living bull itself.

As a matter of plain fact, there is no need at all to turn to Egypt for an explanation, for the depiction of a god in the form of a bull was widespread throughout the entire ancient Near East.[143] That animal was a symbol of lordship, strength, vital energy, and fertility, and was either deified and made an object of worship or, on account of these sovereign attributes, was employed in representation of deity.

Most attractive is the suggestion that the calf made by Aaron was not at all intended to represent the Deity, but was to function as the pedestal of the invisible God of Israel.[144] Here again, we can adduce any number of examples from the art of the ancient Near East wherein gods stand upon animals, mostly bulls and lions.[145] The pedestal elevated the god above the human level,[146] and the particular animal might be suggestive of the god's attributes. Aaron's calf would then be one more example of this practice, in which case Aaron would have followed accepted artistic convention, except that since the God of Israel may not be represented in material form, His Presence on the calf would be left to human imagination.[147] This brings us back once again to the Tabernacle parallel, to the function of the cherubim, as we have explained it. The calf serves the same purpose as they do. But they were hidden from public gaze, and they did not represent any identifiable, existing reality. The calf, on the other hand, was publicly displayed, and was very much an image of a living entity. It was a being, moreover, that would inevitably tend to divert human attention to itself as the focus of consideration and away from the invisible One that it was meant to evoke. In the popular mind, the image-pedestal could not but be endowed with divinity. God was put back into nature. The fundamental, distinctive idea of the religion of Israel was thereby violated and nullified. Instead of the unique, revolutionary idea of the Divine Word enshrined in the Holy of Holies as the token of the immediacy of the Divine Presence, there was a profane, plastic image which could easily be recognized as falling within the orbit of paganism. The situation in the wilderness thus produced two different, contradictory, and mutually exclusive responses: the one illegitimate and distortive, the Golden Calf; the other legitimate and corrective, the Tabernacle. This explains why the story of the Golden Calf intersects the Tabernacle theme.

Not surprisingly, Moses became enraged when he observed, firsthand, the scene in the camp of Israel. It is doubtful, however, that his smashing of the Tablets was an impetuous act. Far more likely, it possessed legal symbolism signifying Israel's abrogation of the Covenant. In Akkadian legal terminology, the term "to break the tablet" (*tuppam ḥepû*) means to invalidate or repudiate a document or agreement. [148]

Moses' subsequent behavior has also been elucidated by ancient Near Eastern documents. [149] Exodus 32:20 describes the burning and pulverizing of the calf and the scattering of the powder over the water. It is now clear from the Ugaritic myth that recounts the destruction of the god Môt by the goddess Anath that the same cumulative series of destructive acts presents a picture of total annihilation. Similar obliterative exercises are featured in both Egyptian and Mesopotamian sources, and there can be no doubt that the purpose was to reduce the obnoxious object to absolute nonexistence.

More enigmatic is the meaning of the ritual of making the Israelites drink the mixture of water and the powder. The duplicate account in Deuteronomy 9:21 identifies the water with the brook that ran down the mountain, but does not mention the drinking. That text as it is seems to imply that the waters of the brook washed away the powder into oblivion. It might, however, be dependent on the Exodus narrative and take for granted that the drinking of the potion was well known. In that case, the account in Deuteronomy would supplement ours. The mountain brook would likely have been the single source of water for the entire camp, so that the idea was that no individual could avoid imbibing the liquid. [150]

This imposition of Moses was quite early connected by commentators with the bitter water ordeal administered to the suspected adulteress. [151]

As described in Numbers 5:11–31, the priest mixed sacral water with dust from the floor of the Tabernacle. He made the woman drink it after he had pronounced a curse on her should the accusation brought against her be the truth. In favor of the association between this ritual and our Golden Calf context is the frequent use of the unfaithful-wife motif in biblical literature as a figure of Israel's apostasy and infidelity to the Covenant with God.[152] It is pertinent to point out that our narrative contains more than a hint of this same metaphor. Three times it stamps the making of and worshipping at the calf a "great sin."[153] It so happens that this phrase is a legal term found in Akkadian documents from Ugarit and in Egyptian marriage contracts, and it always refers to adultery.[154] It is also used in the same context in Genesis 20:9, and a reflex of it appears similarly in Genesis 39:9. Otherwise, all biblical usages of the "great sin" refer to idolatry.[155] It is reasonable, therefore, to perceive in Moses' action a strong intimation of a parallel with the suspected adulteress. Quite likely, the potion administered to all the Israelites had as its purpose to determine the guilty ones, presumably the three thousand who subsequently lost their lives.[156] The two actions of Moses, this and the breaking of the Tablets, are thus seen to be closely connected, both being symbols that express verdicts of infidelity.

As was to be expected, the consequence of the apostasy was alienation from God, a tragic and disastrous condition that Moses sought to repair by prayer and intercession. This was effective, and Moses' role as intermediary between God and Israel was reaffirmed. A renewal of the Covenant took place, and a fresh set of stone Tablets of the Pact bore witness to the reconciliation.[157]

◊   ◊   ◊   ◊

The Book of Exodus closes with an account of the actual construction of the sanctuary. When it was completed,

> the cloud covered the Tent of Meeting, and the Presence of the Lord filled the Tabernacle. . . . For over the Tabernacle a cloud of the Lord rested by day, and fire would appear in it by night, in the view of all the house of Israel throughout their journeys.[158]

Notes

Introduction

1. See Hoffman, 1983:11.
2. Amos 2:10; cf. 3:1.
3. Exod. 5:2.
4. Exod. 12:30–31.
5. Exod. 12:2.
6. Deut. 5:15; cf. Exod. 20:11.
7. Exod. 23:14; Lev. 23:42–43; Deut. 16:9–12.
8. Lev. 11:45.
9. Exod. 22:20.
10. Exod. 23:9.
11. Lev. 19:33–34.
12. Deut. 5:13–15.
13. Deut. 10:17–19.
14. Deut. 15:12–15.
15. Deut. 23:8.
16. Deut. 24:17–18.
17. Deut. 24:20–22.
18. Exod. 3:6, 15, 16; 1:9.
19. Exod. 3:16.
20. Gen. 50:24.
21. Exod. 1:7. The literature on the date of the Exodus is considerable. See Rea, 1960; De Wit, 1960; Wood, 1970; Waltke, 1972; Bimson, 1978. J. H. Hayes and Miller, 1977:151–166, 264–277, is invaluable for a survey of the problems, approaches, and literature.
22. The Septuagint and Samaritan versions include the sojourn in Canaan within the 430-year reckoning. The Seder Olam Rabba 3:2 gives 210 years for the Egyptian episode. See also Hoehner, 1969.

23. Driver, 1935:403; Albright, 1961:50–51.
24. Exod. 6:16, 18, 20; cf. Num. 3:17–19; 26:58–59; 1 Chron. 6:1–3. According to Genesis 46:11, Kohath was born before Jacob migrated to Egypt, and he lived 133 years (Exod. 6:18). His son, Amram, father of Moses, lived 137 years (Exod. 6:20), and Moses was 80 years old at the Exodus (Exod. 7:7).
25. Gen. 50:23; Num. 32:39–41; Deut. 3:14; Josh. 13:31; 17:1. See, however, 1 Chron. 2:22.
26. Num. 1:7; 2:3; 7:12; Ruth 4:18–20; 1 Chron. 2:9–10.
27. Josh. 7:1; cf. 1 Chron. 2:7.
28. The Septuagint reading is 440 years.
29. See Sarna, 1970:81–85.
30. On the number 40, see Roscher, 1909; Davis, 1968:51–54, 122. On the number 12, see de Vaux, 1978:702–3.
31. Gen. 45:10.
32. Gen. 46:28; 47:1–10.
33. Exod. 12:30–31.
34. Exod. 1:11; 12:37. On the location of "Pithom and Raamses," see the next chapter.
35. On the Hyksos, see the next chapter.
36. Joseph, of course, lived many years before Rameses II.
37. On this, see the next chapter.
38. On the "Sea Peoples," see Chap. 3.
39. Text in *ANET*:378; see also Lichtheim, 1976:73–78.
40. For a discussion of the stele and its historical implications, see Wilson, 1951:244–45, 253; Gardiner, 1964:270–75; Faulkner, 1975:232–35; J. H. Hayes and Miller, 1977:152, 248, 251; de Vaux, 1978:390–91, 489–91; Finegan, 1979:312, 413 *n*.41; Spalinger, 1982:206–9.
41. Kitchen, 1966:60.
42. Text in *ANET*:320.
43. See the surveys in Weippert, 1971; J. H. Hayes and Miller, 1977:254–62; Bimson, 1978.

Chapter One

1. Gen. 12:1, 17:2, 28:14, 46:3.
2. Exod. 1:7.
3. Exod. 1:8.
4. On the Hyksos, see Säve-Söderbergh, 1951; van Seters, 1966; Redford, 1970*a*; W. C. Hayes, 1973*a*, 1973*b*; T. G. H. James, 1973.
5. On the site of Avaris, see van Seters, 1966:127–51.
6. *ANET*:231.
7. *Contra Apion* 1:14, 75ff. English translation by H. St. J. Thackeray (Cambridge, Mass.: Loeb Classical Library, 1926, pp. 193ff).

8. Exod. 1:9–10.

9. Gen. 48:3–4, 21.

10. Gen. 50:24–25.

11. Gardiner, 1961:52.

12. On this god, see Velde, 1967.

13. Gardiner, 1918.

14. *ANET*:470–71; Erman, 1966:206, 270.

15. On Goshen, see Montet, 1959:15–17, 53–54, 57–59; 1968:8, 57–59; Vergote, 1959:183–87; Albright, 1968:99, 155 *n*.8; Yeivin, 1971:243–46; Har-El, 1973:90–91, 139, 173, 194–96; Aharoni, 1979:196.

16. Exod. 1:11.

17. On Pithom and Raamses, see Uphill, 1968, 1969; Redford, 1963; Helck, 1965; van Seters, 1966:127–51; Kitchen, 1975:57–59 and notes 5–9.

18. Habachi, 1954.

19. *Bibliotheka Historica* 1:56, translated by C. H. Oldfather (Cambridge, Mass.: Loeb Classical Library, 1933, p. 197).

20. Exod. 3:22; cf. 11:2, 12:35.

21. See Bakir, 1952: esp. 1–4, 7, 88, 114; W. C. Hayes, 1973*b*: 372–81, esp. 375, 377; Baines and Málek, 1980:100.

22. Cf. Deut. 11:10–11.

23. Exod. 1:14.

24. See Erman, 1966:426–27, 434.

25. *ANET*:433; cf. Erman, 1966:69.

26. Lichtheim, 1976:170.

27. Erman, 1971:445; cf. Lichtheim, 1973:184ff.

28. Ibid.

29. Exod. 1:14; 5:7–8, 13–14.

30. See Clarke and Engelbach, 1931.

31. On brickmaking and brickbuilding in Egypt, see L. Lucas, 1962:48–50, 74–75; Kitchen, 1976; id., 1977:77–78; Finegan, 1979:270; Spencer, 1979.

32. *ANET*:433. Cf. Lichtheim, 1973:187; Erman, 1966:69.

33. Exod. 1:12.

34. Exod. 1:15–16.

35. Lichtheim, 1973:220ff; Erman, 1966:36ff.

36. Gen. 38:28–29. See Preuss, 1978:36–39.

37. Cf. Gordis, 1968:230.

38. *ANET*:381; Lichtheim, 1976:107f.

39. See Lambert and Millard, 1969:9, 60–61, 62–63, 153 note to line 259.

40. See Greenberg, 1969:26.

41. Rand, 1970.

42. For the use of the stem *sh-p-r*, cf. Gen. 49:21; Ps. 16:6; Job 26:13; Dan. 3:32, 4:24, 6:2. See Albright, 1954:229 no.233; Kitchen, 1966:144.

43. See *UT*, 19:2081; Albright, 1954:229 *n*.50.

44. Exod. 1:17.

45. Daube, 1972:1–22.
46. Gen. 42:18.
47. Deut. 25:18.
48. Job 1:1, 8.
49. Exod. 1:22.

Chapter Two

1. The stories of Joseph and the Book of Esther are other examples of this biblical literary technique. On the birth story of Moses, see Ackerman, 1974.
2. Cf. Gen. 18:10; 25:23; Judg. 13:3.
3. Exod. 2:1–10.
4. Exod. 12:35–36.
5. Exod. 2:2.
6. Gen. 1:4, 10, 12, 18, 21, 25, 31.
7. Sarna, 1970:49.
8. Lambdin, 1953:149.
9. L. Lucas, 1962:130, 137.
10. See Rank, 1959; Childs, 1965, 1:224–30, and bibliography on p. 380, §78 [1]; Redford, 1967, on which see Greenberg, 1969:199 *n*.3.
11. For fullest text with commentary, see Lewis, 1980.
12. ANET:119; see also Beyerlin, 1978:98–99.
13. Cf. Jacob, 1942.
14. On the *ēntu* (*ēnetu*) priestess, see Harris, 1963; Lewis, 1980:37–38.
15. Cogan, 1968.
16. Exod. 2:6.
17. Erman, 1971:76.
18. Pirenne, 1959; Murray, 1964:68–72; Faulkner, 1975:231.
19. Childs, 1965.
20. Exod. 2:10.
21. Cf. 2 Sam. 22:17; Ps. 18:17.
22. Cassuto, 1967:20–21. See NJPS, Isa. 63:11, fn. j-j.
23. Gardiner, 1936; Černý, 1951; Griffiths, 1953; Albright, 1975*a*:123; de Vaux, 1978:329.
24. Gardiner, 1961:277.
25. Ibid.
26. Williams, 1972; cf. Murray, 1964:73–77.
27. Kitchen, 1965:343–44.
28. Exod. 2:11.
29. Exod. 2:11–12.
30. See Kimelman, 1984.
31. Exod. 2:13–15.
32. Gen. 24:11, 29:2.
33. Exod. 2:16–21.

34. Gen. 25:2, 4; Num. 31:8; Josh. 13:21.

35. Bartlett, 1973; de Vaux, 1978:223, 330–38.

36. Num. 22:4, 7; 25:6–7, 16; 31:1–12; Josh. 13:21; Judg. chaps. 6–8; Isa. 9:3, 10:26; Ps. 83:10.

37. Exod. 2:18. For another solution, see Albright, 1963.

38. Gen. 29:5; cf. Gen. 24:47, 28:5. Cf. also Mephibosheth "son of Saul" in 2 Sam. 19:25, although he was Saul's grandson, and "Jehu son of Nimshi" in 1 Kings 19:16 and 2 Kings 9:20, who is the grandson of Nimshi in 2 Kings 9:2, 14.

39. Exod. 3:1, 18:1.

40. Cf. Gen. 49:3 (Heb. *yeter*).

41. See Abramsky, 1975.

42. Num. 24:21.

43. Exod. 2:22.

44. Exod. 2:17.

45. Exod. 12:39.

46. Exod. 2:23–25.

47. Ibid.

Chapter Three

1. Exod. 3:1.

2. Kitchen, 1975:124.

3. See Clifford, 1972:107–31 for a different view.

4. Exod. 3:2–3.

5. Feliks, 1968:110; see Zohary, 1982:140–41, for a different view.

6. Erman, 1971:226–27; Montet, 1958:31, 155.

7. Cf. Gen. 18:4.

8. Erman, 1971:226.

9. Exod. Chaps. 28–29; Lev. Chap. 8. Cf. Exod. 29:20.

10. On this topic, see Kaufmann, 1942–1956, I–III:245–47; Heschel, 1966.

11. *ANET*: 68–69.

12. On this topic, see further Chapter Nine, pp. 213–15.

13. Exod. 13:21f; Num. 9:15–16, 14:14; Deut. 1:33, 4:24, 9:3; Ps. 78:14; Neh. 9:12, 19.

14. Ezek. 1:4, 13, 27; 8:2.

15. Contrast, however, 1 Kings 19:11–12.

16. The multiple sense of the Scriptures is emphasized in rabbinic literature. Cf. B. Sanhedrin 34a; B. Shabbat 88b; Numbers Rabba, *Naso'*, 13:15.

17. Exod. 3:6.

18. Gen. 17:1.

19. Gen. 26:24.

20. Gen. 46:3.

21. Exod. 20:2; Deut. 5:6. Cf. Exod. 29:46; Lev. 19:36, 25:38.

22. Exod. 6:2.

23. B. Sanhedrin 64b; B. Berakhoth 31b, Nedarim 3a.

24. *KAI*, 181, *l*. 1, p. 33; *ANET*:320.

25. *KAI*, 24, *ll*. 1, 9, pp. 4–5; *ANET*:500, 654.

26. *KAI*, 26, I, *l*. 1, p. 5. *ANET*:499, 653.

27. *KAI*, 13, *l*. 1, p. 2; *ANET*:662.

28. *KAI*, 10, *l*. 1, p. 2; *ANET*:502, 656. Cf. also *KAI*, 54, 57, 59, 276.

29. *KAI*, 202, *l*. 2, p. 37; *ANET*:501, 655. On the name, see Millard, 1978.

30. *KAI*, 214, *l*. 1, p. 38.

31. *KAI*, 216, *l*. 1, p. 40; *ANET*:501, 655. So *KAI*, 217, *l*. 1.

32. On "the God of the Father(s)," see Alt, 1968; Hyatt, 1955; Gemser, 1958; Lewy, 1961; Albright, 1968:68; Haran, 1965 esp. 51–52 *n*.34; Cross, 1973:4–43; de Vaux, 1978:267–82.

33. Gordon, 1949:6; Kitchen, 1975:50, 121.

34. *UT*, 19:493, *b'l*; 19:749, *hd*; 19:761, *hyn*; 19:1335, ktr; 2331 *rkb*.

35. Cf. Tallqvist, 1938.

36. See note 32 above.

37. Lewy, 1961:41f, and note 71.

38. *ANET*:628f.

39. Cited by de Vaux, 1978:270 *n*.14.

40. See Malamat, 1971:987.

41. Cf. Josh. 24:2.

42. See Kaufmann, 1942–1956, IV–V:25–38.

43. Gen. 32:31.

44. Exod. 33:20.

45. Judg. 6:22–23.

46. Judg. 13:22.

47. Exod. 3:7–10.

48. Gen. 12:10; 26:1; 41:54; 43:1; 45:11; 47:4, 13.

49. *ANET*:80. On this tradition, see Fensham, 1966*a*.

50. *ANET*:237–38.

51. Deut. 8:7–8.

52. Judg. 14:8–9.

53. 1 Sam. 14:25–27.

54. Deut. 32:13; Ps. 81:17.

55. See Goor and Nurock, 1968.

56. Josh. Chap. 12.

57. Exod. 3:11.

58. Amos 7:14–15, 3:8.

59. Isa. 6:5.

60. Jer. 1:6.

61. Jer. 20:7, 9.

62. Exod. 3:12.

63. Exod. 3:13.

64. On the problem of the Divine Name, see Childs, 1974:60–80.

65. "Almighty" for *shaddai* is the tradition of the Septuagint and Vulgate. For an extensive bibliography, see Redford, 1970*b*:129 *n.*1., to which add Cross, 1973:52–60.

66. Gen. 17:1, 28:3, 35:11, 43:14, 48:3. Its use in Ruth 1:20f. is due to that book's poetic substratum and archaizing tendencies. See J. M. Myers, 1955; Sasson, 1979:34.

67. Num 1:6; 2:12; 7:36, 41; 10:19.

68. Num. 1:12; 2:25; 7:66, 71; 10:25.

69. Cross, 1973:53.

70. Exod. 6:20; Num. 26:59.

71. Albright, 1968:168–72.

72. Malamat, 1971:982.

73. Evans, 1958; McKenzie, 1959; *TDOT*, 4:122–31; Reviv, 1983.

74. Exod. 12:21, 17:5–6, 18:12, 19:7, 24:14.

75. Exod. 3:18.

76. Exod. 1:15, 16, 19; 2:6, 7, 11, 13. "God of the Hebrews" occurs in Exod. 3:18; 5:3; 7:16; 9:1, 13; 10:3.

77. Cf. Gen. 14:13; Jonah 1:9.

78. Gen. 39:14, 17; 40:15; 41:12; 43:32.

79. 1 Sam. Chaps. 4, 13, 14, and 29:3.

80. On the Habiru, see de Vaux, 1978:209–16 and the literature cited there, to which add Rowton, 1976.

81. Josh. 24:2, 3, 14; see CAD 4, p. 8.

82. Gen. 11:14ff.

83. Gen. 24:10, 25:20, 31:20.

84. Gen. 10:21.

85. Exod. 3:18, 5:1–3, 8:22–25; cf. 10:7–11, 24, 26.

86. Erman, 1971:124; Kitchen, 1975:156–57. See also Meshel, 1982:20; Haran, 1978:300–3; Loewenstamm, 1965:48–49.

87. Exod. 3:21–22.

88. On this topic see Coats, 1968*a*; Childs, 1974:175–77.

89. Exod. 11:2.

90. Exod. 12:35–36.

91. Exod. 3:21, 11:2–3, 12:35–36.

92. Deut. 15:13–15.

93. Exod. 4:2–5, 6–7, 9.

94. Budge, 1962:ix; cf. Frankfort, 1961:3–4.

95. Y. Kaufmann, 1960:21–24, esp. 23 *n.*1.

96. Morenz, 1973:26–27.

97. Budge, 1978; Erman, 1971:143, 308, 353, 355; Breasted, 1961:235–71; Wilson, 1951:243; Murray, 1964:137; Borghouts, 1978.

98. On the "signs," see Kaufmann, 1960:80–87; Greenberg, 1969:87–88; Childs, 1974:67; Fishbane, 1975.

99. So Exod. 15:22–25; Chap. 16; 17:1–7 et al.

100. *TDOT*, 1:167–88.

101. Cf. Isa. 10:5, 24; 14:5; Jer. 48:17; Ezek. 7:11, 19:11–14; Ps. 110:2. See Joines, 1974:85.

102. Erman, 1971:60; Murray, 1964:113.

103. See Preuss, 1978:323–39. Hansen's disease differs from the descriptions given in the Bible in that it does not affect clothing, leather, and walls of a house, or produce whiteness and affliction of the scalp. Also, its progress is very slow and takes years to develop, and no significant changes can be discernible in the course of a seven-day period. On the other hand, the biblical texts do not mention the characteristic symptoms of true leprosy such as swelling and hardening of the skin and the leonine appearance.

104. Cf. Num. 12:10; Deut. 24:8–9; 2 Kings 5:26f; 15:5 = 2 Chron. 26:16–21. See Gaster, 1975, 2:878, §93.

105. Exod. 4:10.

106. See Tigay, 1978.

107. Exod. 4:11–12.

108. Exod. 4:13.

Chapter Four

1. Exod. 3:19.

2. Exod. 4:21.

3. Exod. 7:3; 9:12; 10:1, 20, 27; 11:10; 14:4, 8, 17.

4. Jer. 4:19.

5. Jer. 31:19.

6. Lam. 2:11.

7. Ps. 16:7.

8. Jer. 11:20, 17:10, 20:12; Ps. 7:10.

9. Pedersen, 1926: I–II:102–4, 127, 145, 150, 157, 172, 238, 414, 536, note.

10. Exod. 7:13, 14, 22; 8:11, 15, 28; 9:7, 34, 35; 13:15.

11. See notes 2 and 3, above.

12. Exod. 9:12.

13. Exod. 9:34–35.

14. For a bibliography of recent studies on the hardening of the pharaoh's heart, see Kaiser, 1983:253 *n*.17, to which add Kaufmann, 1960:75–76, and Kaiser's own observations (pp. 251–56). Sarah Ben Reuben, 1984, suggests the Egyptian concept of the "weighing of the heart" as the source of the biblical expression. For a fuller study of the Egyptian background, see Wilson, 1979. For the hardening motif in Ezekiel, see Greenberg, 1983:254, 369.

15. It should be noted that the biblical motif is not identical with the Greek concept of *até* as defined by Dodds, 1957:36ff, for only after the "disease of the

inner-consciousness" has been brought about through the free exercise of a person's will does God utilize this condition for His purposes. An innocent person is not an inescapable victim of God's deliberate deception, as in the Greek concept.

16. Exod. 5:2. On the meaning of *yada'*, "to know," cf. Huffmon-Parker, 1966*a*, *b*.

17. See Nims, 1950.

18. Exod. 5:20–21.

19. Exod. 5:22–23.

20. Exod. 6:2–8.

21. Exod. 5:2.

22. Montet, 1968:91–94; J. H. Hayes and Miller, 1977:194–96.

23. Erman, 1966:36–38; Maspero, 1967:21–27; Simpson, 1972:16–19.

24. Exod. 7:11.

25. Keimer, 1947:16–17; Noerdlinger, 1956:26; Mannix, 1960:32; Gibson, 1967:13.

26. On the plagues narrative as a whole, see Loewenstamm, 1965:25–79; Greenberg, 1969:151–92; Childs, 1974:121–70; J. H. Hayes and Miller, 1977:198–200.

27. Maspero, 1967:165; Lichtheim, 1980:148.

28. *ANET*:441.

29. Kramer, 1963:162–64; Beyerlin, 1978:97.

30. *ANET*:445, l. 35.

31. Lambert and Millard, 1969:98–101.

32. Exod. 10:14–15.

33. *Encyclopaedia Britannica* (Micropaedia) 6:293; (Macropaedia) 12:177–78.

34. Exod. 10:21.

35. Montet, 1968:98.

36. *ANET*:445. The *Encyclopaedia Britannica* (Macropaedia), 13:105, reports that during the spring, sandstorms may persist for three or four days.

37. Hort, 1957–1958.

38. Rofé, 1969:157; Loewenstamm, 1965:30–42, has a different division of the plagues in Ps. 78:42–51.

39. See Greenberg, 1971:606–7; Zevit, 1976.

40. Sarna, 1957.

41. On this theme, see Loewenstamm, 1965:49–51.

42. Wisdom of Solomon 12:23–27, 16:1–14; cf. Jubilees 48:5.

43. Aling, 1981:106–9.

44. See Frankfort, 1978:30–31, 190–92, 290.

45. Frankfort, 1961:132; id., 1978:159.

46. Budge, 1969, 2:378; Frankfort, 1961:150; Montet, 1968:96.

47. Gen. 31:53.

48. Gen. 35:2–4.

49. Exod. 8:14, 9:11.

50. Kaufmann, 1942–1956, I–III:276; ibid., IV–V:41f; id., 1960:223–26.
51. Exod. 20:3.

Chapter Five

1. Exod. 12:2.
2. Finegan, 1959:564–66; E. O. James, 1963:44–69; Bleeker, 1967.
3. Specified in Exod. 13:4, 23:15; Deut. 16:1, 8.
4. Exod. 23:14–17, 34:18–23; Lev. Chap. 23; Deut. 16:1–17.
5. Exod. 13:4, 23:15, 34:18; Deut. 16:1.
6. 1 Kings 6:1, 37.
7. 1 Kings 8:2.
8. 1 Kings 6:38.
9. The inscriptions from Arad mention "the month of *sah*"—Aharoni, 1975:42; cf. Isa. 18:4; Jer. 4:11—Soggin, 1965; on the calendars of biblical Israel, see Morgenstern, 1924, 1935; Van Goudoever, 1961; de Vaux, 1961:190–93; Finegan, 1964.
10. Jer. 36:22–23.
11. Jer. 40:5–12, 41:8.
12. Esther 2:16; 3:7, 13.
13. Exod. 23:16, 34:22.
14. *KAI*, 182; *ANET*:320.
15. Lev. 19:23–25.
16. The four-day interval between securing the lamb and its slaughter is explained by Mekhilta d'R. Yishmael to Exod. 12:6 (edited by Horovitz-Rabin; Jerusalem, 1960, p. 14), as due to the need for the males to be circumcised in time for the *pesah* sacrifice.
17. Josh. 4:19.
18. Lev. 23:27.
19. Lev. 25:9–10.
20. Exod. 12:5–10.
21. Exod. 12:11; cf. 12:27.
22. Exod. 12:15, 17–18, 20.
23. Gen. 19:3.
24. Judg. 6:19–22.
25. 1 Sam. 28:24.
26. Exod. 29:2, 23; Lev. 2:5; 7:12; 8:2, 26 et al.
27. See Segal, 1963:107.
28. Liddell and Scott, 1968:1082, 1072.
29. See Gordon, 1965:296 *n*.4.
30. Exod. 12:13, 23, 27.
31. For the varied traditions, see Brock, 1952; Glasson, 1959; Lieberman, 1962:50–51; Segal, 1963:95; Loewenstamm, 1965:85 and note 21, 130; Weiss, 1981:255–58.

32. Ezek. 45:21.

33. On the character and history of the *pesah*, see Kaufmann, 1942–1956, I–III:122f, 131, 216, 547; ibid., IV–V:132, 430, 460, 481–88, 494; de Vaux, 1961:484; id., 1978:366; Weinfeld, 1972:216f, 230f; Haran, 1978:259f, 317–48; Ginsberg, 1982:42–48, 51–58, 78–83.

34. Lev. 23:9–14.

35. Exod. 12:15.

36. Exod. 12:19–20.

37. Exod. 13:7; cf. Deut. 16:4.

38. Mishnah Pesahim 2:5; cf. Mishnah Hallah 1:1.

39. Exod. 23:18.

40. Lev. 2:11.

41. Lev. 6:9–10.

42. Lev. 7:13.

43. Lev. 23:17–20.

44. B. Berakhoth 17a; cf. Mekhilta d'R. Yishmael, Beshallah 2:2 (edited by Horovitz-Rabin), p. 93; Genesis Rabba 34:12; Yalkut Ruth 60.

45. Matt. 16:6; Mark 8:15; Luke 12:1; 1 Cor. 5:6ff; Gal. 5:9.

46. *Quaestiones Romanae* 109.

47. Cf. Deut. 32:32.

48. See Zohary, 1982:95, 100.

49. B. Pesahim 39a; Y. Pesahim 2:5 (29c).

50. Exod. 12:7, 23.

51. Exod. 12:13, 23.

52. Cf. Gen. 9:4; Lev. 17:11, 14; Deut. 12:23; Ps. 72:14.

53. Cf. Ezek. 9:6.

54. Cf. Lev. 14:4, 6, 49, 51, 52; Num. 19:6, 18; Ps. 51:9.

55. See Zohary, 1982:96.

56. Exod. 12:29.

57. Exod. 13:2, 12, 13, 15; 22:28–29; 34:19; Lev. 27:26; Num. 3:13, 40–46; 18:15; Deut. 15:19.

58. Exod. 23:19; 34:26; Lev. 23:17; Num. 28:26.

59. Exod. 13:2, 13, 15; 22:28; 34:19; Num. 3:12, 13, 40–46; 18:15.

60. Cf. Gen. 43:33; Deut. 21:17.

61. Jer. 2:3.

62. Exod. 4:22f.

63. Exod. 12:32.

64. Exod. 12:37. Hebrew *taf* includes the womenfolk; so Gen. 47:12; Exod. 10:10–11, 24; Num. 32:16, 24.

65. Exod. 12:38.

66. Num. 1:46–47; 2:32.

67. Exod. 30:12–16; 38:25–26.

68. Num. 26:51.

69. Exod. 1:7; cf. Deut. 1:10.

70. Exod. 1:9.

71. Exod. 1:12.
72. Exod. 1:19.
73. Clark, 1955.
74. Exod. 18:13–23.
75. The information given here is based on the article "population" in the *Encyclopaedia Britannica* (Macropaedia), 14:815–16.
76. NWDB:250.
77. *ISBE* (1915), 4:2166ff.
78. Information drawn from *Encyclopaedia Britannica* (Micropaedia), IV:309.
79. Kuznits, 1975:63. These statistics were drawn to my attention by Professor Jonathan D. Sarna.
80. A. Lucas, 1944:164–68.
81. Exod. 6:16, 18, 20.
82. *Wars*, 2:385 (Cambridge, Mass.: Loeb Classical Library edition, 2:475).
83. *Bibliotheka Historica*, I, 31:8 (Cambridge, Mass.: Loeb Classical Library edition, pp. 103–4).
84. Erman, 1971:310; Wilson, 1951:271; Albright, 1975b:108.
85. Finley, 1983:80.
86. See below, chapter VI.
87. See Gray, 1903:12–13.
88. Judg. 6:15; cf. 1 Sam. 9:21; cf. also 1 Sam. 10:19 with v.21; 23:23; Mic. 5:1 for *'elef* as clan or family unit.
89. So Petrie, 1911:40–47; Finegan, 1963:91–95.
90. Mendenhall, 1958; de Vaux, 1978:777–78; Malamat, 1970:9–10.
91. 1 Kings 6:1.
92. Deut. 12:9–11.
93. 1 Kings 5:17–19.
94. 1 Kings 8:16, 56.
95. On the population of Israel at this time, see Albright, 1925; id., 1957:291; Baron, 1971:10–22, 23–73; de Vaux, 1978:20; Shiloh, 1980. Interestingly, already in the fourteenth century C.E., Ibn Khaldun suggested that the figure of 600,000 was based on the population of Solomon's time; see Ibn Khaldun, 1967, 1:18.
96. Cf. Wilson, 1964:339.

Chapter Six

1. Exod. 13:17–18.
2. Gardiner, 1920; Oren, 1973.
3. Katzenstein, 1982:111.
4. Cf. Gen. 49:22; 2 Sam. 22:30 = Ps. 18:30.
5. Gen. 20:1, 25:18; Exod. 15:22; 1 Sam. 15:7, 27:8.
6. ANET:21.
7. ANET:446.

8. See note 2, above; Gardiner, 1961:253; Aharoni, 1979:45–48.

9. Dothan, 1982.

10. On the "Sea Peoples," see Barnett, 1975.

11. For the biblical references to the Cretan connection of the Philistines, cf. Gen. 10:14 = 1 Chron. 1:12; Deut. 2:23; Jer. 47:4; Ezek. 25:16; Amos 9:7; Zeph. 2:5. Cf. also 1 Sam. 30:14, "the Negeb of the Cherethites"; 2 Sam. 15:18 et al., "The Cherethites and Pelethites."

12. Exod. 13:18.

13. See *Encyclopaedia Britannica* (Macropaedia), 14:495, 15:544.

14. Lambdin, 1953:153.

15. Simons, 1959:§417; Towers, 1959; Copisarow, 1962; Snaith, 1965; Batto, 1984.

16. See Har-El, 1973, who carefully examines the various theories relating to the wilderness journeying. See also De Wit, 1960; Rea, 1961; Haran, 1971; G. I. Davies, 1979. An excellent survey of the issues involved is given by Finegan, 1963:77–95.

17. Exod. 13:20, 14:1. Cf. Num. 33:7–8.

18. Ezek. 30:17.

19. Oren, 1984:7–44.

20. See Eissfeldt, 1932; Albright, 1950; Sarna, 1971.

21. *KAI*, 50, ll. 2–3, p. 12; Beyerlin, 1978:253–54.

22. Exod. 14:5.

23. Exod. 14:13–14.

24. Cf. Gottwald, 1979:210–19; cf. Mendenhall, 1962.

25. Exod. 13:21–22.

26. Exod. 14:19–20.

27. Finegan, 1979:94–95.

28. Hab. 3:9–10.

29. Ps. 18:8, 10–12 = 2 Sam. 22:8, 10–12.

30. Mann, 1971:15–30; Cross, 1973:164–66.

31. Plastaras, 1966:186.

32. 1 Kings 8:10–11.

33. Isa. 6:4.

34. Exod. Chap. 15. On the motif of the splitting of the sea, see Loewenstamm, 1965:101–29; Goldin, 1971.

35. Kitchen, 1975:133 *n*.89; Lichtheim, 1976:6, 35, 57–59, 73.

36. Ps. 66:6; 77:17–21; 78:13, 53; 106:9–11, 22; 114:3, 5; 136:13–15.

37. Ps. 66:5–6.

38. Ps. 77:15–21.

39. Josh. 4:22–28.

40. Isa. 51:9–10.

41. Isa. 63:11–13.

42. See Ginzberg, 1946, 6:12 *n*.60.

43. Exod. Chap. 16.

44. Ps. 105:39; cf. Ps. 78:24.

45. Ps. 104:14; cf. Job 28:5.

46. Exod. 16:15.

47. *UT*, 19, 1504.

48. *CAD*, 10, 1:212.

49. Ezra 5:4.

50. See Jastrow, 796, *man*.

51. Exod. 16:35; Num. 11:6; Josh. 5:12, Neh. 9:20–21.

52. Exod. 16:14, 20, 21–31; Num. 11:6–9.

53. See Bodenheimer, 1947; Bates, 1959/60; Orni and Ephrat, 1973:186.

54. Exod. 16:32–34.

55. See Malina, 1968. On the murmuring motif, see Coats, 1968*b*.

56. See Orni and Ephrat, 1973:189–90; see the report of Judith Miller, *New York Times*, 31 October 1984, p. C3.

57. Exod. 17:8–16. On the narrative, see Coats, 1975.

58. Lev. 19:14.

59. Lev. 19:32.

60. Lev. 25:17.

61. Lev. 25:35–36.

62. Lev. 25:39, 43.

63. Exod. 33:11; Num. 13:8; 1 Chron. 7:26–27. Cf. Num. 1:10; 2:18.

64. Exod. 33:11; Num. 11:28.

65. Exod. 24:14.

66. *Antiquities* III, ii, 4 (Cambridge, Mass.: Loeb Classical Library edition, III, 54, p. 235).

67. Exod. 31:2.

68. See Ackerman, 1975: esp. 12.

69. Childs, 1974:315.

70. Cf. the commentary of Samuel b. Meir (RaShBaM, ca. 1080– ca. 1174 C.E.) to Exod. 17:11.

71. On ensigns, see Wevers, 1962.

72. On twelve-tribe confederations, see de Vaux, 1978:695–702, 738–43.

73. Gen. 36:12, 22; 14:6; Deut. 2:12, 22.

74. Num. 13:29.

75. Num. 24:20.

76. Judg. 3:12–13; 6:3–6, 33; 7:12; 10:12.

77. 1 Sam. 14:48; Chap. 15.

78. Cf. 1 Sam. 27:8, 30:18; 2 Sam. 1:1.

79. See Childs, 1962; Eising, 1980; Yerushalmi, 1982: esp. 5–26.

80. Cf. Exod. 20:8; Deut. 5:15; Ps. 103:18.

81. Exod. Chap. 18.

82. Exod. 18:13–27.

83. 1 Kings 5:15–32.

84. *Antiquities* III, iv, 2 (Loeb Classical Library edition, III, 73, pp. 352– 53).

85. Cf. Sifrei, *Beha'alothekha*, §78.

86. See B. Zevahim 116a; Mekhilta d'R. Yishmael, *Yithro* 1:1 (edited by Horovitz-Rabin, p. 188).

87. Exod. 18:5.

88. Exod. 18:16, 20.

89. Num. 10:11, 29–32.

90. Glueck, 1967.

91. Fensham, 1964; Cody, 1968.

92. McCarthy, 1963:162–63, 172.

Chapter Seven

1. Exod. 19:1.

2. Exod. 19:5–6.

3. See Deut. 7:6, 14:2, 26:18; Mal. 3:17; Ps. 135:4; Eccl. 2:8; 1 Chron. 29:3: On this word, see Greenberg, 1971; Landsberger, 1954; Held, 1961; Uffenheimer, 1973:86; Loewenstamm, 1983.

4. On this word, see von Soden, AHW:1041, cf. 1053; Driver and Miles, 1955:221–22.

5. Collon, 1975:12–13, 170–71.

6. On the destruction of Ugarit, see Schaeffer, 1983:74–75.

7. *UT*, 17:1, p. 283, no. 2060, on which, see Huffmon and Parker, 1966*b*:37.

8. On this verse, see Moran, 1962.

9. Exod. 19:8; 24:3, 7.

10. Exod. 19:10–13, 15.

11. Exod. 19:16–19.

12. Isa. 13:13.

13. Joel 2:10.

14. On this phenomenon in the Bible and the ancient Near East, see Kaufmann, 1960:70–72; Kingsbury, 1967; Loewenstamm, 1980:173–89.

15. On the *b'rit*, see Weinfeld, 1975:253–79, and the extensive bibliography given there.

16. McCarthy, 1963:19.

17. Ibid., pp. 15–16; Gadd, 1971:118; *ANEP*, nos. 298–302.

18. McCarthy, 1963:18–19.

19. Ibid., pp. 21–50.

20. Ibid., pp. 51–67.

21. Ibid., pp. 68–79.

22. For the text, see *ANET*:199–203.

23. Cf. the Old Babylonian compendium called *ana ittishu*; see Landsberger, 1937.

24. Mendenhall, 1954*a*, 1954*b*, 1955, has drawn attention to the relevant material. See also Baltzer, 1971; McCarthy, 1963; Hillers, 1969; Kitchen, 1975:90–102; Uffenheimer, 1973:70–94.

25. Exod. 20:2; Deut. 5:6. See above, Chapter Three, for a discussion of this self-identifying formula.

26. Cf. Deut. 10:5; 31:9, 24–26; 1 Kings 8:9 = 2 Chron. 5:10.

27. ANET:205.

28. Deut. 31:10–11, 12–13; cf. Exod. 24:7.

29. Deut. 4:26, 30:19, 32:1.

30. Cf. Josh. 24:19–20.

31. Kaufmann, 1942–1956, has repeatedly made this point; cf. ibid., I–III:185, IV–V:76–77.

32. ANET:412–25.

33. ANET:425–30; Lambert, 1960.

34. Albright, 1957:228–29; Reiner, 1958:13–14; Beyerlin, 1978:131–23.

35. Budge, 1960:572–84; Allen, 1974:97–99; Lichtheim, 1976:124–27; Beyerlin, 1978:63–67; ANET:34–36.

36. ANET:34–36.

37. 2 Chron. 19:5–11.

38. 2 Chron. Chaps. 29–31.

39. 2 Kings Chaps. 22–23 = 2 Chron. Chaps. 34–35.

40. See Kaufmann, 1942–1956, IV–V:587f.

41. ANEP no. 515.

42. ANET:165, 177, 178.

43. Cf. Exod. 21:1; Deut. 31:1, 10–13; Neh. 8:1–8.

44. See ANET:331.

45. Exod. 20:3–5.

46. Säve-Söderbergh, 1961:124.

47. Gen. 2:2–3.

48. Exod. 20:8–11.

49. Exod. 31:13–17.

50. Exod. 16:5, 23, 25, 29.

51. Lewy and Lewy, 1942–1943.

52. Barton, 1929:253.

53. Lambert and Millard, 1969:63.

54. ANET:91.

55. ANET:94.

56. ANET:134.

57. ANET:104.

58. ANET:149–50.

59. Hooke, 1962:53.

60. Barton, 1917:258–59.

61. Hallo, 1977.

62. On the Sabbath, see de Vaux, 1961:475–83; Andreasen, 1972; Tsevat, 1972; Bacchiocchi, 1977, 1980; Tigay, 1978; Zerubavel, 1985.

63. Gen. 11:26.

64. Exod. 6:20–26; Num. 26:59. On the question of the pre-Israelite use of *YHVH* as a phrase, see Barr, 1959.

65. This was noted by Maimonides, *Guide*, 1:63.

66. See Kaufmann, 1960:221–41.

67. See Radin, 1957:343–74, esp. 364, 366, 368–69; Albright, 1957:257–58; Finley, 1959:147.

68. On this theory, see Rowley, 1950:149–55; id., 1963:48–57; Kaufmann, 1960:242–44; Meek, 1960:93–96; de Vaux. 1978:330–38. See also Abramsky, 1975:35–39.

69. *N.B.*: Exod. 18:10–12 has Jethro bring sacrifices to *'elohim*, even though he acknowledges YHVH.

70. Freud, 1959.

71. The following sketch of the Akhenaten phenomenon is based on Wilson, 1951:206–35; Bratton, 1961; Steindorff and Seele, 1963:201–21; Gardiner, 1964:212–46; Redford, 1967:88–169, 170–82; Breasted, 1961:272–78, 297; Manchip-White, 1970:80–81, 96–98, 169–74; Giles, 1970; Finegan, 1963:101–16; 1979:279–87; Collier, 1972; W. C. Hayes, 1973*b*; Aldred, 1975; Redford, 1984.

72. Cf. Jer. 46:25; Ezek. 30:14–16.

73. Sauneron, 1960:55; T. G. H. James, 1979:143–44.

74. *ANET*:371; Erman, 1966:288–91; Lichtheim, 1976:96–100.

75. See, however, Žabkar, 1954:87–101, esp. 94–96.

76. On this issue, see Weiss-Rosmarin, 1939; Baron, 1972; Kaufmann, 1940; id., 1960:226, and note 6; Albright, 1957:12–13, 218–23.

Chapter Eight

1. See Thompson, 1952; Paul, 1970; Boecker, 1980:135–75.

2. Cf. Lev. 19:2.

3. For a list of the major parallels, see Greengus, 1976:533–34.

4. Cf. Paul, 1970:102.

5. See Finkelstein, 1961:71; Speiser, 1963; Paul, 1970:3–26; Boecker, 1980:53–56.

6. *ANET*:523–25. See Kramer, 1963:83–85; Finkelstein, 1968–69; Boecker, 1980:57–58.

7. *ANET*:159–61. See Kramer, 1963:87–88; Gadd, 1971:634–35; Boecker, 1980:58–60.

8. *ANET*:161–63; Goetze, 1956; Yaron, 1969. See Gadd, 1971:635; Boecker, 1980:60–65.

9. *ANET*:163–80; Driver and Miles, 1952, 1955. See Gordon, 1957; Wiseman, 1962; Gadd, 1973:184–208; Boecker, 1980:67–133.

10. See Speiser, 1958; Finkelstein, 1970:249; Boecker, 1980:78.

11. *ANET*:180–88; Driver and Miles, 1935. See Smith, 1976:104–8.

12. *ANET*:188–97; Neufeld, 1951. See Gütterbock, 1954; Gurney, 1964:88–103.

13. See Wilson, 1951:49–50; id., 1954:172–73; Hawkes-Woolley, 1963:488; W. C. Hayes, 1973*b*:357; Lorton, 1979:464.

14. Diodorus Siculus I, 79, 1. See M. Smith, 1978:39* and notes.

15. Boecker, 1980:55; see also next note.

16. Finkelstein, 1961:101–3; Wiseman, 1962:166; Oppenheim, 1964:23, 158; Paul, 1970:25–26.

17. Cassuto, 1967:254–316.

18. See Sarna, 1970:185–87.

19. Num. 27:1–11.

20. Cf. Gen. 24:59; Exod. 2:7; 2 Kings 11:2.

21. Cf. Prov. 6:1, 11:15, 17:18, 20:16–17, 27:13.

22. Jer. 32:6–12.

23. For recent studies on Israelite law, see Daube, 1947; Kaufmann, 1960:166–72; Greenberg, 1960; de Vaux, 1961:143–63; Falk, 1964; Noth, 1966; Paul, 1970; Loewenstamm, 1971; Jackson, 1975; Greengus, 1976; Boecker, 1980; Sonsino, 1984.

24. Exod. 22:21–23.

25. Exod. 22:24–26.

26. Exod. 22:27–30.

27. Exod. 23:1–3.

28. Exod. 23:4–5.

29. Exod. 19:6.

30. Exod. 19:8; 24:3, 7.

31. Exod. 21:1, 24:3–4.

32. Cf. Ps. 1, 19, 119.

33. Gemser, 1953; Sonsino, 1980.

34. For Eshnunna, see ANET:162, §§12, 13, 24, 34, 50.

35. ANET:175, §§209, 211.

36. ANET:185, A §55.

37. ANET:175, §210.

38. ANET:176, §§229–31.

39. See Deut. 25:11–12.

40. ANET:525, §22 (B §29).

41. ANET:175, §202.

42. ANET:175, §195.

43. ANET:175, §218.

44. ANET:175, §205.

45. ANET:177, §282.

46. ANET:175, §192–93.

47. ANET:175, §194.

48. ANET:180, A §4.

49. ANET:180, A §5.

50. ANET:181, A §9.

51. ANET:181, A §§15, 19, 20.

52. ANET:181, A §§7, 18, 19, 21; B §§7, 8, 9, 14, 15, 18; C §§2, 3, 8; F §1; N §2. Judicial flogging is permitted in Deut. 25:1–3 (cf. Deut. 22:18), but is limited to a maximum of forty strokes.

53. ANET:181, A §18.

54. ANET:183, A §40.

55. ANET:187, F §1.

56. Cf. Driver and Miles, 1952:494.

57. ANET:166–67, §§6, 7, 10, 15, 16, 19.

58. ANET:170, §108.

59. ANET:176–77, §§253–56.

60. Good, 1967.

61. Exod. 22:24; Lev. 25:35–37; Deut. 23:20–21.

62. Lev. 25:35–38.

63. Deut. 23:20.

64. On this topic, see van Selms, 1950; Finkelstein, 1973, 1981; Yaron, 1971; Jackson, 1975:108–52.

65. Num. 35:31–33.

66. On slavery, see Mendelsohn, 1949; Driver and Miles, 1952: 221–30, 306–9; de Vaux, 1961: 80–90; Van der ploeg, 1972; Lipinsky, 1975; Lemche, 1975; Japhet, 1978; Phillips, 1984.

67. Exod. 21:2–11, 20–21, 26–27, 32.

68. Cf. Eshnunna, §§51, 52 = ANET:163; Hammurabi, §§146, 226–27 = ANET:172, 176.

69. Hammurabi, §§199, 252 = ANET:176; cf. Hittite, §§8, 12, 14–16, 18 = ANET:189–90.

70. Driver and Miles, 1952:215–18.

71. Cf. Oppenheim, 1964:75.

72. The Samaritan text reads: "He shall surely be put to death."

73. Exod. 21:26–27.

74. Cf. Lipit Ishtar, §§12–13 = ANET:160; Eshnunna, §§49–51 = ANET:163. Cf. Ur-Nammu, §14 = ANET:524; Driver and Miles, 1952:105–8.

75. Exod. 12:44.

76. Job 31:13–15.

77. For studies on this subject, see Daube, 1947:102–53; Finkelstein, 1961:98; Hawkes and Woolley, 1963:487, 492; Cassuto, 1967:272–78; Good, 1967:953–54; Doron, 1969; Phillips, 1970:96–99; Paul, 1970:71–77; Jackson, 1973:75–107; Childs, 1974:420–74; Boecker, 1980:171–75; J. H. Hayes, 1982: 8–13.

78. Ur-Nammu, §§16–17 = ANET:524.

79. Eshnunna, §§42–48 = ANET:163.

80. Hittite, §7 = ANET:189.

81. Hammurabi §§196–97, 200 = ANET:175.

82. Diamond, 1935:8–45, 102–26; id., 1957.

83. Lambert, 1960:12–13; id., 1965:289.

84. Gen. 42:4, 38; 44:29.

85. The sole exception is Deut. 25:11–12 which, of course, is conditioned by a specific situation and has nothing to do with any other judicial penalties.

86. Mekhilta, Mishpatim, 8; edited by Horovitz-Rabin, pp. 274–78; Mishnah Bava Qama 8:1; b. Bava Qama 83b–84a.

87. *ANET*:175, §§196–97, cf. §198; §200, cf. §201; §§209–10, cf. §§211–12.

Chapter Nine

1. For the most thorough descriptions of the Tabernacle, see Kennedy, 1902; Haran, 1978:149–88.

2. Levine, 1965; Cross, 1981:169; Hurowitz, 1985.

3. Kaufman, 1984, fixes the cubit of Moses at 42.8 centimeters.

4. For a similar tripartite arrangement in a temple uncovered at Tainat in northern Syria, see Wright, 1941: esp. 20; Albright, 1969:138, 215 *nn*.43–44.

5. Exod. 27:9–19, 38:9–20.

6. Exod. 27:13–16. The Tainat temple, that of King Solomon, and the one covered at Arad also had an east-west axis, with a westward orientation; see Aharoni, 1968:21.

7. Exod. 26:36, 27:16.

8. See, however, Friedman, 1980, for a possible different reconstruction.

9. Exod. 26:31–33.

10. Exod. 27:9–19.

11. On the *qerashim*, see Friedman, 1980, and Cross, 1981:171.

12. Exod. 26:15–29, 36:20–34.

13. Exod. 26:1–6.

14. Exod. 26:7–14.

15. So NJPS, on which see Cross, 1981:172. Greenberg, 1983:278, seriously questions this translation.

16. Exod. 26:31–33, 36:35–36.

17. Exod. 27:1–8; 38:1–7; 40:6, 29.

18. Exod. 29:38–42.

19. Exod. 30:17–21; 40:7, 30–32.

20. Exod. 38:8.

21. On bronze mirrors, see Barrois, 1962.

22. Exod. 25:23–30, 37:10–16, 40:22; Lev. 24:5–9. Cf. Num. 4:7; 1 Chron. 9:32.

23. Exod. 25:31–40, 37:17–24, 40:24; Lev. 24:2–4; Num. 8:2–4. On the Menorah, see Yarden, 1971; C. L. Myers, 1976.

24. Exod. 30:1–10; 37:25–29; 39:38; 40:5, 26–27; Num. 4:11.

25. Exod. 25:10–22, 37:1–9, 40:20–21.

26. Cf. Exod. 35:12; Lev. 16:2, 14–15; 1 Chron. 28:11.

27. Wellhausen, 1957:38–51; see Cross, 1947; cf. Cross, 1981:169–70; see the convenient list of problems in Hyatt, 1980:260; Hurowitz, 1985:21; and the careful survey of the major issues by Childs, 1974:529–38.

28. So calculated by Professor Albert Schild, *Jewish Press*, New York, 23 September 1977, p. 45.

29. See above, p. 57.

30. Num. Chap. 7, passim.

31. Kitchen, 1960:12–14.

32. 2 Sam. 7:6–7. See Cross, 1981:173–74.

33. Num. 24:5; Isa. 54:2; Jer. 30:18; Ps. 78:60. Cf. Isa. 13:20; Ps. 15:1; 78:55, 60; Job 11:14, 18:15, 21:28.

34. Num. 16:26–27; Ezek. 25:4, with which, cf. Judg. 6:3–5; Song 1:8.

35. *UT*, 128, iii:18f; 2 Aqht v:32f.

36. *CAD* 10, i, 369, s.v. *maškanu* 4.

37. E.g., Gen. 4:20, 12:8, et al.

38. Isa. 16:5; Ps. 26:8; 27:5; 43:3; 46:5; 74:7; 84:2; 132:5, 7. Cf. Ezra 7:15. On this topic, see Cross, 1973:97, 245, 298–99.

39. On this topic, see Hartman, 1917–1918; Lammens, 1919; Morgenstern, 1942–1943, 1943–1944; Jomier, 1953; de Vaux, 1961:296–97; Woudstra, 1970:90–91.

40. Cf. Num. 10:35–36; 1 Sam. Chap. 4.

41. Exod. 26:14.

42. Ingholt, 1936.

43. English translation by R. M. Geer (Cambridge, Mass., and London: Loeb Classical Library, 1933, 10:321).

44. Albright, 1968:223–26.

45. Cross, 1947:55 and *n.*17; Piankoff, 1955:41; Kitchen, 1960:7–13; Harrison, 1969:403–5. It should be added that the excavations of B. Rothenberg at Timna yielded a Midianite tented shrine; see Rothenberg, 1975, 1:16, 2:11.

46. Exod. 25:9.

47. Exod. 25:40; cf. Num. 8:4.

48. Exod. 27:8.

49. Exod. 38:22, Chap. 39 passim, Chap. 40 passim.

50. Exod. 31:1–11, 35:30–36:1.

51. Exod. 40:1–33.

52. This was drawn to my attention by Professor Marvin Fox.

53. So Deut. 4:16–18; Josh. 22:28; 2 Kings 16:10; Isa. 44:13; Ezek. 8:3, 10; 10:8; Ps. 106:20, 144:12; cf. 1 Chron. 28:11, 12, 18; see, however, Hurowitz, 1985:22 *n.*4.

54. Ezek. 40:1ff.

55. 1 Chron. 28:11–12, 19.

56. See Patai, 1947:107–39; Eliade, 1959:6–7; Kapelrud, 1963; Hurowitz, 1985:22 *n.*4, 25–28.

57. See Jacobsen, 1976:80–81, 84, 156; Frankfort, 1978:255–56; Beyerlin, 1978:112.

58. *Enuma elish* VI:51–70; *ANET*:68–69.

59. Frankfort, 1978:274 and Fig. 48; id., 1939:76.

60. Frankfort, 1978:269–71; Reymond, 1969:4, 6, 43, 302, 304–5, 310–12, 323.

61. Exod. 19:17, 23; Deut. 4:11; Exod. 24:4–5. Cf. Exod. 27:1–8; 38:1–7; 40:6, 29.

62. Exod. 19:22; 24:1, 14. Cf. Num. 18:1–7.

63. Exod. 19:20–22, 24:2; cf. 34:2–3.

64. Exod. 25:22, 29:42–43; Num. 7:89; Exod. 24:15–16, cf. 40:34; Exod. 24:17, cf. 40:35.

65. Exod. 25:1–9.

66. Exod. 36:5–7.

67. Exod. 25:8.

68. Exod. 29:45.

69. Exod. 25:22.

70. Exod. 28:9–12, 21, 29; 39:6–7, 14.

71. Exod. 30:11–16.

72. Exod. 39:42.

73. See Haran, 1978:158–65, 175–88.

74. Exod. 30:10; Lev. 16:1–34.

75. Num. 1:53, 2:1–34.

76. Cf. Oppenheim, 1964:58.

77. 1 Kings 8:27. Cf. Isa. 66:1.

78. Cf. Gen. 9:27; 14:13; Num. 24:2; Judg. 8:11; Ps. 78:55, 60; 120:5; Job. 11:14; 18:15. See Cross, 1973:37, 245, 298–99.

79. Exod. 25:8.

80. Exod. 29:45–46.

81. Exod. 33:9, 40:34–36; cf. Num. 11:25, 12:5.

82. Exod. 19:11, 18, 20.

83. Exod. 26:6, 11; 36:13, 18. Cf. Exod. 25:36; 36:9, 15; 37:22.

84. Breasted, 1906:163–74, §§367–391: *ANET*:199.

85. Exod. 24:12.

86. Exod. 31:18.

87. Exod. 34:28.

88. Exod. 24:12, 31:18, 34:4; Deut. 4:13, 5:19, 9:9–11, 10:1–3; 1 Kings 8:9.

89. Deut. 9:9, 11, 15; cf. Deut. 4:13.

90. Exod. 31:18, 32:15, 34:29. *'Edut* alone is used in Exod. 25:16, 21; 27:21; 30:6, 36; 38:21; 40:20; Lev. 16:13; 24:3; Num. 17:19, 25. In Num. 1:50 and 53, and 10:11, the Tabernacle is termed *mishkan ha-'edut*, and in Num. 9:15, 17:22 and 23, 18:2, and 2 Chron. 24:6, *'ohel ha-'edut*.

91. *CAD* I, i, 131–34 s.v. *Adû*.

92. *KAI*, no. 222 I, A §7. See Albright, 1957:16–17; id., 1968:104 *n*.128, 106 *n*.136; Cross, 1973:267, 300, 312–14; McCarthy, 1963:97.

93. Kitchen, 1975:108.

94. Cf. Ps. 99:7 *'edut* ǁ *ḥoq* with Ps. 105:10 *b'rit* ǁ *ḥoq*. See Clements, 1965:119; Haran, 1978:272.

95. Exod. 25:22; 26:33, 34; 30:6, 26; 39:35; 40:3, 5, 21; Num. 4:5; 7:89; Josh. 4:16.

96. Num. 10:33, 14:44; Deut. 31:9, 25, 26; Josh. 3:3, 6, 8, 11; 4:7, 9, 18; 6:6, 8; 8:33 et al.

97. Exod. 25:16, 21; 31:7; 40:20–21; Deut. 10:1–5; 1 Kings 8:9, 21; 2 Chron. 5:10.

98. ANET:205.

99. Mendenhall, 1954b:60.

100. de Vaux, 1961:299; id., 1971:148; Haran, 1978:303.

101. Hermann, 1908:299; Budge, 1960:441, appendix to Chap. 30b; Allen, 1936:151 §20.

102. G. H. Davies, 1962:309; Fabry, 1978:325–34.

103. Exod. 25:21–22.

104. Num. 7:89.

105. 1 Sam. 4:4; 2 Sam 6:2; 2 Kings 19:15 = Isa. 37:16; Ps. 80:2, 99:1; 1 Chron. 13:6. Cf. Jer. 3:16–17.

106. See ANEP nos. 332, 371, 415–17, 451, 456, 458, 460, 463, 477, 493, 515, 525, 537, 849.

107. Cf. 2 Sam. 6:6–7.

108. Clements, 1965:28–29, has made a strong case against viewing the Ark itself as the throne.

109. Exod. 25:15; 1 Kings 8:7–8; cf. Num. 4:15.

110. Albright, 1938:1–3; Wright, 1941:23–25; Haran, 1959:30–38, 89–94; Kaufmann, 1960:72, 237, 239–40, 286; de Vaux, 1961:300, 304, 326, 333; Clements, 1965:31–34, 65.

111. Exod. 25:18–20, 37:7–9.

112. Exod. 25:22; Lev. 16:2; Num. 7:89.

113. Exod. 26:1, 31; 36:8, 35.

114. 1 Kings 6:23–25, 7:36, 8:6–8.

115. Ezek. 41:18–20, 25.

116. Ps. 68:5.

117. Ps. 104:3.

118. Isa. 66:15. Cf. Hab. 3:8.

119. Cf. Ben Sira 49:8 (11).

120. Exod. 25:20; 1 Kings 6:24–27.

121. Ezek. 1:6, 8, 10, 23, and 10:21; cf. 41:18f. See, however, the explanation of Haran, 1959:93 n.16.

122. B. Sukkah 5b; Hagigah 13b.

123. CAD, 8:559, s.v. Kurību.

124. See ANEP nos. 644, 646, 647, 649–55, 855. See also Dever, 1984:24–25.

125. Plastaras, 1966:269, suggests that the poles being permanently fixed to the Ark expresses the "quintessence of mobility."

126. Exod. 25:1; 30:11, 17, 22, 34; 34:1, noted by Kearney, 1977:375–87. On this topic, see also Cassuto, 1967:476; Blenkinsopp, 1977:57, 60–66,

75; Weinfeld, 1968:105–32, esp. 109–10; id., 1977:188–93; id., 1981:501–11, esp. 502 *n.*5 and 503 *n.*1.

127. Exod. 31:12–17.

128. Gen. 1:31; cf. Exod. 39:43.

129. Gen. 2:2; cf. Exod. 40:33.

130. Gen. 2:3; cf. Exod. 39:43.

131. Exod. 40:2, 17; cf. Exod. 12:2. Cf. also Frankfort, 1978:274.

132. Gen. 8:13.

133. I owe this observation to Dr. Chaim Potok.

134. Exod. 35:1–3.

135. Lev. 19:30, 26:2.

136. On this topic, see Lewy, 1959; Beyerlin, 1965:126–33; Cassuto, 1967:407–10; Aberbach and Smolar, 1967; Loewenstamm, 1967; Coats, 1968*b*:184ff; Bailey, 1971; Sasson, 1973; Childs, 1974:552–638; Brichto, 1983; Ginsberg, 1982:84–91.

137. Brichto, 1983, considers the entire pericope to Chapters 32–34 to be the work of a single author.

138. Exod. 32:4. It is clear that the plural verb in v.1 and the plural demonstrative pronoun and verb in v.4 are nothing but a stylistic device intended to express the incompatibility of the image with monotheism. After all, Aaron only made one calf.

139. Cf. Plasteras, 1966:238–39; Haran, 1978:29 *n.*28; Ginsberg, 1982:87–88. Cf. the similar use of *'elohim* to refer to the representative image in Gen. 31:30.

140. Kaufmann, 1942–1956, I–II:279, 609.

141. It is to be noted that in Ps. 106:19–20 the image is variously termed "a calf" and "a bull."

142. See Murray, 1964:98–99; Morenz, 1973:20, 103, 143–44, 148, 157, 259, 265, 268; *CAH*, II, 2:874.

143. Mazar, 1982:29–32.

144. Albright, 1957:266; id., 1968:151.

145. *ANEP* nos. 470–74; 479, 486, 522, 525, 526, 531, 534, 537, 830, 835.

146. Oppenheim, 1964:186.

147. See Kaufmann, 1942–1956, IV–V:259–61; Phillips, 1970:170.

148. Hammurabi, §37 = *ANET*:167; *CAD*, 6, H, pp. 170–72; McCarthy, 1963:39 *n.*47; Weinfeld, 1977:265, 276.

149. Loewenstamm, 1980:236–45, 503–16; Fensham, 1966b:191–93; Watson, 1972:60–64.

150. Ginsberg, 1982:89 *n.*110.

151. B. Avodah Zarah 44a.

152. Exod. 34:16; Num. 15:39; Jer. 3:1–5, 8; 5:7–9; Ezek. Chap. 16, passim; 23:27; Hos. Chap. 2. For the use of *b'rit* to express the marital bond, cf. Prov. 2:17; Mal. 2:14.

153. Exod. 32:21, 30, 32.

154. Rabinowitz, 1959:73; Moran, 1959:280; Milgrom, 1976:132–35.
155. Exod. Chap. 32 and 2 Kings 17:21.
156. Brichto, 1983:16.
157. Exod. 32:30–34:35. On the prophet as intercessor, see Rhodes, 1977; Muffs, 1978.
158. Exod. 40:34–38.

Abbreviations

AASOR	*Annual of the American School of Oriental Research*
ABR	*Australian Biblical Review*
ANEP	*The Ancient Near East in Pictures Relating to the Old Testament* (Princeton, N.J., 1954, 1968)
ANET	*Ancient Near Eastern Texts Relating to the Old Testament* (Princeton, N.J., 1955, 1968)
AO	*Archiv Orientalni*
AOAT	*Alter Orient und Altes Testament*
ASAE	*Annales du Service des Antiquités de l'Égypt* (Cairo)
ASTI	*Annual of the Swedish Theological Institute in Jerusalem*
BA	*Biblical Archaeologist*
BAR	*Biblical Archaeologist Reader*
BARev	*Biblical Archaeology Review*
BASOR	*Bulletin of the American Schools of Oriental Research*
BETS	*Bulletin of the Evangelical Theology Society*
BIFAO	*Bulletin de l'Institut Français d'Archéologie Orientale* (Cairo)
BIJS	*Bulletin of the Institute of Jewish Studies*
BS	*Bibliotheca Sacra*
CAD	*Chicago Assyrian Dictionary*
CAH	*Cambridge Ancient History* (3rd ed.)
CBQ	*Catholic Biblical Quarterly*
EJ	*Encyclopaedia Judaica* (1972)
GJ	*Grace Journal*
HDB	*Hastings Dictionary of the Bible* (5 vols.)
HTR	*Harvard Theological Review*
HUCA	*Hebrew Union College Annual*

IDB	*Interpreter's Dictionary of the Bible*
IEJ	*Israel Exploration Journal*
ISBE	*International Standard Bible Encyclopaedia*
JANES	*Journal of the Ancient Near Eastern Society*
JAOS	*Journal of the American Oriental Society*
JBL	*Journal of Biblical Literature*
JCS	*Journal of Cuneiform Studies*
JEA	*Journal of Egyptian Archaeology*
JESHO	*Journal of the Economic and Social History of the Orient*
JNES	*Journal of Near Eastern Studies*
JPOS	*Journal of the Palestine Oriental Society*
JQR	*Jewish Quarterly Review*
JSOT	*Journal for the Study of the Old Testament*
JSS	*Journal of Semitic Studies*
JTS	*Journal of Theological Studies*
JTVI	*Journal of the Transactions of the Victoria Institute*
KAI	*Kanaanäische und Aramäische Inschriften*
MIE	*Mémoires de l'Institut d'Égypt*
NBD	*New Bible Dictionary*
NJPS	New Jewish Publication Society Version
NWDB	*New Westminster Dictionary of the Bible*
OTS	*Oudtestamentische Studiën*
PAH	*Perspectives in American History*
PAPS	*Proceedings of the American Philosophical Society*
PEQ	*Palestine Exploration Quarterly*
PFES	*Publications of the Finnish Exegetical Society*
RSJB	*Recueils de la Societé Jean Bodin*
SLR	*Stanford Law Review*
SOTS	*Society for Old Testament Study*
SVT	Supplement to *Vetus Testament*
TDOT	*Theological Dictionary of the Old Testament*
TGUOS	*Transactions of the Glasgow University Oriental Society*
THB	*Tyndale House Bulletin*
TLQ	*Temple Law Quarterly*
TUSR	*Trinity University Studies in Religion*
UT	*Ugaritic Textbook*
VT	*Vetus Testamentum*
WHJP	*World History of the Jewish People*
ZAW	*Zeitschrift für die alttestamentliche Wissenschaft*

Bibliography

Aberbach, M., and Smolar, L. 1967. "Aaron, Jereboam and the Golden Calves." *JBL* 86:129–40.

Abramsky, S. 1975. "On the Kenite-Midianite Background of Moses' Leadership" [Hebrew]. *Eretz-Israel* 12:35–39.

Ackerman, J. S. 1974. "The Literary Context of the Moses Birth-Story." In *Literary Interpretations of Biblical Narratives*, edited by K. R. R. Gos Louis, with J. S. Ackerman and T. S. Warshaw. Nashville: Abingdon, pp. 74–119.

————. 1975. "Prophecy and Warfare in Early Israel: A Study of the Deborah-Barak Story." *BASOR* 220:5–13.

Aharoni, Y. 1968. "Arad: Its Inscriptions and Temple." *BA* 21:2–32.

————. 1975. *Arad Inscriptions* [Hebrew]. Jerusalem: Mosad Bialik.

————. 1979. *The Land of the Bible: A Historical-Geography*, rev. and enlarged ed., translated from the Hebrew and edited by A. F. Rainey. Philadelphia: Westminster.

Albright, W. F. 1925. "The Administrative Divisions of Israel and Judah." *JPOS* 5:17–24.

————. 1938. "What Were the Cherubim?" *BA* 1:1–3.

————. 1950. "Baal Zaphon." In *Festschrift Alfred Bertholet sum 80 Geburtstag*, edited by W. Baumgartner. Tübingen: Mohr, pp. 1–14.

————. 1954. "Northwest Semitic Names in a List of Egyptian Slaves from the Eighteenth Century B.C." *JAOS* 74:222–33.

————. 1957. *From the Stone Age to Christianity*, 2nd ed. Garden City, N.Y.: Doubleday Anchor.

————. 1961. "Abram the Hebrew: A New Archaeological Interpretation." *BASOR* 163:36–54.

————. 1963. "Jethro, Hobab and Reuel in Early Biblical Tradition, with Some Comments on the Origin of 'JE.' " *CBQ* 25:1–11.

————. 1968. *Yahweh and the Gods of Canaan: A Historical Analysis of Two Contrasting Faiths*. Garden City, N.Y.: Doubleday.

————. 1969. *Archaeology and the Religion of Israel*, 5th ed. Garden City, N.Y.: Anchor Books.

————. 1975a. "Moses in Historical and Theological Perspective." In

Magnalia Dei, Essays in Honor of George Ernest Wright. New York: Doubleday & Co.

—————. 1975*b*. "The Amarna Letters from Palestine." *CAH*, II, 2:98–116.

Aldred, C. 1975. "Egypt: The Amarna Period and the End of the Eighteenth Dynasty." *CAH*, II, 2:49–97.

Aling, Ch. F. 1981. *Egypt and Bible History from Earliest Times to 1000 B.C.* Grand Rapids, Mich.: Baker.

Allen, T. G. 1936. "Types of Rubrics in the Egyptian Book of the Dead." *JAOS* 56:145–54.

—————. 1974. *The Egyptian Book of the Dead*. Chicago: University of Chicago Press.

Alt, A. 1968. "The God of the Fathers." In *Essays on Old Testament History and Religion*, translated by R. A. Wilson. Garden City, N.Y.: Doubleday Anchor, pp. 3–100.

Andreason, N. E. A. 1972. *The Old Testament Sabbath: A Tradition-Historical Approach*. Missoula, Mont.: Scholars Press, S.B.L. Dissertation Series No. 7.

Bacchiocchi, S. 1977. *From Sabbath to Sunday, A Historical Investigation of the Rise of Sunday Observance in Early Christianity*. Rome: Pontifical Gregorian University.

—————. 1980. *Divine Rest for Human Restlessness*. Rome: Pontifical Gregorian University.

Bailey, L. R. 1971. "The Golden Calf." *HUCA* 42:97–115.

Baines, J., and Málek, J. 1980. *Atlas of Ancient Egypt*. Oxford: Phaidon.

Bakir, A. 1952. *Slavery in Pharaonic Egypt*. ASAE Supplement No. 18.

Baltzer, K. 1971. *The Covenant Formulary*, translated by David E. Green. Philadelphia: Fortress Press.

Barnett, R. 1975. "The Sea Peoples." *CAH*, II, 2:359–78.

Baron, S. 1971. "Population." *EJ* 13:866.

—————. 1972. *Ancient and Medieval Jewish History, Essays by Salo Baron*, edited by L. A. Feldman. New Brunswick, N.J.: Rutgers University Press.

Barr, J. 1959. "The Problem of Israelite Monotheism." *TGUOS* 17:52–62.

Barrois, G. A. 1962. "Mirror" in *IDB* vol. 3:402–3.

Bartlett, J. R. 1973. "The Moabites and Edomites." In *Peoples of Old Testament Times*, edited by D. J. Wiseman. Oxford: Clarendon, pp. 229–58.

Barton, G. A. 1917. *Archaeology and the Bible*. Philadelphia: American Sunday-School Union.

—————. 1929. *The Royal Inscriptions of Sumer and Akkad*. New Haven, Conn.: Yale University Press.

Bates, M. 1959–1960. "Insects in the Diet." *American Scholar* 24:46–49.

Batto, B. F. 1984. "Red Sea or Reed Sea." *BARev* 10, no. 4:56–63.

Beyerlin, W. 1965. *Origins and History of the Oldest Sinaitic Tradition*, translated by S. Rudman. Oxford: Blackwell, pp. 126–33.

—————. 1978. *Near Eastern Texts Relating to the Old Testament*, translated by J. Bowden. Philadelphia: Westminster.

Bimson, J. J. 1978. *Redating the Exodus and Conquest*. JSOT Supplement Series No. 5.

Blackman, A. M. 1921. "On the Position of Women in the Ancient Egyptian Hierarchy." *JEA* 8:30.

Bleeker, C. J. 1967. *Egyptian Festivals: Enactments of Religious Renewal*. Leiden: Numen Supplement XIII.

—————. 1973. *Hathor and Thoth: Two Key Figures of the Ancient Egyptian Religion*. Leiden: Numen Supplement XXVI.

Blenkinsopp, C. J. 1975. "The Position of the Queen in Ancient Egypt." *Rainbow*. Leiden: Brill.

—————. 1977. *Prophecy and Canon*. Notre Dame, Ind.: University of Notre Dame Press.

Bodenheimer, F. S. 1947. "The Manna of Sinai." *BA* 10:2–6.

Boecker, H. J. 1980. *Law and the Administration of Justice in the Old Testament and Ancient East*. Minneapolis: Augsburg Publishing House.

Borghouts, J. F. 1978. *Ancient Egyptian Magical Texts*. Leiden: Brill.

Bratton, F. G. 1961. *The First Heretic: The Life and Times of Ikhnaton the King*. Boston: Beacon Press.

Breasted, J. H. 1906. *Ancient Records of Egypt*, vol. 3. Chicago: University of Chicago Press.

—————. 1961. *The Dawn of Conscience*. New York: Charles Scribner's (reprint).

Brichto, H. Ch. 1983. "The Worship of the Golden Calf: A Literary Analysis of a Fable on Idolatry." *HUCA* 54:1–44.

Brock, S. P. 1952. "An Early Interpretation of *pāssah: 'aggēn* in the Palestinian Targum." In *Interpreting the Hebrew Bible*, edited by J. A. Emerton and S. C. Reif. Cambridge: Cambridge University Press.

Budge, W. 1960. *The Book of the Dead*. New York: University Books (reprint).

—————. 1969. *The Gods of the Egyptians*. New York: Dover (reprint).

—————. 1978. *Egyptian Magic*. Secaucus, N.J.: Citadel (reprint).

Cassuto, U. 1967. *A Commentary on the Book of Exodus*. Jerusalem: Magnes.

Černý, J. 1951. "The Greek Etymology of the Name of Moses." *ASAE* 51: 349–54.

Childs, B. S. 1962. *Memory and Tradition*. London: Studies in Biblical Theology No. 37.

—————. 1965. "The Birth of Moses." *JBL* 84:109–22.

—————. 1974. *The Book of Exodus: A Critical Theological Commentary*. Philadelphia: Westminster.

Clark, R. E. D. 1955. "The Large Numbers of the Old Testament." *JTVI* 87:82–92.

Clarke, S., and Engelbach, R. 1930. *Ancient Egyptian Masonry: The Building Craft*. London: Oxford University Press; reprinted Boston; Milford House, 1974.

Clements, R. E. 1965. *God and Temple*. Philadelphia: Fortress Press.

Clifford, R. J. 1972. *The Cosmic Mountain in Canaan and the Old Testament*. Cambridge, Mass.: Harvard University Press.

Coats, G. W. 1968a. "Despoiling the Egyptians." *VT* 18:450–57.

—————. 1968b. *The Murmuring Motif in the Wilderness Traditions of the Old Testament: Rebellion in the Wilderness*. New York: Nashville.

—————. 1975. "Moses versus Amalek: Aetiology and Legend in Exod. XVII:8–16." *SVT* 28:29–41.

Cody, A. 1968. "Exodus 18:12: Jethro Accepts a Covenant with the Israelites." *Biblica* 49:153–66.

Cogan, M. 1968. "A Technical Term for Exposure." *JNES* 27:133–35.

Collier, J. 1972. *The Heretic King*. New York: John Day.

Collon, D. 1975. "The Seal Impressions from Tell Atchana/Alalakh." *AOAT* 27:12–13, 170–71.

Copisarow, M. 1962. "The Ancient Egyptian, Greek, and Hebrew Concept of the Red Sea." *VT* 12:1–13.

Cross, F. M. 1947. "The Tabernacle: A Study from an Archaeological and Historical Approach." *BA* 10:45–68 (reprinted and slightly revised as "The Priestly Tabernacle," in *BAR*, 1961, edited by G. Ernest Wright and D. N. Freedman. New York, pp. 201–28).

—————. 1973. *Canaanite Myth and Hebrew Epic: Essays in the History of the Religion of Israel*. Cambridge, Mass.: Harvard University Press.

—————. 1981. "The Priestly Tabernacle in the Light of Recent Research." In *Temples and High Places in Biblical Times*, edited by A. Biran. Jerusalem: Hebrew Union College–Jewish Institute of Religion.

Daube, D. 1947. *Studies in Biblical Law*. Cambridge: Cambridge University Press.

—————. 1963. *The Exodus Pattern in the Bible*. London: Faber and Faber.

—————. 1972. *Civil Disobedience in Antiquity*. Edinburgh: Edinburgh University Press.

David, M. 1950. "The Codex Hammurabi and its Relation to the Provisions of Law in Exodus." *OTS* 7:149–78.

Davies, G. H. 1962. "Footstool." *IDB* 2:309.

Davies, G. I. 1979. *The Way of the Wilderness: A Geographical Study of the Itineraries in the Old Testament*. Cambridge: SOTS Monograph Series 5.

Davis, J. J. 1968. *Biblical Numerology*. Grand Rapids, Mich.: Baker.

Dever, W. G. 1984. "Asherah, Consort of Yahweh?" *BASOR* 255:21–37.

De Wit, C. 1960. *The Date and Route of the Exodus*. London: Tyndale.

Diamond, A. S. 1935. *Primitive Law*. London: Longmans, Green and Co.

—————. 1957. "An Eye for an Eye." *Iraq* 19:15–55.

Dodds, E. R. 1957. *The Greeks and the Irrational*. Boston: Beacon Press.

Doron, P. 1969. "A New Look at an Old Lex," *JANES* 1, no. 2:21–27.

Dothan, T. 1982. "Gaza Sands Yield Lost Outpost of the Egyptian Empire," *National Geographic*, December, pp. 739–68.

Driver, G. R. 1935. "Notes and Studies," *JTS* 36:403.

—————, and Miles, J. C. 1935. *The Assyrian Laws.* Oxford: Clarendon.

—————. 1952, 1955. *The Babylonian Laws* (2 vols.) Oxford: Clarendon.

Eichrodt, E. 1961, 1967. *Theology of the Old Testament.* Translated by J. A. Baker. (2 vols.) Philadelphia, Pa.: Westminster.

Eising, H. 1980. "Zākhār," in *Theological Dictionary of the Old Testament*, edited by C. J. Botterwick and H. Ringgren. Translated by D. E. Green. Grand Rapids, Mich.: Eerdmans, vol. 4: pp. 64–82.

Eissfeldt, O. 1932. *Baal Zephon, Zeus Kasios und der Durchzug der Israelitan durchs Meer.* Beiträge zur Religionsgeschichte des Altertums, Heft 1. Halle: Niemayer.

Eliade, M. 1959. *Cosmos and History: The Myth of the Eternal Return.* New York: Harper Torchbooks.

Erman, A. 1966. *The Ancient Egyptians: A Sourcebook of their Writings.* New York: Harper Torchbooks (reprint).

—————. 1971. *Life in Ancient Egypt.* New York: Dover (reprint).

Evans, G. 1958. "Ancient Mesopotamian Assemblies." *JAOS* 78:1–11.

Fabry, H. J. 1978. "Hᵃdhōm." *TDOT* 3:325–34.

Falk, Z. 1964. *Hebrew Law in Biblical Times.* Jerusalem: Wahrman Books.

Faulkner, R. O. 1975. "Egypt from the Inception of the Nineteenth Dynasty to the Death of Ramesses III." *CAH*, II, 2:217–51.

Feliks, J. 1968. *Plant World of the Bible* [Hebrew]. Ramat Gan: Massada Ltd.

Fensham, F. C. 1964. "Did a Treaty between the Israelites and the Kenites Exist?" *BASOR* 175:51–54.

—————. 1966a. "An Ancient Tradition of the Fertility of Palestine." *PEQ* 98:166–67.

—————. 1966b. "The Burning of the Golden Calf and Ugarit." *IEJ* 16:191–93.

Finegan, J. 1959. *Light from the Ancient Past.* Princeton, N.J.: Princeton University Press.

—————. 1963. *Let My People Go.* New York: Harper and Row.

—————. 1964. *Handbook of Biblical Chronology: Principles of Time Reckoning in the Ancient World and Problems of Chronology in the Bible.* Princeton, N.J.: Princeton University Press.

—————. 1979. *Archaeological History of the Ancient Middle East.* Boulder, Colo.: Westview.

Finkelstein, J. J. 1961. "Ammisaduqa's Edict and the Babylonian Law Codes." *JCS* 15:103–4.

—————. 1968–69. "The Laws of Ur-Nammu," *JCS* XXII:66–82.

—————. 1970. "On Some Recent Studies in Cuneiform Laws," *JAOS* 90:243–56.

—————. 1971. "Law, Mesopotamia." *EJ* 16:1505.

—————. 1973. "The Goring Ox: Some Historical Perspectives on Deodands, Forfeitures, Wrongful Death and the Western Notion of Sovereignty." *TLQ* 46:169–290.

——————. 1981. "The Ox That Gored." *TAPS* 46:1–47.

Finley, M. I. 1959. *The World of Odysseus*. New York: Meridian.

——————. 1983. *Ancient Slavery and Modern Ideology*. Middlesex, England: Penguin.

Fishbane, M. 1975. "The Biblical *'ot*" [Hebrew]. *Shnaton* 1:213–34.

Frankfort, H. 1939. *Cylinder Seals*. London: Gregg Press.

——————. 1961. *Ancient Egyptian Religion*. New York: Harper (reprint).

——————. 1978. *Kingship and the Gods: A Study of Ancient Near Eastern Religion as the Integration of Society and Nature*. Chicago: University of Chicago Press (reprint).

Freud, S. 1959. *Moses and Monotheism*, translated by K. Jones. New York: Vintage (reprint).

Friedman, R. E. 1980. "The Tabernacle in the Temple." *BA* 43:241–47.

Frymer-Kensky, T. 1980. "Tit for Tat: The Principle of Equal Retribution in Near Eastern and Biblical Law." *BA* 43:230–34.

Gadd, C. J. 1971. "The Cities of Babylonia." *CAH*, I, 2:93–144.

——————. 1973. "Hammurabi and the End of the Dynasty." *CAH*, II, 1:176–227.

Gardiner, A. H. 1918. "The Delta Residence of the Ramessides." *JEA* 5:127–38, 179–200, 242–71.

——————. 1920. "The Ancient Military Road between Egypt and Palestine." *JEA* 6:99–116.

——————. 1936. "The Egyptian Origin of Some English Personal Names." *JAOS* 56:192–94.

——————. 1961. *Egypt of the Pharaohs*. Oxford: Clarendon.

Gaster, Th. H. 1975. *Myth, Legend and Custom in the Old Testament*. (2 vols.) New York, Evanston, San Francisco and London: Harper and Row.

Gemser, B. 1958. "God in Genesis." *OTS* XII:1–21.

——————. 1953. "The Importance of the Motive Clause in the Old Testament Law." *SVT* 1:50–66.

Gibson, W. 1967. *Secrets of Magic: Ancient and Modern*. New York: Grosset and Dunlap.

Giles, F. J. 1970. *Ikhnaton: Legend and History*. Rutherford, N.J.: Fairleigh Dickinson University Press.

Ginsberg, H. L. 1982. *The Israelian Heritage*. New York: Jewish Theological Seminary.

Ginzberg, L. 1946. *The Legends of the Jews*. Philadelphia: Jewish Publication Society.

Glasson, T. F. 1959. "The 'Passover,' a Misnomer: The Meaning of the Verb *pāsāch*." *JTS* 10(n.s.):79–84.

Glueck, N. 1967. *Hesed in the Bible*. Translated by A. Gottschalk. Cincinnati: Hebrew Union College.

Goetze, A. 1956. *The Laws of Eshnunna*. AASOR 21:1–197.

Goldin, J. 1971. *The Song at the Sea*. New Haven and London: Yale University Press.

Good, E. M. 1967. "Capital Punishment and Its Alternatives in Ancient Near Eastern Law." *SLR* 19:947–77.

Goor, A., and Nurock, M. 1968. *The Fruits of the Holy Land*. Jerusalem: Israel Universities Press.

Gordis, R. 1968. *Koheleth: The Man and His World*, 3rd augmented ed. New York: Schocken Books.

Gordon, C. H. 1949. *Ugaritic Literature: A Comprehensive Translation of the Poetic and Prose Texts*. Rome: Pontifical Biblical Institute.

————. 1957. *Hammurabi's Code: Quaint or Forward-Looking?* New York: Rinehart and Co.

————. 1965. *The Ancient Near East*, 3rd rev. ed. New York: W. W. Norton.

Gottwald, N. K. 1979. *The Tribes of Yahweh: A Sociology of the Religion of Liberated Israel, 1250–1000 B.C.* Maryknoll, N.Y.: Orbis.

Goudoever, J. van. 1961. *Biblical Calendars*, 2nd rev. ed. Leiden: Brill.

Gray, G. B. 1903. *A Critical and Exegetical Commentary on Numbers* (ICC). Edinburgh: T. & T. Clark.

Greenberg, M. 1951. "Hebrew s^egulla: Akkadian sikiltu." *JAOS* 71:172–74.

————. 1960. "Some Postulates of Biblical Criminal Law." In *Yehezkel Kaufmann Jubilee Volume*, edited by M. Haran. Jerusalem: Magnes, pp. 5–28.

————. 1969. *Understanding Exodus*. New York: Behrman House.

————. 1971. "Plagues of Egypt." *EJ* 13:604–13.

————. 1983. *Ezekiel, 1-20*. New York: Anchor Bible.

Greengus, S. 1976. "Law in the Old Testament." *IDB* Supplementary Volume, pp. 532–37.

Griffiths, J. G. 1953. "The Egyptian Derivation of the Name Moses." *JNES* 12:225–31.

Gurney, O. R. 1964. *The Hittites*. Baltimore, Md.: Penguin Books, pp. 88–103.

Gütterbock, H. G. 1954. "Authority and Law in the Hittite Kingdom." *JAOS* Suppl. 17:16–24.

Habachi, L. 1954. "Khata 'na-Qantir." *ASAE* 52:443–559.

Hallo, W. W. 1977. "New Moons and Sabbaths: A Case-Study in the Contrastive Approach." *HUCA* 48:1–8.

Haran, M. 1959. "The Ark and the Cherubim: Their Symbolic Significance in Biblical Ritual." *IEJ* 9:30–38, 89–94.

————. 1965. "The Religion of the Patriarchs, an attempt at Synthesis." *ASTI* 4:30–55.

————. 1971. "The Exodus Routes in the Pentateuch Sources." [Hebrew]. *Tarbiz* 40:113–43.

————. 1978. *Temples and Temple Service in Ancient Israel*. Oxford: Clarendon.

Har-El, M. 1973. *The Sinai Journeys: The Route of the Exodus in the Light of the Historical Geography of the Sinai Peninsula*. Tel-Aviv: Am Oved.

Harris, R. 1963. "The Organization and Administration of the Cloister in Ancient Babylonia." *JESHO* 6:122–57.

Harrison, R. K. 1969. *Introduction to the Old Testament*. Grand Rapids, Mich.: Eerdmans.

Hartman, R. 1917–1918. "Zelt und Lade." ZAW 37:209–44.

Hawkes, Y., and Woolley, L. 1963. *Prehistory and the Beginnings of Civilization*, vol. 1 of *History of Mankind*. New York and Evanston, Ill.: Harper & Row.

Hayes, J. H. 1982. "Restitution, Forgiveness and the Victim in Old Testament Law." *TUSR* 2:1–23.

——————, and Miller, J. M. 1977. *Israelite and Judaean History*. Philadelphia: Westminster.

Hayes, W. C. 1973*a*. "Egypt: From the Death of Ammenemes III to Seqenenre II." *CAH*, II, 1:54–73.

——————. 1973*b*. "Egypt: Internal Affairs from Tuthmosis I to the Death of Amenophis III." *CAH*, II, 1:313–416.

Helck, W. 1965. "*Tkw* und die Ramsesstadt." VT 15:35–48.

Held, M. 1961. "An Old Babylonian Dialogue." *JCS* 15:11–12.

Hermann, J. 1908. "Ägyptische Analogien zum Funde des Deuteronomiums." ZAW 28:299–302.

Heschel, A. J. 1966. *The Sabbath*. New York: Harper Torchbooks.

Hillers, D. R. 1969. *Covenant: The History of a Biblical Idea*. Baltimore: Johns Hopkins Press.

Hoehner, H. W. 1969. "The Duration of the Egyptian Bondage." BS 126:306–16.

Hoffman, Y. 1983. *The Doctrine of the Exodus in the Bible* [Hebrew]. Tel-Aviv: Tel Aviv University.

Hooke, S. H. 1962. *Babylonian and Assyrian Religion*. Oxford: Blackwell.

Hort, G. 1957–1958. "The Plagues of Egypt." ZAW 69:84–103, 70:48–59.

Huffmon, H. B. 1966*a*. "The Treaty Background of Hebrew *yada'*." *BASOR* 181:31–37.

——————, and Parker, S. B. 1966*b*. "A Further Note on the Treaty Background of Hebrew *yada'*." *BASOR* 184:36–38.

Hurowitz, V. 1985. "The Priestly Account of the Building of the Tabernacle." *JAOS* 105:21–30.

Hyatt, J. P. 1955. "Yahweh as the God of My Father." VT 5:130–36.

——————. 1980. *Exodus*, New Century Bible Commentary. Grand Rapids, Mich.: Eerdmans.

Ingholt, H. 1936. "Inscriptions and Sculptures from Palmyra." *Berytus* 3:83–88.

Jackson, B. S. 1973. "The Problem of Exodus XXI:22–5 (*ius talionis*)." VT 23:273–304 (reprinted in *Essays*, 1975, pp. 75–107).

——————. 1975. *Essays in Jewish and Comparative Legal History*; Leiden: Brill.

Jacob, B. 1942. "The Childhood and Youth of Moses, the Messenger of God." In *Essays Presented to J. H. Hertz*, edited by I. Epstein et al. London: Edward Golston.

Jacobsen, Th. 1976. *The Treasures of Darkness: A History of Mesopotamian Religion*. New Haven and London: Yale University Press.

James, E. O. 1963. *Seasonal Feasts and Festivals*. New York: University Paperback.

James, T. G. H. 1973. "Egypt: From the Expulsion of the Hyksos to Amenophis I." *CAH*, II, 1:289–312.

——————. 1979. *An Introduction to Ancient Egypt*. New York: Farrar Straus Giroux.

Japhet, S. 1978. "The Laws of Manumission of Slaves" in *Studies in the Bible and the Ancient Near East Presented to Samuel Loewenstamm*, edited by Y. Avishur and J. Blau. Jerusalem: Rubinstein, vol. 1:231–49.

Jastrow, M. 1926. *A Dictionary of the Targumim, the Talmud Babli, Yerushalmi and the Midrashic Literature*. New York, Berlin and London: Shapiro and Vallentine.

Joines, K. R. 1974. *Serpent Symbolism in the Old Testament*. Haddonfield, N.J.: Haddonfield House.

Jomier, J. 1953. *Le Mahmal et la caravane égyptienne du pèlerinage de la Mecque*. Cairo.

Kaiser, W. C. 1983. *Toward Old Testament Ethics*. Grand Rapids, Mich.: Zondervan.

Kapelrud, A. S. 1963. "Temple Building, a Task for Gods and Men." *Orientalia* 30:56–62.

Katzenstein, H. J. 1982. "Gaza in the Egyptian Texts of the New Period." *JAOS* 102:111–13.

Kaufman, A. S. 1984. "Determining the Length of the Medium Cubit." *PEQ* 116:120–32.

Kaufmann, Y. 1940. "Freud's Book on Moses and Monotheism" [Hebrew]. *Moznaim* 10:199–211.

——————. 1942–1956. *History of the Religion of Israel* [Hebrew]. Tel-Aviv: Mosad Bialik.

——————. 1972. *The Religion of Israel*, translated and abridged by M. Greenberg. New York: Schocken Books.

Kearney, P. J. 1977. "Creation and Liturgy: The P Redaction of Exodus 25:40." *ZAW* 89:375–87.

Keimer, L. 1947. "Histoires de serpents dans L'Égypt ancienne et moderne." *MIE* vol. L (Cairo): Imprimerie de l'Institute français orientale.

Kennedy, A. R. S. 1902. "Tabernacle." HDB 4:653–68.

Ibn Khaldun. 1967. *The Muqaddima: An Introduction to History*, translated by F. Rosenthal, 2nd ed. Princeton, N.J.: Princeton University Press.

Kimelman, R. 1984. "Torah against Terror." *The Jewish Monthly*, October, pp. 16–22.

Kingsbury, E. C. 1967. "The Theophany *Topos* and the Mountain of God." *JBL* 86:205–10.

Kitchen, K. H. 1960. "Some Egyptian Background to the Old Testament." *THB* 5–6:7–13.

—————. 1965. "Egypt." In *The New Bible Dictionary.* Grand Rapids, Mich.: Eerdmans, pp. 337–53.

—————. 1975. *Ancient Orient and the Old Testament.* Downers Grove, Ill.: Intervarsity Press.

—————. 1976. "From the Brickfields of Egypt." *THB* 27:136–47.

—————. 1977. *The Bible in Its World.* Downers Grove, Ill.: Intervarsity Press.

Kramer, S. N. 1963. *The Sumerians: Their History and Culture.* Chicago: University of Chicago Press.

Kuznets, S. 1975. "Immigration of Russian Jews to the United States: Background and Structure." *PAH* 9:35–126.

Lambdin, T. O. 1953. "Egyptian Loan Words in the Old Testament." *JAOS* 73:145–55.

Lambert, W. G. 1960. *Babylonian Wisdom Literature.* Oxford: Clarendon.

—————. 1965. "A New Look at the Babylonian Background of Genesis." *JTS* 16:287–300.

—————, and Millard, A. R. 1969. *Atra-Hasis, with the Sumerian Flood Story by M. Civil.* Oxford: Clarendon.

Lammens, H. 1919. "Le culte des bétyles et les processions religieuses chez les Arabes préislamiques." *BIFAO* 17:39–101.

Landsberger, B. 1937. *Materialien zum Sumerischen Lexikon,* vol. 1. Rome: Pontifical Biblical Institute.

—————. 1954. "Assyrische Königsliste und 'Dunkles Zeitalter'," *JCS* 8:47–73.

Lemche, N. P. 1975. "The Hebrew Slave." *VT* 25:129–44.

Levine, B. A. 1965. "The Descriptive Tabernacle Texts of the Pentateuch." *JAOS* 85:307–18.

Lewis, B. 1980. *The Sargon Legend.* Cambridge, Mass.: ASOR Dissertation Series, No. 4.

Lewy, H., and Lewy, J. 1942–1943. "The Origin of the Week and the Oldest West Asiatic Calendar." *HUCA* 17:1–152.

Lewy, J. 1959. "The Story of the Golden Calf Reanalysed." *VT* 9:318–22.

—————. 1961. "Amurritica." *HUCA* 32:31–74.

Lichtheim, M. 1973, 1976, 1980. *Ancient Egyptian Literature* (vols. 1–3). Berkeley: University of California Press.

Liddel, H. G., and Scott, R. 1968. *A Greek-English Lexicon,* revised and augmented by H. S. Jones. Oxford: Clarendon Press.

Lieberman, S. 1962. *Hellenism in Jewish Palestine.* New York: Jewish Theological Seminary.

Lipinski, E. 1975. "L'esclave hébreu." *VT* 26:120–24.

Loewenstamm, S. E. 1957. Review of A. Goetze, 1956. *IEJ* 7:192–98.
───────. 1964. "The Trembling of Nature during the Theophany" [Hebrew]. In *Oz LeDavid*. Jerusalem: Kiryat Sepher, pp. 508–20 (English translation, 1980, pp. 173–89).
───────. 1965. *The Tradition of the Exodus in Its Development* [Hebrew]. Jerusalem: Magnes.
───────. 1967. "The Making and Destruction of the Golden Calf." *Biblica* 48:481–90 (reprinted in *AOAT*, 204 [1980]:236–45.)
───────. 1971. "Law." *WHJP* 3:231–67.
───────. 1975a. "The Making and Destruction of the Golden Calf—a Rejoinder." *Biblica* 56:330–43 (reprinted in *AOAT* 204 [1980]:503–16).
───────. 1975b. "New Proposals to Analyse the Composition of the Plagues Pericope" [Hebrew]. *Shnaton* 1:183–88.
───────. 1980. *Comparative Studies in Biblical and Ancient Oriental Cultures* = *AOAT* 204, Neukirchen-Vluyn.
───────. 1983. *"am segulah."* In *Hebrew Language Studies Presented to Professor Zeev Ben-Hayyim*, edited by M. Bar Asher et al. Jerusalem: Magnes, pp. 321–28.
Lorton, D. 1979. "Towards a Constitutional Approach to Ancient Egyptian Kingship." *JAOS* 99:460–65.
Lucas, A. 1944. "The Number of Israelites at the Exodus." *PEQ* 76:164–68.
Lucas, L. 1962. *Ancient Egyptian Materials and Industries*, 4th ed., revised and enlarged by J. R. Harris. London: Edward Arnold.
Malamat, A. 1970. "The Danite Migration and the Pan-Israelite Exodus-Conquest: A Biblical Narrative Pattern." *Biblica* 51:1–16.
───────. 1971. "Mari." *EJ* 11:972–89.
Malina, B. J. 1968. *The Palestinian Manna Tradition: The Manna Tradition in the Palestinian Targums and Its Relationship to the New Testament Writings*. Leiden: Brill.
Manchip-White, J. E. 1970. *Ancient Egypt*. New York: Dover.
Mann, T. W. 1971. "The Pillar of Cloud in the Reed Sea Narratives." *JBL* 90:15–30.
Mannix, D. P. 1960. "Magic Unmasked." *Holiday*, November, p. 32.
Maspero, G. 1967. *Popular Stories of Ancient Egypt*. New York: University Books (reprint).
Mazar, A. 1982. "The 'Bull Site'—An Iron Age I Open Cult Place." *BASOR* 247:27, 42.
McCarthy, D. J. 1963. *Treaty and Covenant: A Study in Form in the Ancient Oriental Documents and in the Old Testament*. Rome: Pontifical Biblical Institute.
McKenzie, J. L. 1959. "The Elders in the Old Testament." *Biblica* 40:522–40.
Meek, Th. J. 1960. *Hebrew Origins*. New York: Harper.
Mendelsohn, I. 1949. *Slavery in the Ancient Near East*. New York: Oxford University Press.

Mendenhall, G. E. 1954a. "Ancient Oriental and Biblical Law." *BA* 17:26–46.
––––––––––––. 1954b. "Covenant Forms in Israelite Tradition." *BA* 17:50–76.
––––––––––––. 1955. *Law and Covenant in Israel and the Ancient Near East.* Pittsburgh, Pa.: Biblical Colloquium.
––––––––––––. 1958. "The Census Lists of Numbers 1 and 26." *JBL* 77:52–66.
––––––––––––. 1962. "The Hebrew Conquest of Palestine." *BA* 25:66–87.
Meshel, Z. 1982. "An Exploration of the Journeys of the Israelites in the Wilderness." *BA* 45:19–20.
Milgrom, J. 1976. *Cult and Conscience: The Asham and the Priestly Doctrine of Repentance.* Leiden: Brill.
Millard, A. R. 1978. "Epigraphic Notes, Aramaic and Hebrew." *PEQ* 110:23–26.
Montet, P. 1958. *Everyday Life in Egypt in the Days of Ramesses the Great,* translated by A. R. M. Hyslop and M. S. Drower. London: E. Arnold.
––––––––––––. 1959. *L'Egypt et la Bible.* Neuchâtel: Delachaux et Niestlé.
––––––––––––. 1968. *Egypt and the Bible,* translated by L. R. Keylock. Philadelphia: Fortress Press.
Moran, W. L. 1959. "The Scandal of the 'Great Sin' at Ugarit." *JNES* 18:280.
––––––––––––. 1962. "A Kingdom of Priests." In *The Bible in Current Catholic Thought,* edited by J. McKenzie. New York: Herder and Herder; pp. 7–20.
Morenz, S. 1973. *Egyptian Religion,* translated by A. E. Keep. Ithaca, N.Y.: Cornell University Press.
Morgenstern, J. 1924. "The Three Calendars of Ancient Israel." *HUCA* 1:13–78.
––––––––––––. 1935. "Supplementary Studies in the Calendars of Ancient Israel." *HUCA* 10:1–148.
––––––––––––. 1942/43, 1943/44. "The Ark, the Ephod and the Tent of Meeting." *HUCA* 17:153–266, 18:1–52.
Muffs, Y. 1978. "Reflections on Prophetic Prayer in the Bible" [Hebrew]. *Eretz-Israel* 14:48–55.
Murray, M. 1964. *The Splendour that was Egypt.* London: Sidgwick and Jackson.
Myers, C. L. 1976. *The Tabernacle Menorah: A Synthetic Study of a Symbol from the Biblical Cult.* Missoula, Mont.: Scholars Press, ASOR Dissertation series No. 2.
Myers, J. M. 1955. *The Linguistic and Literary Form of the Book of Ruth.* Leiden: Brill.
Neufeld, E. 1951. *The Hittite Laws.* London: Luzac.
Nims, C. F. 1950. "Bricks without Straw." *BA* 13:22–28.
Noerdlinger, H. S. 1956. *Moses and Egypt: The Documentation to the Motion Picture* The Ten Commandments. Los Angeles: University of Southern California Press.

Noth, M. 1966. *The Laws in the Pentateuch and Other Studies,* translated by D. R. Ap-Thomas. Edinburgh and London: Oliver and Boyd.

Oppenheim, A. L. 1964. *Ancient Mesopotamia.* Chicago and London: University of Chicago Press.

Oren, E. D. 1973. "The Overland Route between Egypt and Canaan in the Early Bronze Age." *IEJ* 23:198–205.

——————. 1984. "Migdol: A New Fortress on the Edge of the Eastern Nile Delta." *BASOR* 256:7–44.

Orni, E., and Efrat, E. 1973. *Geography of Israel,* 3rd rev. ed. Philadelphia: Jewish Publication Society.

Patai, R. 1947. *Man and Temple.* London: Thomas Nelson.

Paul, S. 1970. *Studies in the Book of the Covenant in the Light of Cuneiform and Biblical Law.* Leiden: Brill.

Pedersen, J. 1926, 1940. *Israel: Its Life and Culture* (2 vols.). London and Copenhagen: Geoffrey Cumberlege and Branner og Korch.

Petrie, F. 1911. *Egypt and Israel.* London: Society for Promoting Christian Knowledge.

Phillips, A. 1970. *Israel's Criminal Law: A New Approach to the Decalogue.* New York: Schocken Books.

——————. 1984. "The Laws of Slavery: Exodus 21:2–11." *JSOT* 30:51–66.

Piankoff, A. 1955. *The Shrines of Tut-Ankh-Amon.* New York and Evanston: Harper Books.

Pirenne, J. 1959. "Le statut de la femme dans l'ancienne Égypt." *RSJB* 11:63–77.

Plastaras, J. 1966. *The God of Exodus: The Theology of the Exodus Narratives.* Milwaukee: Bruce.

Preuss, J. 1978. *Biblical and Talmudic Medicine,* translated and edited by F. Rosner. New York and London: Sanhedrin.

Rabinowitz, J. J. 1959. " 'The Great Sin' in Ancient Egyptian Marriage Contracts." *JNES* 18:73.

Rad, G. von. 1962, 1965. *Old Testament Theology* (2 vols.), translated by D. M. G. Stalker. New York: Harper.

Radin, P. 1957. *Primitive Man as a Philosopher.* New York and London: D. Appelton.

Raïsänen, H. 1972. *The Idea of Divine Hardening.* Helsinki: PFES No. 25.

Rand, H. 1970. "Figure-Vases in Ancient Egypt and Hebrew Midwives." *IEJ* 20:209–12.

Rank, O. 1959. *The Myth of the Birth of the Hero,* edited by P. Freund. New York: Vintage Books.

Rea, J. 1960. "The Time of the Oppression and the Exodus." *BETS* 3:58–69.

——————. 1961. "New Light on the Wilderness and Conquest." *GJ* 2:5–13.

Redford, D. B. 1963. "Exodus I, II." *VT* 13:401–18.

—————. 1967. "The Literary Motif of the Exposed Child." *Numen* 14:209–28.

—————. 1970a. "The Hyksos Invasion in History and Tradition." *Orientalia* 39:1–51.

—————. 1970b. *A Study of the Biblical Story of Joseph.* Leiden: Brill.

—————. 1984. *Akhenaton the Heretic King.* Princeton, N.J.: Princeton University Press.

Reiner, E. 1958. *Šurpu: A Collection of Sumerian and Akkadian Incantations.* Graz: Afo. 11.

Reuben, S. Ben 1984. "And He Hardened the Heart of Pharaoh" [Hebrew]. *Beth Mikra* 97:112–13.

Reviv, H. 1983. *The Elders in Ancient Israel: A Study of a Biblical Institution* [Hebrew]. Jerusalem: Magnes.

Reymond, E. A. E. 1969. *The Mythical Origin of the Egyptian Temple.* Manchester and New York: Manchester University Press.

Rhodes, A. B. 1977. "Israel's Prophets as Intercessors." In *Scripture in History and Theology,* edited by A. L. Merrill and T. W. Overholt. Pittsburgh: Pickwick Press, pp. 107–28.

Rofé, A. 1969. *Israelite Belief in Angels in the Pre-Exilic Period as Evidenced by Biblical Traditions.* Doctoral Dissertation, Hebrew University.

Roscher, W. H. 1909. *Die Zahl 40 in Glauben, Brauch und Schriften der Semiten.* Leipzig: Teubner.

Rothenberg, B. 1975. *BARev* 1, no. 1:16 (reference to Rothenberg in unsigned article), no. 2:11 (letter by Rothenberg to editor).

Rowley, H. H. 1950. *From Joseph to Joshua.* Oxford: Oxford University Press.

—————. 1963. *From Moses to Qumran.* New York: Association Press.

—————. 1967. *Worship in Ancient Israel: Its Form and Meaning.* Philadelphia: Fortress Press.

Rowton, M. B. 1976. "Dimorphic Structure and the Problem of the 'Apirû-'Ibrim." *JNES* 35:13–20.

Sarna, N. M. 1957. "Epic Substratum in the Prose of Job." *JBL* 76: 13–25.

—————. 1970. *Understanding Genesis.* New York: Schocken Books.

—————. 1971. "Ṣaphon." In *Encyclopaedia Biblica Hebraica* 6:747–51.

Sasson, J. M. 1973. "The Worship of the Golden Calf." In *Orient and Occident: Essays Presented to Cyrus H. Gordon.* AOAT 22:151–59.

—————. 1979. *Ruth: A New Translation with a Philological Folklorist Interpretation.* Baltimore and London: Johns Hopkins University Press.

Sauneron, S. 1960. *The Priests of Egypt.* New York: Grove Press.

Säve-Söderbergh, T. 1951. "The Hyksos Rule in Egypt." *JEA* 37:53–71.

—————. 1961. *Pharaohs and Mortals,* translated by R. E. Oldenburg. New York: Bobbs Merrill.

Schaeffer, C. F. A. 1983. "The Last Days of Ugarit." *BARev* 9, no. 5:74–75.

Segal, J. B. 1963. *The Hebrew Passover.* London and New York: Oxford University Press.

Selms, A. van. 1950. "The Goring Ox in Babylonian and Biblical Law." *Ar. Or* 18:321–30.

Seters, J. van. 1966. *The Hyksos: A New Investigation.* New Haven: Yale University Press.

Shiloh, Y. 1980. "The Population of Iron Age Palestine in the Light of a Sample Analysis of Urban Plans, Areas and Population Density." *BASOR* 239:25–35.

Simons, J. 1959. *The Geographical and Topographical Texts of the Old Testament.* Leiden: Brill.

Simpson, W. K., ed. 1972. *Literature of Ancient Egypt.* New Haven: Yale University Press.

Smith, M. 1978. "East Mediterranean Law Codes of the Early Bronze Age." *Eretz-Israel* 14:28–43.

Smith, S. 1976. "Assyrian Law." *CAH,* II, 2:104–8.

Snaith, N. 1965. " סוף ים The Sea of Reeds: The Red Sea." *VT* 15:395–98.

Soggin, J. A. 1965. "Zum Wiederentdeckten Altkanaanäischen Monat." *ZAW* 77:83–86.

Sonsino, R. 1980. *Motive Clauses in Hebrew Law.* Ann Arbor, Mich.: SBL Dissertation Series No. 45.

—————. 1984. "Characteristics of Biblical Law." *Judaism* 33:202–9.

Spalinger, A. J. 1982. *Aspects of the Military Documents of the Ancient Egyptians.* New Haven and London: Yale University Press.

Speiser, E. A. 1958. "The Muškenum." *Orientalia* 27:19–28.

—————. 1963. "Cuneiform Law and the History of Civilization." *PAPS* 107:536–41.

Spencer, A. J. 1979. *Brick Architecture in Ancient Egypt.* Warminster, Wiltshire, England: Aris and Phillips.

Steindorff, G., and Seele, K. C. 1963. *When Egypt Ruled the East.* Chicago: Phoenix Books.

Tallqvist, K. 1938. *Akkadische Götterepitheta.* Helsinfors, Finland: Societas Orientalis Fennica.

Thompson, J. A. 1952. "The Book of the Covenant in the Light of Modern Archaeological Research." *ABR* 2:97–107.

Tigay, J. H. 1978. "Notes on the Development of the Jewish Week." *Eretz-Israel* 14:111*–21.*

Towers, J. R. 1959. "The Red Sea." *JNES* 18:150–53.

Tsevat, M. 1972. "The Basic Meaning of the Sabbath." *ZAW* 84:447–59.

Uffenheimer, B. 1973. *Ancient Prophecy in Israel* [Hebrew]. Jerusalem: Magnes.

Uphill, E. P. 1968, 1969. "Pithom and Raamses: Their Location and Significance." *JNES* 27:291–316, 28:15–39.

Van der Ploeg, J. 1972. "Slavery in the Old Testament." *SVT* 22:72–87.

Vaux, R. de. 1961. *Ancient Israel: Its Life and Institutions,* translated by J. McHugh. New York: McGraw-Hill.

—————. 1971. *The Bible and the Ancient Near East*, translated by D. McHugh. Garden City, N.Y.: Doubleday.

—————. 1978. *The Early History of Israel*, translated by D. Smith. Philadelphia: Westminster.

Velde, H. T. E. 1967. *Seth, God of Confusion: A Study of His Role in Egyptian Mythology and Religion*. Leiden: Brill.

Vergote, J. 1959. *Joseph en Égypt*. Louvain, Belgium: Orientalia et Biblica Lovaniensia III.

von Soden, W. 1972. *Akkadishes Handwörterbuch*. Wiesbaden: Otto Harrasowitz.

Waltke, B. K. 1972. "Palestinian Artifactual Evidence Supporting the Early Date for the Exodus." *BS* 129:33–47.

Warshaver, G. 1973. "The Hardening of Pharaoh's Heart in the Bible and Qumranic Literature." *BIJS* 1:1ff.

Watson, P. L. 1972. "The Death of 'Death' in the Ugaritic Texts." *JAOS* 92:60–64.

Weinfeld, M. 1968. "The Creator God in Gen. 1 and in the Prophecy of Second Isaiah" [Hebrew]. *Tarbiz* 37:105–32.

—————. 1972. *Deuteronomy and the Deuteronomic School*. Oxford: Clarendon.

—————. 1975. "B'rith." *TDOT* 2:253–79.

—————. 1977. "Sabbath, Temple Building and the Enthronement of the Lord" [Hebrew]. *Beth Mikra* 69:188–93.

—————. 1981. "Sabbath, Temple and the Enthronement of the Lord, The Problem of the *Sitz-im-Leben* of Gen. 1:1–2:3." In *Festschrift Cazelles* (AOAT 212), Neukirchen-Vluyn, pp. 501–11.

Weippert, M. 1971. *The Settlement of the Israelite Tribes in Palestine: A Critical Survey of the Recent Scholarly Debate*, translated by J. D. Mardin. Naperville, Ill.: A. R. Allenson.

Weiss, R. 1981. *Studies in the Text and Language of the Bible* [Hebrew]. Jerusalem: Magnes.

Weiss-Rosmarin, T. 1939. *The Hebrew Moses*. New York: The Jewish Book Club.

Wellhausen, J. 1957. *Prolegomenon to the History of Ancient Israel*. Cleveland and New York: Meridian Books (reprint).

Wevers, J. W. 1962. "Banner." *IDB* 1:347–48.

Williams, R. J. 1972. "Scribal Training in Ancient Egypt." *JAOS* 92:214–21.

Wilson, J. A. 1951. *The Culture of Ancient Egypt*. Chicago: Phoenix Books.

—————. 1954. "Egypt." In *Authority and Law in the Ancient Orient*, *JAOS* Supplement No. 17, pp. 1–7.

—————. 1964. "Egypt—The Kingdom of the 'Two Lands,' " in *The World History of the Jewish People*, vol. 1, edited by E. A. Speiser. Tel-Aviv: Massada.

—————. 1979. "The Hardening of Pharaoh's Heart." *CBQ* 41:18–36.

Wiseman, D. J. 1962. "The Laws of Hammurabi Again." *JSS* 8:161–72.

Wood, L. T. 1970. "The Date of the Exodus." In *New Perspectives on the Old Testament*, edited by J. B. Wayne. Waco, Texas: Word Books, Evangelical Theological Society, pp. 66–87.

Woudstra, M. H. 1970. "The Tabernacle in Biblical Theological Perspective." In *New Perspectives on the Old Testament*, edited by J. B. Payne. Waco, Texas: Word Books, Evangelical Theological Society, pp. 88–103.

Wright, G. E. 1941. "Solomon's Temple Resurrected." *BA* 4:19–31.

Yarden, L. 1971. *The Tree of Light: A Study of the Menorah, the Seven-Branched Lampstand*. Ithaca, N.Y.: Cornell University Press.

Yaron, R. 1969. *The Laws of Eshnunna*. Jerusalem: Magnes.

—————. 1971. "The Goring Ox in Near Eastern Law." In *Jewish Law in Ancient and Modern Israel*, edited by Haim Cohn. New York: Ktav, pp. 50–60.

Yeivin, S. 1971. *The Israelite Conquest of Canaan*. Istanbul: Nederlands Historisch-Archaeologisch Instituut in het Nabije Oosten.

Yerushalmi, Y. H. 1982. *Zakhor: Jewish History and Jewish Memory*. Seattle, Wash.: University of Washington Press.

Žabkar, L. V. 1954. "The Theocracy of Amarna and the Doctrine of the BA." *JNES* 13:87–101.

Zerubavel, E. 1985. *The Seven Day Circle: The History and Meaning of the Week*. New York: The Free Press.

Zevit, Z. 1976. "The Priestly Redaction and Interpretation of the Plagues Narrative in Exodus." *JQR* 66:193–211.

Zohary, M. 1982. *Plants of the Bible*. Cambridge: Cambridge University Press.

Index